LIVING THE JAZZ LIFE

LIVING THE JAZZ LIFE

Conversations with Forty Musicians about Their Careers in Jazz

W. ROYAL STOKES

OXFORD
UNIVERSITY PRESS

OXFORD
UNIVERSITY PRESS

Oxford   New York
Auckland   Bangkok   Buenos Aires
Cape Town   Chennai   Dar es Salaam   Delhi   Hong Kong   Istanbul
Karachi   Kolkata   Kuala Lumpur   Madrid   Melbourne   Mexico City   Mumbai
Nairobi   São Paulo   Shanghai   Singapore   Taipei   Tokyo   Toronto

and an associated company in
Berlin

Copyright © 2000 by W. Royal Stokes

First published by Oxford University Press, Inc., 2000
198 Madison Avenue, New York, New York 10016

First issued as an Oxford University Press paperback, 2002

Oxford is a registered trademark of Oxford University Press

Library of Congress Cataloging-in-Publication Data
Stokes, W. Royal
Living the jazz life: Conversations with forty musicians
about their careers in jazz
p. cm.
Includes index
ISBN 0-19-508108-0 (cloth)   ISBN 0-19-515249-2 (pbk.)
1. Jazz musicians—Interviews. I. Title.
ML394.S86 2000 781.65'092'2—dc21 00-022593

9 8 7 6 5 4 3 2 1
Printed in the United States of America

For Erika, Sutton, and Neale

Contents

Contents

Introduction

As I made clear in the Introduction to my 1991 *The Jazz Scene: An Informal History from New Orleans to 1990*, I am not a musicologist and make no claim of being equipped to analyze music closely. While I have published three books and several thousand pieces on jazz in my nearly three decades of writing on the art form, the work has been for the most part of a descriptive, not critical, nature.

All the profiles contained here were based on my interviews. A major emphasis—perhaps *the* major emphasis—of this book is on early development, as early as I could *drag* out of the interviewees (often annoying the dickens out of them with my importuning to "stop jumping ahead"). It is, I think, extremely important to learn about these formative years. I have rarely seen much attention paid to this period of a jazz artist's life, except in a few full-length biographies or autobiographies.

This volume, like its predecessor, is a sort of oral history, and not just an oral history of jazz, for there is much Americana in the accounts that these individuals provide of their lives and careers. Whereas the earlier work was more a continuous history from New Orleans to the beginning of the final decade of the millennium, this book is divided into nine categories into which the individual stories quite naturally fell—although many of the profiles could have fitted just as naturally into categories other than those where they are.

Those readers who wish to quibble will no doubt notice that there is a chapter on saxophonists but none on trumpeters or trombonists, one on string players but none on percussionists, and one on singers that contains no men—and so on and so forth, as the immortal Jelly Roll Morton was fond of saying. So what? Several trumpeters and trombonists are profiled as are a drummer, a couple of bassists, a violinist, a harpist, four singers, fifteen pianists, a slew of guitar players, and a half dozen male instrumentalists who sing.

In defense of the organization of the book and my choices of whom to include, I set out neither to write a history of the jazz idiom (or of blues) nor to profile musicians whose presence in this type of compilation and in the jazz press is too often ubiquitous. My objective was only to provide portraits, largely in their own words, of forty or so artists who have played significant roles in the development of the music or who display the potential of doing that and whose personal and professional histories make for interesting, often riveting, reading.

Everyone who opens the book will soon notice that this is, in its way, a very personal collection of accounts. I make no apology for that slant, for I came both to know the individuals profiled here and to love their artistry. I treasure the moments spent talking with them and I try to bring the reader into those scenes. I also cherish the memories of the beautiful and moving sounds I have heard these artists execute, both in live performance and on record, and I try to describe some of those sounds.

So, here is a series of accounts about the speakers and their art and about the societies and cultures from whence they sprang.

LIVING THE JAZZ LIFE

1

Musical Families

"I tell my students, 'It's an important tradition and you have to go back and hear this music and learn its language all the way through. How are you going to know what's new to play, if you haven't listened to everything that's old?'"

Jackie McLean

"My destiny and dedication is to really put the grin back on the groove and help people to feel a certain love for the American art form of jazz and its history."   Duffy Jackson

A jazz musician's education generally consists of a combination of some, most, or all of the following: listening to records, radio, and live performance; classroom instruction; participation in school bands; private lessons; membership in combos with one's peers while still in school; jam sessions; and on-the-job training with professionals.

"I was very fortunate to have met these guys and to have heard them play," trumpeter Doc Cheatham told the author a decade and a half before he died at the age of ninety-one, citing Freddie Keppard, King Oliver, Louis Armstrong, Bix Beiderbecke, and Bunny Berigan. "That's how I got my education."

Of all the elements listed above, exposure to real artists is clearly the most significant learning experience a musician can enjoy, and it

3

is one that all young musicians strive for as often as possible. Still, one important element is missing from that list—namely, the family. The family has played a crucial role not only in nurturing, from an early age, the musical potential of its members but also in handing down a family musical tradition from one generation to another or from one musician to a younger brother or sister. One has only to browse in the standard jazz encyclopedias to compile an impressively lengthy roster of families. To cite three from New Orleans alone, there are the Morgan brothers, four of whom were in the same band in the 1920s; the Humphrey clan, which stretches from turn-of-the-century formally trained James (Professor Jim) Humphrey through four generations of family musicians, including grandsons Percy and Willie of the Preservation Hall Jazz Band; and pianist Ellis Marsalis and his sons, trumpeter Wynton, saxophonist Branford, trombonist Delfeayo, and drummer Jason. To these add the bandleading pianist Duke and trumpeter and leader Mercer Ellington; the Dorsey brothers—trombonist Tommy and reed player Jimmy; the Marsala brothers—trumpeter Marty and clarinetist and saxophonist Joe; the Jones brothers—pianist Hank, cornetist Thad, and drummer Elvin; the Heath brothers—bassist Percy, saxophonist Jimmy, and drummer Tootie; father and son saxophonists Von and Chico Freeman; pianist Jimmy and daughter Stacy Rowles, a trumpeter and flugelhorn player; the Brecker brothers—trumpeter Randy and saxophonist Michael; the Roney brothers, trumpeter Wallace and saxophonist Antoine.

"Well, yeah, it's following a tradition," agreed saxophonist and educator Jackie McLean, whose father John McLean played guitar in the band of Tiny Bradshaw and whose godfather Norman Cobbs, a saxophonist, presented him with his first instrument, a soprano saxophone. "There's the Heath family and the Joneses, so many families that have passed the tradition down. It's beautiful, in the case of René and me, because I discovered that his writing is the kind of vehicle I need in order to express myself in the way that I want to now. So what a pleasure it is to have him write these pieces." He added, in reference to the *Generations of Jazz* concert at the Kennedy Center that mid-1980s evening, "It's also a real pleasure that we're getting together with the Roneys, the Freemans, and the Marsalis family."

René McLean joined in the conversation: "My dad and I, we've been doing this for quite a while now, ever since my playing ability was at a level that I could perform with him. But all the while I was learning with him at home and he would give me the opportunity to come and sit in with his band whenever they were playing on pieces that I knew. So the tradition has been passed on to me in that sense. I also feel that there's a unique relationship between my father and me in the fact that we can relate on a musical level. Our ideas are somewhat compatible and our interests, too, so there's not what you'd call a generation gap there. Because I was raised in a particular household, I was exposed to the music and I saw my dad's broadmindedness, his ability not to be locked into the music of a particular period."

"We're coming to a period now," chimed in Jackie, who since the late 1960s has been on the faculty of Hartford's Hartt College, "where I think younger musicians are more aware of the history and speak of it, as Wynton Marsalis does all the time. I tell my students, 'It's an important tradition and you have to go back and hear this music and learn its language all the way through. How are you going to know what's new to play if you haven't listened to everything that's old?' I was fortunate to come up in a period when I had real heroes, real live heroes, that were as important to me as any you could think of at the time, like Joe Louis or Paul Robeson. I had heroes like Charlie Parker and Bud Powell, Thelonious Monk, Kenny Clarke, and they were real heroes for me and all my peers. So they kind of passed it to us as a kind of extended family. Charlie Parker and those musicians of that era were very serious; they had no shenanigans. Bird was very straightforward in the presentation of the music. I think it is a classical music, and it's a long time coming, this understanding that it is."

A small item in the *Washington Post* in 1993 caught my attention and reminded me that Louie Bellson was soon coming to town. When I had seen him at the North Sea Jazz Festival a couple of years before I had asked him to be in my next book. The news item alluded to was an announcement that Carmen McRae, Ahmad Jamal, and Bellson were being named Masters of Jazz by the National Endowment for the Arts.

"I was very fortunate, Royal, to come from a musical family," Louie began. "We had a music store in Moline, Illinois, for years. I started playing when I was three years old. Dad took me to a parade, and I pointed at the drum section and said, 'That's what I want to play.' The music store was a joy because we were four girls and four boys, and we all worked there. I got an education right off the bat. I get a little chuckle when I hear people say I'm a jazz drummer when I had, really, a strictly legit background, because Dad taught us almost every aria from every opera by the time we were thirteen, and I sat in conducting for fifteen years with him. So we were well versed, all of us, in classical music and symphonies, as well as jazz and everything.

"My father, Louis Sr., was born in Naples, Italy, and he spent a lot of time in Florence. My mother was born in Milano. They came over about 1918, and both of them spoke a little broken English and very good Italian, naturally. My father went through all that marvelous training right from childhood, where they sing solfeggio and read scores, and he played every instrument just wonderfully. He was a great musician, and he was a great teacher. He taught keyboards and guitars, mainly. His biggest thing was string instruments; that's what he excelled in. He got so busy that we finally had to bring in a trumpet teacher, a trombone teacher, and one for the saxophones. I took care of the drum section. My two uncles, Julius and Albert, and my father were very prominent with the Gibson guitar factory in Kalamazoo, Michigan. In fact, if you look at the Gibson book, you'll see the name of Bellson very prominent throughout the years. They helped design guitars. To give you an idea of what a virtuoso my uncle Albert was, when Andrés Segovia came to St. Paul, Minnesota, they got together and played duets.

"All the girls came first, then the four boys. Saxophone, clarinet, and, would you believe, three boys wound up playing drums. We were taught to play guitar and a little bit about every instrument so that we could teach. I gave many a trumpet and trombone lesson. We knew all about embouchure, we knew the scales, we knew the valves.

"They let me join the union in Moline at the age of fourteen, which was unheard of. But they gave me the card on one condition—that whatever date I played I had to be accompanied by a grown-up to make sure that he got me there and got me back home, because the venues all sold liquor. I had a very dear friend, Warren Graham, who had a truck. We'd load up the drums, and he'd take me there and sit with me all night long and then get me back home.

"At the time I started working in the music store and when I started giving lessons, from thirteen years old, I got real interested in the classics—a lot of Ravel, a lot of Stravinsky, a lot of Shostakovich. Later on I got into Bartók, and of course, the old masters, Beethoven and Bach. We learned how to study the scores, we deciphered all the scores bar by bar. Dad was very meticulous in his learning and his teaching, but very patient.

"I started getting records of Louis Armstrong and Benny Goodman and Duke Ellington and Count Basie. When these records came in I jumped at the opportunity to play 'em, and that's when I started my collection. I really got into that. But the biggest thing that happened to me was while I was in Moline and fourteen years old, at a place called the Rendezvous Nightclub. They had a typical Kansas City swing band in there and I'll never forget those guys. The piano player was named Spec Redd, from Des Moines, Iowa; Francis Bates was the bass player, Steiner was the saxophone player, and the drummer, his name was Percy Argo Walker, all black musicians. Percy taught me so much. He was from the Jo Jones school. They let me play a whole set every Tuesday night. Those guys taught me what swing was all about. I did that for almost three years.

"The Gene Krupa contest in 1942 was nationwide. They had maybe 40,000 drummers involved. It was local, regional, semifinalists, and finalists. You had to be eighteen or younger to be in this contest. When I won the regional in Chicago, one of the parents of one of the guys—who played very well, by the way—got jealous and said, 'Oh, he's twenty years old!' So I had to go get a birth certificate and prove that I was eighteen at that time. The last five players were sent to New York, and Gene was the judge for those, at the Wurlitzer Music Store. And that was quite a thrill.

"I used to go up to Chicago to study with Roy Knapp—he was Gene's teacher, too—and I saw Gene at the College Inn or the Panther Room in the Sherman Hotel. A couple of times I kinda shook hands with him, but at the finals of his contest I got to sit down and really talk to him, and we got to know one another. Then of course we became good friends and even recorded together. I think he was an influence on almost every drummer, and I think all of us owe him a certain debt. He was the person who brought drums to the foreground and made them a very important part of the band or orchestra. Before his time the drummers *should* have been recognized, but everyone just took those guys for granted. When you start with Baby Dodds and Zutty Singleton and then you come up to Chick Webb, then Big Sid Catlett and Jo Jones, and then you bring Kenny Clarke and Max Roach in there, I mean, those guys were not only great, they were innovators. They taught all of us. Everything I know today, I have to give credit to all those players.

"Then I joined Ted Fio Rito's band in California, and that was a great experience for me, but it only lasted three months because Benny's brother Freddy walked into the place and said, 'You want to go down and audition for Benny Goodman?' He was doing a picture at Paramount"—the 1942 *The Powers Girl* —"so my audition was actually playing in the movie. Benny said, 'Hey, put the tuxedo on and put the makeup on and I'll see you on the set.' So I played one tune, a segment with Benny and Jess Stacy, and he said, 'Okay, we leave Thursday for New York.' And that was it.

"I stayed with Benny for a year and then Uncle Sam got me. I was stationed in Washington, D.C., with a very good band, so I played all during my three years. When I came out I rejoined Benny for a year. Then in 1947 I joined Tommy Dorsey out in California. He was a marvelous guy to work for, one of the *toughest* bandleaders. I mean, when you got an itinerary from him it was about a hundred pages long. You went out there and did one-nighters and never came back. He always had a good band and *loved* drummers. He was used to Gene and Buddy Rich and all those guys, so you had to be prepared; you had to be in good shape to play with that band. Not only did you have to swing, but you had to be a good soloist, too.

"Actually, Tommy's the guy who pinpointed the two-bass drum thing for me. When I told him about the idea he said, 'Oh, that's fantastic!' So he and I worked out a device to put the drums on a revolving platform so that my set would go around, my back would be to the audience, and they could see that I operated not one bass drum but two. Ordinary laymen could look and see that from the front and they didn't know what's goin' on. This way it spelled out the whole thing. Tommy was a great one for theatrics, but it had to be something good musically, not just a gimmick. I had always wanted to get another big sound beside the hi-hat with the left foot and I had designed the two-bass drum thing in art class when I was in high school, and my teacher passed me on that.

"I left Tommy's band after three years. I was very happy with that band but I wanted to come out and join Harry's band because they were only working Fridays and Saturdays, and the rest of the time I wanted to study composition with Buddy Baker. Harry James was one of the most phenomenal men. I don't know whether people realize that Harry came from circus training. He was also a very good drummer, besides being a great trumpet player. He was a joy to work with, a perfectionist. All those guys were: Tommy, Harry, Benny, Jimmy Dorsey, Basie, and Duke. They were all perfection-ists, they demanded good quality, they were very particular about the way the band looked and the way the band sounded. Tommy Dorsey would walk up to you if you had a tuxedo on and make sure you didn't have on white socks. I was with Harry for about a year, and that was right before joining Duke.

"And then when Duke called, three of us out of Harry James's band—Juan Tizol, Willie Smith, and myself—went to Harry and we said, 'Harry, we got a chance to join Duke's band. In view of the fact that we're only doing two days a week with you, would you mind if we did that?' So he looked at all three of us and about five seconds later he said, 'Take me with you.'" Louie chuckled at the memory. "That's exactly what he said! He was a great guy, a great player. He passed away in July 1983 and he wanted to do a concert the begin-ning of August at the Hollywood Bowl and he wanted me to do it with him. I had been talking to him in June. He was very sick and I said, 'Hey, I'll come and play for nothing, just to play with you.' And we didn't get the opportunity. He always had a good band and he always featured me. We got along so beautifully. He used to call me Apples 'cause I always ate apples, ate a lot of fruit all the time.

"Without a doubt, probably the greatest experience I had was with Duke's band, because we did so many different things. The other bands did theaters; we did ballrooms, we did television, radio. With Ellington I would see on the agenda, next week we're gonna be playing with Toscanini's NBC Orchestra in New York. And then the first performance of the first sacred music that Duke wrote, at Grace Cathedral in San Francisco. These were things that you put in your record book, just absolutely giant musical things that you never forget. He was always doing stuff like that. It was always just a lot of excitement with him. Boy! Harry Carney, Russell Procope, Jimmy Hamilton, Paul Gonsalves, Cat Anderson and Clark Terry, Britt Woodman, Lawrence Brown, Juan Tizol, you go right on down. My goodness, they taught me so much, Billy Strayhorn and Duke, about composition. At first, they were very standoffish, as far as people knowing what their techniques were. They had certain codes, and they didn't like to tell anybody what their codes were. But they finally let me in on a few secrets. It's all God-given talent, you know; they didn't go to school to learn all that stuff, it's just things that God gave them."

Sometimes the transmission of the family tradition from one member to the other takes a more subtle form.

"If there had not been a Nat Cole, there may not be a Freddy Cole," Freddy conceded to me some years ago. "It hasn't been a hindrance being the brother of Nat Cole and I'd be telling lies saying it hasn't been a benefit, but I keep it in proper perspective. The situation that it created was basically that everybody figured I was going to be doing Nat Cole. But you have to prove what *you* can do and let the chips fall where they may and don't worry about it."

Singer and pianist Freddy Cole was once dubbed by Washington, D.C., jazz deejay Ron Sutton "the Cole nobody knows." It took a few years for him to shed the mantle of his late brother, whom he refers to as "one of the greatest persons who ever lived," but after more than four decades of performing here and abroad and recording many albums under his own name, he has finally come into his own as one of the several leading jazz voices of the 1990s. He has established an identity apart from the shadow of his older brother. As Billy Strayhorn biographer David Hajdu wrote in a recent *New York Times* profile of Freddy, "Overall, he is the most maturely expressive male jazz singer of his generation, if not the best alive" and "one of the few male jazz singers these days who still, at sixty-seven, is at the height of his powers."

It is not as if Nat took his younger brother under his wing, Freddy pointed out. "We were both in music, but he was, like, almost thirteen years older than I, so he was gone from home when I was still growing up. He would come home every now and then, but he was out there struggling, trying to get a career going, and when we got together music would be the last thing we would talk about."

All of which says much for a theory of musical osmosis.

"Yes, I did come from a musical family," Nat Adderley told me a decade after the death at forty-six of his brother Julian. "My father played cornet and all of his brothers and sisters—and there were five of them—were musical. The truth is, my brother actually started me playing trumpet because my father bought *him* a trumpet. Cannonball was a good trumpet player but didn't have any endurance and no range and was wise enough when we were kids to know that. So he switched to alto. But he also started teaching me to play trumpet so that Pop wouldn't be disappointed that neither one of the boys played the instrument that he played.

"Basically, I think it is the environment that influences what someone does," he said. "Across the street from where we lived was the Tabernacle Baptist Church that had a little band. My brother and I used to come home from our church and stand outside the Tabernacle Church and listen to the music most of Sunday afternoon when we were little boys because we just liked the feeling—tambourine and trombone and I think they had a blind man playing piano. We were studying the classical forms in the Episcopal church, with its Gregorian chants, and standing in front of the Tabernacle church with its sanctified feeling. So you put it all together and play what your background tells you to play."

That early routine goes far in explaining the depth of feeling in the art of the two brothers. "We just had a kind of bluesy feeling, I guess. The blues became an integral part of whatever we did. I could no more get rid of the blues than I could get rid of the me. I think the blues is going to be there no matter what. It's a cry that comes through in the music because that is the way you feel.

"I think that in the years since Julian's death he is gaining more respect," Nat Adderley reflected. "By now, Julian is almost becoming revered by musicians. He was really a tremendous player. For example, I just returned from a trip to Scotland and England, after having come back from Europe earlier in the summer, and there were British musicians on that tour who were asking me about particular records from the Riverside catalogue of 1960 to 1965. So I get the feeling that there's almost like a renaissance going on and it's a great pleasure for me."

Keeping alive the legacy of his brother motivates Nat, but he hastens to clarify that re-creation is not his way. "The music that we played, the straight-ahead kind of music, that is the music that I love, that is the music that I enjoy and the music that has the most in it for me. So since 1980 I've had a regular working unit, with Walter Booker on bass, Jimmy Cobb on drums, Larry Willis on piano most of the time, Sonny Fortune alto, Junior Cook tenor, either one or the other or both." In reference to that weekend's gig, he continued, "It was Julian's philosophy that you can play concerts, and certainly make more money playing concerts, but if you're going to get your music together, you have to play clubs, like the One Step Down."

Overseas gigs were taking up much of his time. "Of course, we earn *far* more money in other countries than we do here, so it becomes a matter of earning money there in order to subsidize yourself for playing music in this country.

"It isn't like it used to be, where you did one tour overseas," Nat Adderley continued. "Now you can go and come back and go again—concerts and clubs, except in the summer when you get all the festivals. It's all concerts in Japan, maybe one or two clubs, and little coffee houses. It's funny, these coffee houses; I don't know how they do it. I think the people who own them are probably so wealthy they just pay for you to play in their place."

Nat also had some observations to make on the status of the music and its future.

"I think it is the avant-garde nature of this music, the fact that it is in front and remains in front, that causes it to be in a perennially financially unhealthy state. Jazz *has* to remain creatively in front in order for pop music to have somewhere to go in later years. But jazz is gaining an artistic recognition that it has not had before. It's a great pleasure for me to tell you that the reception of the music is not only improving tremendously by leaps and bounds, but there are young players today—I'm talking about those who don't go into that hybrid fusion, electronic kind of music—who play straight-ahead jazz, no funny business at all. I'm so very happy to see many young people who are playing jazz for jazz's sake. I've had occasion to notice—especially in Europe and Japan—that on the same festivals where you have fusion groups playing, where you would normally expect great crowd reactions for that, the straight-ahead music gets a far bigger reception now than ten years ago. Obviously the general jazz listening public is reverting to form.

"I believe that when we had big bands—*lots* of big bands—to get started in, I think it made for more discipline in young players. I wish we still had big bands so that young players could come through them and get that discipline that is very important. It does help you to play better because you have to fit within a given structure and at the same time in order to be creative you must also play with other people. Sometimes young players play solos well but they don't play with each other very well; that is one of the functions of big bands, to give you that kind of disciplinary training.

" What I think is that the music will continue. It will always continue, unless we stop having regard for the music of this country. It isn't about money. It's about self-satisfaction and about creating music that one honestly believes is good music for posterity's sake."

Nat Adderley died of complications of diabetes on January 2, 2000. He was sixty-eight.

A few months after the legendary trumpeter Dizzy Gillespie died in early 1993, Wolf Trap Farm Park, America's only national park for the performing arts, located in Vienna, Virginia, hosted a tribute to him and titled the event Dedicated to Dizzy. It was a star-studded extravaganza of a concert featuring Slide Hampton and the Jazz Masters, Paquito D'Rivera and the United Nation Orchestra, and the Roy Hargrove Quintet. It was a long and quite thrilling summer evening, capped by a marathon, no-holds-barred jam session for which some of Slide's big band and the quintet's leader returned to the stage and joined the UNO. I especially recall that finale's fierce cutting contest between trumpeters Hargrove and Byron Stripling.

"I was born in Jeannette, Pennsylvania," Slide Hampton began an interview we did a few months later, "and I was raised in Indianapolis. I was fortunate to be born into a musical family. My mother and father were musicians and all my brothers and sisters were. There were five brothers, four sisters, my mother and father, and we had a family band and played many different kinds of musical affairs. The band also went to Carnegie Hall in the 1950s and the Apollo Theatre and also the Savoy Ballroom and had big successes.

"I actually started at twelve years old on trombone. Our father taught all the kids in the family and then a lot of our training actually was just in our practical experiences. Two of my sisters and two brothers played saxophone, two brothers played trumpet, one sister played piano and one played bass, my father played tenor saxophone and drums, my mother played harp. We had some friends that would augment the band so we could play the arrangements of Count Basie and Duke Ellington, Stan Kenton, Fletcher Henderson, Glenn Miller, Dizzy Gillespie, and all of those guys.

"We all went to Crispus Attucks High School, and Indianapolis was a musical center at the time. Many bands were coming from all over the country because there was a booking agent there who booked all of them. So we had a chance to hear a lot of music. We were too young to go in some of the clubs but we would stand in the back and listen and we played in some of the dance halls with our family band. We had a real good musical environment to grow up in and had a teacher in the high school, Mr. Brown, who was very influential with all the young people interested in becoming musicians.

"At that time jazz was the popular music of the day. I mean, on the radio when you heard Count Basie it was playing all over town, or Glenn Miller or Benny Goodman or Duke Ellington. Jazz was actually what everybody was listening to. So we grew up listening to it. The whole country was aware of jazz. We finally started getting records, especially my brother and I; we were getting the Charlie Parker records first and Dizzy Gillespie and J. J. Johnson, who was born in Indianapolis. We were listening to music all the time. From the time we woke up in the morning we'd put on whatever records we had. Mayfield Hampton, my brother, was more fanatic about music than I was. We were very influenced by Charlie Parker.

"When I finally left the family band in the mid-1950s I joined

Buddy Johnson's band, and he's the one who actually brought me to New York City. That was a beautiful experience for me. Buddy gave me a chance to do some writing and I had an outlet for trying to develop my compositional skills. And Buddy himself was a great composer and a very beautiful person. We traveled always, throughout the South. It was a great experience musically. We played the Savoy Ballroom and his sister Ella was there in the band and also Arthur Prysock. It was a very popular band. A lot of people don't know about him, but Buddy was a very, very fine pianist, a wonderful composer, and on top of all that, a helluva nice guy.

"Then I went with Lionel Hampton's band and stayed with him for two years," Slide Hampton recounted, naming trombonist Julian Priester and Oscar Dennard ("a great pianist and a real genius that most people never heard of") as two in that band whom he was especially close to. "By this time I guess I was in my middle twenties. And I went overseas for the first time, with Lionel Hampton—England and Sweden and Germany. That was fabulous; I was just so in awe. I mean, I was so overtaken by it, the wonderful attitude from the people over there about music. All I could think of after that was getting back to spend some time in Europe, when I had the chance. It was a very good band." Laughing, he added, "We just didn't make any money. They paid us very little."

"And then I went to Maynard Ferguson in the late 1950s and I stayed for about two years and got a chance to develop my writing skills a little more, did a few arrangements, and got to do quite a bit of soloing, too. That was a good outlet for me. And then I joined Dizzy Gillespie's big band in the early '60s. I stayed with Dizzy for about a year. This was the band that Lee Morgan was in and Benny Golson and Wynton Kelly; Melba Liston was the musical director—a *fabulous* band! From there I joined Art Blakey. When I joined that band it was McCoy Tyner, Joe Henderson, Bill Hardman, Joony Booth, Art, and myself, a tremendous band.

"Then I did several other things in my musical career, stayed at Motown Records for a while and worked as musical director for the Four Tops and Stevie Wonder and people like that, and then I joined Woody Herman's band in the late '60s and went overseas with him for two weeks in England. He asked me to stay on, but I had the opportunity to go over to the continent and do concerts, and I left the band and was off to France with my own group. I only intended to stay for a short period, but the experience I had and the attitude I found toward musicians and music was so tremendous that I stayed in Europe for eight years. It was something I never imagined to ever experience in music. It was overwhelming. I originally settled in Paris and all the trombone players there gave me a big dinner; they opened up possibilities for me for all kinds of work—television, radio, concerts, clubs, everything. And the people, they felt as though art is so important and culture is so important; their attitude was just really beautiful.

"I worked with Dexter Gordon over there, Johnny Griffin, Benny Bailey, Arthur Taylor, and a really important musician, Sacha Distel, a popular music singer who's a jazz guitarist. We did albums together. See, in every city in Europe there is an orchestra that is subsidized by the government, usually radio orchestras, but they do television, too, and they have a budget for jazz. Every year they have to record a certain amount of jazz. Like they have a certain amount of classical music they record, they record a certain amount of popular music, and every year they have a certain budget for jazz. So I worked with most of the radio orchestras in the major cities doin' my own compositions and arrangements.

"When I first came back I did the World of Trombones because the trombone had been kind of excluded from the musical scene. We started with four and then we had five and then six and we ended up with nine and we did an album called *The World of Trombones*. Our first trombone was Janice Robinson and we had Steve Turre, Curtis Fuller, Robin Eubanks, and Papo Vasquez. Albert Dailey was on piano, Ray Drummond on bass, and Leroy Williams on drums. And the opportunity to work with Jimmy Heath started opening up to me and we did that album *Mad about Tadd* and played several engagements featuring the music of Tadd Dameron."

I asked Hampton to tell me how the renewed association with Dizzy Gillespie came about at the end of the 1980s and to look back on his long career and cite the most significant influences on him.

"Charlie Fishman, who was Dizzy's manager at the time, came up with the idea of putting a band together, and he and Dizzy called it the Dizzy Gillespie United Nation Orchestra. They wanted to get guys from all of the Latin countries together and develop music comin' out of that whole experience. We had people from Brazil, from Cuba, from Puerto Rico. We put those musicians together and started developing a repertoire based on Dizzy's music with new arrangements. Dizzy was fronting the band and we were doing the arrangements—myself and a few other guys.

"Charlie Parker, Lester Young, Louis Armstrong, and Dizzy are my main influences concerning improvisation. For trombone, if I went way back to the beginning, it would start with Lawrence Brown and Trummy Young and Tommy Dorsey. My *biggest* influences on the trombone have been J. J. Johnson and Curtis Fuller." He added Kid Ory, Jim Robinson, Jack Teagarden, Jimmy Harrison, Sandy Williams, and J. C. Higginbotham as a few of the other trombonists he has listened to.

"I listen all the way back as far as the recordings go; I listen to all of that 'cause those guys were great players. People today couldn't imagine how great those guys were. They were the ones who were actually *creating* the whole concept. Man, I don't know how they made so much advancement without having somebody to follow. As I get older I realize how all those styles have so much in common, and the more of them that you can employ in *your* way of playing, the stronger your whole voice, your whole concept of playing will be.

"I think art music is gonna be as popular as the musicians want it to be, if they're willing to relate to the audiences with whatever their music is, and that's what we try to do. We really think the audience is very important; we want the audience to feel like once they come and hear us, the next time they see us somewhere they'll say, 'Yeah, I want to go do that again, 'cause that was a beautiful experience for us.' I think when musicians can start thinking about it like that, we can develop even more jazz audience."

"My uncles Bobby and Peter Domenick, from Paterson, New Jersey, taught me guitar," Bucky Pizzarelli, the acknowledged master of the seven-string version of the instrument, told me when I interviewed him in the mid-1970s in the studios of Georgetown University's WGTB-FM. "Bobby played with a lot of dance bands in the old days, played with Buddy Rogers, Clyde McCoy, Joe Mooney, Bob Chester. He played all over. In those days it was just rhythm guitar. Funny enough, during the war he was in the Air Force band at Bolling Field. I visited him once, when I had just gotten into the service myself in 1944. He spent a lot of time here in Washington and everybody knew him here in those days. He played at the Shoreham Hotel after the war. He stayed there for a while, then he came back to New Jersey."

Bucky Pizzarelli's career dates from 1943 when he was seventeen and was asked to occupy the guitar chair of the Vaughan Monroe Orchestra. In his two years in the army, he was in Europe playing with the band of the 86th Division. Rejoining the Monroe band after his discharge, he stayed with it until 1952 and then settled in New York. For the rest of that decade he toured for a while with the Three Suns, started doing studio work, and made himself available for free-lance gigs. In the '60s he began a long association with Benny Goodman. Over the years, Bucky has performed and recorded with hundreds of jazz greats, including Lionel Hampton, Benny Carter, Joe Venuti, Stephane Grappelli, Red Norvo, Bob Haggart, Bobby Hackett, Bud Freeman, Milt Hinton, Joe Mooney, Flip Phillips, Clark Terry, Ruby Braff, Hank Jones, Zoot Sims, Gene Ammons, and the Doc Severinsen Tonight Show Orchestra. Singers he has accompanied include Helen Ward, Maxine Sullivan, Lee Wiley, Frank Sinatra, Sarah Vaughan, and Rosemary Clooney.

"I used to listen to Carl Kress and Dick McDonough and to Joe Venuti and Eddie Lang," he said, pointing out that duos have loomed big in his musical life—for example, collaborations with guitarist George Barnes and bassist Slam Stewart. "The guitar duo carried over from my uncles. That was always the big thing with us. Whenever we would think musically of doing something, we always included two guitars, like if you want to play some pretty piano music it's playable with two guitars.

"All of us play," Bucky picked up the account in a later talk. He was referring to his four children, of whom three play guitar and one piano. Mary has recorded guitar duos with her father; John Jr. has been established in his own right for two decades; and Martin is bassist in his brother's trio. "We did it around the house a lot for fun. My uncles gave John some banjo lessons and he learned 'Bye-Bye Blues' and things like that. And then he picked up the guitar. There's so many hangin' around my house you can't miss 'em." He laughed. "So he learned his chords and then I gave him the seven-string to play and it was very easy for him. Little by little he figured it out and he became accompanist for me. In fact, he's a real good accompanist. We made a duet album together on Stash Records."

Another decade went by, and I found myself spending an afternoon and evening in Annapolis interviewing John Pizzarelli Jr. and checking him out at the King of France Tavern in the Maryland Inn.

"My father's guitars were in the house, but they were never in cases," John explained. "They were just *out* and you could always get to them. So there was always something to plunk along on even if you didn't know what you were doing. I must have been six or seven, first grade or second grade. I remember it was Sunday and my father came down and said, 'You're going to learn how to play the tenor banjo'—because his uncles were banjo players who taught *him* how to play. One of 'em was Pete Domenick. Pete basically stayed in his hometown and worked and raised his brothers and sister. But he played on the weekends and he was technically one of the best musicians I ever knew; he was unbelievable. His younger brother Bobby was the one who went out on the road. You can see him in some of those Bob Chester soundies playing rhythm guitar, and he played banjo, too.

"So they gave me a banjo and I went for lessons with Bobby at the local music store and learned how to play chord solos on tenor banjo. I played in talent shows—'Bye-Bye Blues' and 'Bye-Bye Blackbird' and songs like that. And they had a record out called *Banjorama* with Carmen Mastren, where Pete did most of the solos and he was just marvelous to hear. You'd go to family parties and you would play. It gave you an opportunity to be able to do something on Sunday.

"So I took lessons from Bobby for a year and then I dropped the banjo for a while and came back to it when I was about ten. I took lessons in Pete's kitchen with him. My dad would sit there and watch because he liked being around Pete. He adored him. It was the first time I ever played 'Yes Sir! That's My Baby,' and Pete wouldn't just play it with me, like Bobby would; he would play something else that made my playing sound really great. I was thinking, 'Gee, I never sound this good with Bobby.' Pete really knew how to harmonize all the things around what I was doing. And after the lesson, my dad and Pete would fake something. The kitchen was tiled halfway up the wall and it was really loud. It was always amazing and I remember thinking that I was hearing something really special.

"Right after that Pete died and the banjo sort of went south. I just picked up the guitar and realized you could open the book to solos and find the fingerings and things on little tablatures, and I started teaching myself guitar. My dad would show me a few chords on it and he'd get frustrated because I had no guitar savvy. I didn't know where anything fell and I didn't know if I played a certain fingering this way it was a flat five or plus five augmented or whatever. I didn't know the chord names, the really intricate chord names. That took me a while, as I really learned by myself, and he would say, 'That's it!' He'd get frustrated and *I'd* get frustrated. He was trying to play Art Tatum records for me and I was going to his gigs. I was watching Benny Goodman and Joe Venuti and George Barnes and people like that. I'd go to record dates every once in a while, around the New York area. We always thought it was a big deal that he had records out and it was always neat to see my dad playing.

"Around 1976 he played a Django Reinhardt record for me. 'Roseroom' was on it and"—he chuckled at the memory—"and I'm going, 'Gee, this guy's nuts!' He was really great and my dad said he would give me $5 if I learned the three or four choruses right at the beginning of the song. I think I only learned a chorus and a half and I had to play it, so I never got the $5. It was my introduction. The point is that he said, 'If you can learn all that Peter Frampton stuff off the records, whyn't you try and learn *this* off the record?' And I was, like, 'Gee, what a great idea!' I had never thought of that. I got that mind set, 'Gee, you can learn jazz this way! This is great!' I had never thought of it, and that's when I really began to start thinking about listening to those records differently and actually as an education, as opposed to my own enjoyment; it really turned my whole head around. I was playing the trumpet every day and practicin', and really getting into that. But also, coming back to the room and sittin' down with the guitar and trying to learn things and lookin' at the guitar and goin', 'Wait a second, here's a chord I haven't played before, look at that voicing.' And all of a sudden, things were falling into place and I started to write songs.

"I ended up with another record that influenced me at that time, because I was singing, too, singing and playing in all these rock bands. It was an album Kenny Rankin made called *The Kenny Rankin Album*, with Don Costa arrangements, 'Here's That Rainy Day' and 'Sunny Gets Blue,' songs like that. 'On and On' was on it, the Steven Bishop song; 'You Are So Beautiful,' the Joe Cocker hit. They were arranged in this gorgeous setting with this orchestra. And I started to learn all the chords to those things and sing them. Then I was starting to sing standards and I played the guitar at some coffee houses, startin' to put those kinds of things together. That was when I began getting interested in Pat Metheny. His *Bright Size Life* album had been out for a couple of years, but that's when it finally got to me, and I could sing every song on that album. I probably still can. It was really a whole other world now, a whole other sound from what I had grown up with. It was modern jazz guitar playing. Still, he was playing great melodies and his solos were melodic and there were great things to learn and to try and put together on the guitar now. It was starting to change everything for me from just playing open G chords on the Jackson Brownes and the Eagles. Now I'm trying to learn Pat Metheny's things, see what he's doing. It was really great."

Those coffee house gigs, some dances, and a few club dates had come John Pizzarelli's way while he was at college, and when he returned home to Saddle River, New Jersey, his father invited him to join him in a duo performance.

"'Why don't we try two seven-strings for this concert today?' he says. 'That way, if you play I can back you up and when I play, you can back me up.' I had an idea of how it worked because I had had a guitar duo with a friend and I had backed him up à la the Bucky and George Barnes thing. It was really simple for me to learn because I knew what he did with it. So I played this library gig with him and it really seemed to work out. All of a sudden, we were two seven-string guitars.

"The big gig was shortly after that on February 12, 1980. We played Highlights of Jazz in New York City for Jack Kleinsinger, a running series; Zoot Sims was the guest of honor, the secret surprise guest. It was something, hearing him play, and Zoot and I became friends on that gig. He really took a shine to me and I fell in love with him, which was easy because he was such a lovable guy. So we played our numbers up front and then Zoot came out and joined us and we played 'Stompin' at the Savoy.' Bucky was playing and I was backin' him up and when Bucky finished his solo he looked back at Zoot, who'd already played his solo; Zoot pointed over to me, like, 'We're not done yet, there's another guy on the bandstand's gotta play a solo yet.' And my dad's like, 'Oh, my God!' He wasn't ready for that. So I got to play my solo and I got applause and everything. It was really fun. And that's how I started to learn.

"At the beginning of '81 I was playing in a restaurant, singing a lot of Michael Franks songs, and my girlfriend played for me a record of a guy named Frank Webber singing 'Straighten Up and Fly Right.' I learned it off the record. Bucky said, 'You gotta get a hold on that whole thing. Those are perfect songs for you—really, it's great!' Then it happened that Capitol released *The Best of Nat King Cole*. I said, 'This is it, this is what I want to do. That's it! It's jazz and it's entertainment and it's funny and it's slick!' That was ter- rific and I learned all the songs and that's what started me in that direction. It gave me a niche that I wanted to be part of. I could play jazz, I could entertain. I could do the entertainment that I did in the high school band and play jazz, so I had something I could latch onto for this style of music."

Bucky and John Pizzarelli regularly played together throughout the 1980s. "We worked anywhere, we worked any club that would have us, and we didn't care if they talked; we didn't care if they lis- tened. It got steadier as we went along. We did parties and houses where they'd be right on your knees. We did where we'd be on one side of the room and they'd be over there, and it was great because you didn't care what *they* thought. We were playing together and we were learning, we were shaping. When we would have to do a big concert we were ready, we were ready to do anything we had to do. That's followed me; I'll play 8 P.M. to 1 A.M.; I'll do whatever you want to do. It's preparation for the half hour you gotta do in front of Frank Sinatra, or like last week in front of Herbie Hancock. We were Benny Goodman's opening act on about seven or eight gigs. He would say, 'Bucky, why'nt you bring your kid and open the show.' We had a whole night of material, five hours of it, we can pick our best stuff and we're ready to go; that was what my father's mentality was. Sometimes we'd play two hours without a break at some of these places, without ever repeating. And that was all preparation for what I was starting to do at the end of the '80s. All that came from working with my dad throughout. We made our first album in 1980, 2 X 7, and in '83 I made my first singing album."

John's performing career as a leader of his own group took off in the 1990s with steady gigs, concert dates, festival appearances here and abroad, and a string of albums.

"When I look at the things that I've gotten from Bucky that I think are the most important," he said, "I think of the time his hometown of Paterson gave an award for service to him and to five other people one night. And I've only realized this, say, in the last five years, just from being around him a little more, watching him a little more, but with more of a psychologist's eye as opposed to a son's eye, or maybe more from a son's eye than a musician's eye. A lot of people were getting up and saying, 'Strive to be number one, you can be number one,' and all this. And when my father got up, I heard him say that it never was a goal of his to be number one, that his goal was to be part of an organization that did its best and played together. I didn't realize how heavy it was until my wife sort of hit me in the arm and said, 'You realize what he just said?' To be in a band and contribute to a bigger goal was more important to him than being soloist in a band.

"And I think the other thing that I realized was that there wasn't anybody saying anything bad about him, and it wasn't because he was just a nice guy; it was because he did his job so well and thoroughly and was a respected musician—*is* a respected musician. Personalities didn't matter to him; he wanted to get on. He would work with the most difficult people. He got along with Benny Goodman!

"So it really has given me a different outlook. I'm not as concerned with making hit records as I am with making records that are good, so that people will say, 'That's a really good jazz record,' or that things are done well here, this was executed well, this is good, as opposed to something that's gonna sell a million copies. I'd rather sell a decent amount of records and be a respected musician, because of what he's meant to me through the years. It's because of his dedication. I don't know if I can do it like my father did it. He made sacrifices to be a great musician. I don't know if I can do that, but I know what it took for him to do it, to give to us what he gave us. He gave us a beautiful house and a great life and that kind of example to go on as a successful musician—which is not an easy thing. I'm very proud of that."

On an evening in the fall of 1979, I reviewed the Count Basie Orchestra at Rockville (Maryland) High School for the *Washington Post*. Among the many pleasures I anticipated as I sat waiting for the musicians to assemble on the stage were the understated keyboard approach of its leader, the unit's tight ensemble attack, the solo prowess of members of its horn sections, and the power of its rhythm section, which since 1975 had been driven by drummer Butch Miles. To my disappointment, Miles was not occupying the drummer's stool. In his place was a heavyset youth wearing glasses; I'd never seen him before. Of course, when the first number kicked off, my letdown was replaced by pure delight. I learned that Butch's replacement was Duffy Jackson, son of Chubby Jackson, the great bass player of Woody Herman's First Herd. Since that night I have never missed a chance to catch Duffy in action. He is not only one of the best timekeepers in the business, he is also a spectacular sight to behold in action.

"I was born July 3, 1953, in Freeport, Long Island," he began his story, "and two weeks after I was born we moved to Chicago. I didn't have too much choice in the matter. My father at that time was doing his *Little Rascals* TV show. I think that was around 1954, '55. He had played with Woody Herman in the '40s and with Louis Armstrong in the '50s for a short while, but my mom said, 'Hey, I have three kids here; I need you to take care of them,' that sort of thing. So he came off the road and we settled in Chicago and he went into a TV phase.

"My father used to wake me up in the middle of the night when I was three years old to play brushes on a chair and scat sing for all his friends." Duffy chuckled at the memory. "So I feel that through just hanging with all the cats late at night I had a nice little education as a jazz baby. When I was four, Don Lamond saw me playing some congas and keepin' a beat and he said to my dad, 'Hey, he's keepin' time with these records here!' So they went and got me a bass drum and a little snare and a hi-hat and cymbal and Don taught me how to keep some time."

Now, mind you, so far we are only at about age four of Duffy's life.

"So my mom gave my dad a set of bongos for his birthday. My dad always hated the bongos because they used to cover up the bass sound. So they stayed on the mantelpiece most of the time, and I used to climb up there and get 'em down all the time to play on 'em. When I was around five years old, Gene Krupa gave me a drum lesson on television. I didn't even know who he was; he just said, 'Play the tom-tom.' So we did a bit together on my dad's show. When I was six years old Roy Burns worked out with me for a little while. I did drum clinics with Louie Bellson for Rogers Drums when I was eight years old. I was on TV many, many times through my childhood, on shows like *I've Got a Secret* and the *Mike Douglas Show* and the *Jerry Lewis Telethon*, as a child prodigy playing piano and bass and drums and scatting and all that stuff. I used to stand on a chair and play the bass. I could play the blues in C when I was five or six." He also studied with drummers Ray McKinley and Buddy Rich.

"Now the thing is, I had a unique approach to learning drums. I just gave you a little insight to the drummers who helped me. I was really taught rhythms and accents by Steve Condos, the late, great jazz tap dancer of the Condos Brothers, and also by my dad. I learned rhythms and accents from a tap dancer and the pulse and the groove and musically blending in with other people and with other instruments from my dad. To be taught by a tap dancer and a bass player how to play drums—that's a little bit of a different approach as far as just tryin' to be sensitive to other people playing other instruments. It's also rhythmically stimulating—the groove, rhythms, and accents.

"So I think like a tap dancer. Years ago, when I was playing with Ray Brown and Milt Jackson and Monty Alexander in San Francisco—I think this was '73—Jon Hendricks was reviewing for the newspaper at that time and he did three paragraphs on me, saying that I sounded like Steve Condos tap dancing. He said, 'Yeah, Duffy thinks like a tap dancer when he plays.' I've jammed with Gregory Hines and Maurice Hines and Sammy Davis Jr. and a whole bunch of great jazz dancers, and I feel that I can be sympathetic to them rhythmically because of my teachings from Steve Condos. He had a tremendous influence on my life as a man and as an artist. Just in the last few years of his life was he really appreciated for everything that he could do. He was in France two years ago doing a big festival of dance where he was one of the true artists and stars; he did his big number, got a standing ovation, went back to his dressing room, and dropped dead.

"I appeared with Woody Herman's band as a guest soloist around twenty-five times in my life. I was playing bongos with the band when I was five and I played drums with the band when I was seven. I jammed with Basie when I was twelve. There's a very funny story about that. You remember the Riverboat in the Empire State Building? Don Lamond was filling in for Sonny Payne for the two-week engagement and it was the last set of the night on a Thursday. There weren't really a lot of people there but all the cats were there, all the mainstays of the band at that time. So I get up there and there were no drum charts. I should've known 'Shiny Stockings' at that point. So, anyway, we're playing it and Basie's stretchin' out and Sweets [Harry Edison] is taking extra choruses and all of a sudden the dance floor is flooded and it's happening, everybody's swinging, and it gets to that real soft part where the ensemble comes in and it builds up to that peak—'*dadadadadahwowwowwow!*' Now when it got to that point everybody stopped playing, and so so did I, and Basie looked at me and said, '*Play, boy!*' and I went"—he fluttered his lips—"and '*crash bang!*' And I got through the rest of the chart. Basie wouldn't let me sit in for seven years after that!

"But when I was nineteen the band was in Florida doing a dance benefit for the Heart Association. My dad and I were playing with Pete Candoli at the Boca Raton Hotel, so after our show we went up to catch the last two sets. Sonny Payne, unfortunately, was a little bit too juiced to play, so Basie got me up there and the first tune I played was 'Shiny Stockings.' He looked at me and I looked at him and I did what I had to do. And he kept me up there for the rest of the night. I played fifteen tunes with the band!" He laughed. "And it was one of the joyous moments of my life.

"Now, lemme back up a little bit here. When I was nine years old I was spiked playing Little League baseball and it developed into osteomyelitis. The doctors had no idea what I had the first two months I was in the hospital. They almost amputated my leg at one point. They would call my dad and mom every day sayin' I had different diseases and stuff. They ended up taking out half of my right hip because if the disease had spread to my heart it would have killed me!

"Then I went to Detroit in the summer of '63 with my dad because my mom and dad divorced at that point. My two sisters stayed with my mom and I went with my father, because, hey, we had a father-son act. In Detroit I saw a specialist and found that it had not been necessary to have the bone removed. But it had already been done and this has prompted around five other surgeries. I've had my right hip replaced twice and my left hip is breaking down because of it. But I'm very grateful that I can play and I count my blessings that I have four limbs when there're people with no arms and no legs that are makin' it in this world. So, I've had a lot of tragedy in my life, with my surgeries and stuff, but I've come back.

"My dad and I lived together and we traveled all over the world. I was in twenty schools, kindergarten through high school, man! We went all over the country making music together with our father-son act—Chubby and Duffy, and then it was Duffy and Dad. We were vagabond jazz musicians. We had to move around because in a world of rock 'n' roll, Dad and I had a very difficult time tryin' to play jazz. We would put together whatever we could—trios or quintets, piano and trumpet and tenor, and sometimes we'd have another drummer or percussionist. We played with all the heavyweights in New York. Dad had the best musicians money could buy. Mainstream through bebop. Straight-ahead swinging. I even had Dad in the later years singin' and playin' some Stevie Wonder and Chick Corea stuff. He was very progressive. At times, one of the horn players could keep enough time and then I would get out front and scat and play the piano and the bass, and Dad and I would do our little bits together on the mike. It's a very loving thing when you see Dad and me talking on the mike together, having fun with each other. It's cute.

"We were down in Florida from '67 through '71, and when I was fourteen I sat in with Duke's band in West Palm Beach. Duke, as you remember, would never get off the piano during intermission; he always composed. So he's sitting at the piano and I'm in the wings. There's a big crowd there, like 15,000 people or something, big West Palm Beach Auditorium thing. Duke says, 'Hey, Duffy, get up here!' And Cootie [Williams] was juiced and says, 'Aw, Duke, don't let that kid play, man!' —you know, that kind of thing.

"So I got up there and we just started playing with the rhythm section. Jeff Castleman was the bassist at that time; he was only nineteen or twenty and a great bass player. I was fourteen. Just bass and piano and drums. I started just playing time on the hi-hat, real soft and easy, and none of the guys in the band, except for Cootie, were on the bandstand yet; they all trickled off whenever they felt like it." He chuckles at this reference to the notorious independence of the Ellington band members.

"So, anyway, Duke and the bass player and myself, we started playing around forty choruses of blues and it got cookin'. I never even went to the ride-cymbal, I just stayed right on the hi-hats, but I opened the bump just a little bit. Al McKibbon taught me this years ago; there's an old trick, if you open up the hi-hat cymbals just slightly, all of a sudden the hi-hats start to shimmer and glimmer and sizzle and it creates a very interesting atmosphere. And we started swingin' a nice easy tempo, a little bit slower than 'Rockin' in Rhythm' or somethin' like that. By the time the whole band came on we were cookin' so hard it was ridiculous and there was a whole new feeling to Duke's band. All of a sudden, Johnny Hodges started playing, and Paul Gonsalves started playing, and Cootie got up there, and he was laughin' and smilin' and groovin' with me. It was just such a—a joyous, fantasy experience, I'll never forget it. My old drum teacher taped it and the tape got caught up in the machine and got crunched. It wasn't meant to be preserved. Duke wrote my dad a nice little note sayin', 'Dear Chubby, Thanks for letting Duff play with the band. Love, Duke.' "

I asked Duffy how he got along with Basie and if Basie had liked the idea of his presence in his band.

"Well, he chose me," he replied, "and he treated me the greatest. He was such a beautiful man to me." As for the rest of the band, he added with a laugh, "Let me put it this way; they tolerated my sense of humor. I mean, hey, I'm still Chubby's kid. My over-zealousness or whatever it is—I don't know what aggravates certain musicians from the cool, slick, laid-back school. I mean, hey, I'm very proud to be a vaudevillian of jazz. I'm into entertaining people. The most exquisite jazz in the world might be boring to watch sometimes. So you gotta give people a show. People remember me. They may not know my name but they say, 'Oh yeah, I remember that big fat drummer with the Basie band.'

"I'm tryin' to carry on the tradition of the Chubby Jackson groove in this business—I mean, when Dad was kickin' Woody's band without a bass amp and you felt that groove on 'Caldonia' and 'Apple Honey' and 'Your Father's Moustache' and all that." He interrupted his train of thought for an aside. "That was, like, almost the first rap record, huh?

"That period and the energy and the drive and the love for swingin' hard, that's the groove my dad was known for. My destiny and dedication is to really put the grin back on the groove and help people to feel a certain love for the American art form of jazz and its history. That's all I'm attempting to do now, to fit that into working with other people.

"Through my association with my father, I was permitted an opportunity to at least get a shot up there. I had to earn it once I was up there. I mean, if I wasn't makin' it as a player, they wouldn't have let me back again. Through my dad's association I was permitted at least an opportunity to prove myself. But since the age of seven, I decided I did not want to be Chubby Jackson Jr.; I wanted to be Duffy. My dad said, 'Hey, man, don't be Chubby.' Dad always influenced me about that. So I do have a purpose; I'm trying not to sound like anybody else. Individuality is a very special thing with me. I want to hear the person play; I don't want to hear him imitate a master. I mean, I could barely imitate myself! I'm constantly proving myself, even at this age. I've been playing since 1957, so down deep I'm very proud to be on the last tip-end of the old-school concepts, which I respect totally, and I give a lot of respect to the grand masters of this music. I'm not really part of the yuppie jazz era."

2

Saxophonists

"I wonder if it would surprise the women instrumentalists of the 1930s and '40s to hear that some fifty and sixty years after their days as young players facing stereotypes and ignorance, I still hear that I'm the first woman saxophonist someone has ever seen."
Leigh Pilzer

"If you're living in the middle of nowhere you can live in a fantasy world of being someone else. In New York you have to find yourself really quick."
Lew Tabackin

"I found early on that not a lot of people were transcending the color line. I realized I was different in that respect and I was very proud of the fact that I was."
Ron Holloway

Nearly two decades ago I spent an evening in Washington, D.C.'s, One Step Down, a jazz club ten blocks up Pennsylvania Avenue from the White House, where, a few years later, an amateur saxophonist would take up residence for the remainder of the century. On this particular evening, however, I sat enthralled by a professional saxophonist who, for these ears, has not many present-day peers on his instrument, the tenor.

"I was born in Little Rock, Arkansas, in 1945; I was a war baby," was how John Stubblefield began telling me the story of his life. "My father was in the navy and served as a mess attendant on the USS Lexington. He was injured on active duty in the Atlantic Ocean. After his injuries he came back to Norfolk, to the naval hospital there; he got his release from the service and came to Little Rock, where he lived before, and married my mother in 1944.

"I realized very early that my father loved music," Stubblefield continued. "I never forget that in 1975, when Mary Lou Williams recorded two of my songs, my father told me how he used to dance on 9th Street in Little Rock to Andy Kirk and the Clouds of Joy." John chuckled. "He *knew* Mary Lou Williams! He did the Lindy Hop, saw Basie when his band would come through. My father was *there*!

"I grew up on the South Side of Little Rock and attended Booker T. Washington Elementary School and Dunbar Junior High School—named after Paul Laurence Dunbar, of course. That's where I became interested in band instruments. There were all kinds of musicians in my neighborhood because one of the best schools of the blind was in Little Rock, the Conservatory for the Blind. Ray Charles would come through there. Al Hibbler, too, who also was born in Little Rock and grew up there and studied there. Well, there was a blind lady who was a pianist in my church. She went to the blind school with Al, and she and my mother were tight. Sister Howard was her name, a wonderful pianist, wonderful player. She was the musical director of our choir. As a kid, when my mother would step out of the room, she'd play Fats Waller, some blues, or something like that, because I was interested in the blues, and then my mother'd come back and Sister Howard would play some spirituals.

"In '53, the piano came into the house because my second grade teacher used to see me doin' this"—he drummed on the table—"and I was about to flunk the third grade; she told my mother, she said, 'You let this kid study piano; maybe this will give him some incentive to do the school work.' So my mother got me started on piano lessons from a wonderful teacher in my neighborhood, Miss Douglas, who had graduated from the Chicago Conservatory. Her job in the community, which she felt very proud of and was very dedicated to, was to train pianists to function in church. I started playing the saxophone in 1957 and she would see me passing by comin' home from school and she'd look at me and say, 'Oh, what a waste!' She was disappointed because I'd stopped my studies with her. I was talented as a pianist. Before I was ten years old I could span ten keys.

"I remember my father bought a television set for our family around '52, I think it was. Okay, so, '53, '54, I'm studyin' piano and the *Liberace Show* would come on, a fifteen-minute television show; after that was the *Jimmy Dorsey Show*, which I loved. I would see these saxophones bent like this"—he shaped the curve with his hands—"in the saxophone section. My father was a Baptist, my mother was from the Holiness Church, and my mother brought me to her church. There was a choir and there was also a piano. So as a kid I would see these instruments, and I'm studyin', you know, learnin' the rudiments of piano. I think it was '55, '56, there was a lady who played saxophone in the church and one of the ministers played trombone. She was a *mean* lady, *mean* to the kids. She was so mean, everybody would get out of her way. But she could *wail* on that saxophone! And for certain songs, when the congregation would sing, man, she would break that horn out of the case; I remember how she would put the neck on it and you'd look at her and she'd look at you. Mean to kids, man! But she could play! And I used to think, as a kid, 'Man, she must have bent that saxophone up like that.' So I felt sorry for that instrument. I had a passion in terms of my sorrow for that instrument, just the image of it.

"We used to have music periods in the school in first grade, second grade, all the way to the third grade. All my teachers would have a music session about rhythm and they would give a person a tambourine, they would give a person a bell, a triangle; they had all these little percussion instruments, and we would sing. I remember the first song I ever learned"—he sang—"'Clouds, clouds, riding the sky, now you are blue, now you are grey, tell me as you float by, will you be true today?' Now I learned that in '51, right? But I'm also hearing the songs that we sang in our church, I'm also hearing all the different hymns.

"I've done a lot of research on this. Thomas Dorsey played with Ma Rainey in the '20s, and when he discontinued his work in that circuit and became the father of gospel music, he used a lot of the forms that were used in African-American music and he took those forms and used them in sacred music, in gospel. So a lot of the blues forms that were sung at the turn of the century, we sing those songs in the church. But the whole thing was, a lot of people didn't realize this. Like my mom, she used to say that blues and all that was 'devil music,' and she really was opposed to me getting in the music that had that. My father had no problem with it, being Baptist. The hymns from the Baptist church, and the chants, those same chants go back to West Africa. I can sing all of those chants because my father's church was a block from my house.

"All these things were in my head when I was a very young kid, hearing all the forms of the Holiness church, hearin' the music of the Baptist church, these were some of the first things I heard. As far as pop music of that time, they had the Hit Parade in the early '50s, and we all know, at that time in America, everybody, young and teenagers alike, we all listened to the same hits. We used to watch the *Dinah Shore Show*, we used to watch Perry Como, and we *lo-o-oved* to watch the *Nat King Cole Show*.

"The television we got—and I never forget, it was a Zenith—had a radio on top and a phonograph under the bottom, and I can remember listening to the radio. I was hearing *The Lone Ranger* and shows like that. And music. I would check out the lab bands that would play on the radio. I used to get the North Texas State big band, out of Denton, Texas. I don't know how it came about but I knew where to find it. All the records that my mother had were Sister Rosetta Tharpe, the Soul Stirrers, all great gospel kinds of things. I don't remember my father ever buyin' a record, but he loved Count Basie, he loved Duke Ellington and Mary Lou Williams and the Clouds of Joy. But we didn't have that kind of music at home.

"One of the first jazz records that I bought was called *Jazz Under The Dome*, recorded right here in Washington by Rob and Earl Swope, and Al Seibert was the tenor saxophone player. I was always a fan of his—man, I was really into Al Seibert. This is around '59 or so I bought that record, and so we're talkin' when I was, like, fourteen.

"When I went to junior high school, they asked us if we would like to participate in the band, and I got down to the band room and that was *it*! I selected a bass clarinet, thinkin' it was a saxophone. It had the curved neck and it had a bell; I picked it based on my sorrow for that instrument that this mean lady in our church played. And my friend Tyrone Shaw, who went on to sing lead with the Vibrations, he and I were partners—we were in the Boy Scouts together and we were tight—he selected the tenor saxophone. Within a day or two I realized that I had selected the wrong instrument, so he was gracious enough to exchange with me. The band director, Mr. Adams, who was a graduate of Tennesse State University, told me that if you play saxophone you should play clarinet, and he tried to push the clarinet down my throat. I wasn't going for that, I said, 'I want to play the tenor.' So he didn't bother me that first year. I was lucky to be with some very bright kids in the band and we were able within one year to go and play with the ninth graders, we learned that fast. We were taught to read and were able to read fast.

"Around that time I met John Bush III, who now is a magistrate judge. His great-grandfather was a great man of the community and John's father was a saxophone player. John came in with this old silver saxophone and we used to laugh at him, 'cause it wasn't gold. But as it turned out, John Bush was way ahead of everybody; he was not only a straight-A student, his family was *culturally* ahead of a lot of people. Turns out that John's aunt had married Don Byas. As a kid I saw all kinds of photos of Don Byas holdin' John Bush. John's parents had a record library you wouldn't believe. I mean, it was a *wall* of records. So as a kid I heard a *lo-t-t* of stuff. I heard Benny Goodman, I heard King Oliver, they had everything that Don Byas had recorded with the Basie band. I mean, I got a wealth of education from a very young age.

"I was in a little band we had in the eighth grade, maybe a six-piece band. We were playing for school affairs and whatever. And my band directress at this time was Mrs. Clay. We used to play the pop songs, the latest rhythm and blues songs of the day. We had stock arrangements of the jazz kinds of things. We used to do 'Woodchoppers' Ball' and a lot of Count Basie stuff. There was a thing that John Bush and I used to do—'Honky Tonk' by Bill Doggett, a big hit back in '58. We had that down.

"So from that it went on until the ninth grade and I'm becoming associated with cats who were before me. I met Pharoah Sanders in '57. Ray Charles would come to Little Rock. Stevie Wonder also came to Little Rock, to the braille school. There was a band of all sightless men and they played at the El Dorado. I could name so many musicians. Richard Boone was from Little Rock. At the time he was with Della Reese he gave me my first arrangement lesson.

"If I could paint a picture of what 9th Street was like, I know of at least twelve clubs along this whole long strip. Just recently the Little Rock Jazz Society had a concert to save a building that was about to be torn down, a dance hall where Duke Ellington played, Billie Holiday, Count Basie, Stan Kenton played. Now, 9th Street is torn down. There are freeways through there now. I first started working at the Flamingo Club, the largest black club on 9th Street. It was *the* club." Tracing a grid on the table, he continued, "9th Street ran into State Street. Flamingo is right here, a church is right here, El Dorado is here. And down here was the Safari, Chez Paris, and King's Court. It was the mainstream, right in the heart of town.

"I started working on 9th Street when I was in my teen years, fifteen, sixteen, with the band of York Wilborn. We took over the Flamingo with our band around '61. I played my last job there a little bit after the assassination of President Kennedy. Had a chance to play with everybody there—Jackie Wilson, Al Hibbler, Peg Leg Bates, vaudeville shows, every big act that came through.

At Agriculture, Mechanical, and Normal College, Pine Bluff, Arkansas, John was in school bands and worked in local clubs, supporting such acts as the Drifters, Solomon Burke, "all the rhythm-and-blues people." After graduation in 1966 he relocated to Chicago.

At a recording session at Chess Records he met trumpeter Lester Bowie, who invited him to attend a concert by the Art Ensemble of Chicago. This initiated his introduction to the Association for the Advancement of Creative Musicians (AACM), which he had already heard about. He soon joined and began playing concerts and recording with fellow members. He also taught band in the public schools and still traveled with rhythm and blues bands.

"My former wife and I moved to New York in July of '71. There was an eight-month telephone strike going on and Mary Lou Williams sent me a Western Union telegram—I still have it in one of my scrapbooks—asking me to join her quartet and perform a mass. She found out about me because Milton Suggs, her bass player, had played in one of my bands in Chicago and he recommended me. He told her about my writings and about me as an orchestrator. She helped me immensely and was actually the first person to hire me in New York.

"I worked with the Collective Black Artists' big band for a number of years and I made a lot of contacts there—Stanley Cowell, Charles Tolliver, Reggie Workman, Albert Dailey, Jimmy Owens. I had a chance to play with Kenny Dorham and Harold Vick in that band. And then in '73 I got a call from from Charles Mingus and I joined his quintet. That led to Roy Brooks's Artistic Truth Band for a year or so. Then I got the call from Miles Davis and got a chance to record with him on *Get Up with It*."

John Stubblefield also established an ongoing relationship with McCoy Tyner and worked with the Thad Jones–Mel Lewis Orchestra, Tito Puente, Anthony Braxton, Roy Haynes, Abdullah Ibrahim, Gil Evans, Lester Bowie, Nat Adderley, Freddie Hubbard, Teo Macero, Sonny Phillips, Billy Taylor, Cecil McBee, Kenny Barron, George Russell, Sam Woodings's Orchestra, and the World Saxophone Quartet. He led his own combos, did Hollywood studio work for a year in the late 1970s, participated in such educational efforts as Jazzmobile and workshops at universities, and frequently perfomed overseas during the 1970s and through the 1990s. His most recent CD as leader is *Morning Song* on Enja Records.

In the early 1980s I again found myself in the One Step Down, listening to a trio. Saxophonist and flutist Lew Tabackin, bass player Michael Moore, and drummer Joey Barron were producing some of the most swinging sounds I had recently heard. My companion at the bar was Lew's wife, Toshiko Akiyoshi, and she was all smiles as the trio dug in its heels and, well, just plain blew! In a review of the performance I did for the *Washington Post*, I alluded to Lew's "mammoth tenor sound" as "coming out of the Coleman Hawkins school, enhanced by a melodic imagination from which ideas tumble one after the other."

"I grew up in south Philadelphia," Lew Tabackin told me in an interview we did when he was in town a decade later for a gig at Blues Alley. "It was not a musical family; it was a blue-collar kind of a family just trying to survive. In Philadelphia you could actually borrow an instrument from school and take lessons. I wasn't really that serious, but for some strange reason that I don't quite understand I thought I might like to play a clarinet. I tried to borrow one from school—this was in late elementary school—and there were no clarinets available. The only thing that was available was the flute, which nobody really wanted. I grew up in a fairly rough neighborhood—Irish Catholics, mainly, and some Italians—and it wasn't the macho thing to play flute. To play the trumpet, I guess that was cool, but a flute, well, that's pretty wimpy.

"It was a relatively poor neighborhood," Lew went on, "almost violent in a sense. For me to get back and forth from school was a trauma because I had to get past a Catholic school to get to my public school. The Catholic school went to a slightly higher grade than the elementary school I went to, so the Catholic kids were bigger and tougher; they were so repressed during the school hours that after school they were ready to kick ass, especially if you were a Jew. I mean, it was like they were being told that Jews killed Christ, and they were looking for some outlets. It was a trauma almost every day to deal with that kind of a situation, being from a minority group. Those were the days when blacks and Jews kind of had a feeling of brotherhood out of necessity.

"My only awareness of music was just a subliminal kind of thing. There wasn't much music in the family, although my grandmother had one of those 78 rpm things that you put the needles in and wound up, one of those big consoles; my grandfather kind of liked music. My grandparents were immigrants, Russian Jews, and weren't exactly cultured. A lot of jazz musicians are descended from Eastern European immigrants. My grandfather was what they called a huckster in those days. He would get a horse and a carriage and sell fruits and vegetables and he used to make sour pickles and tomatoes and stuff. He didn't make much money. In the very beginning I remember living with my grandparents. Later, we moved but stayed in the same neighborhood. I have one sister, who is not musical.

"My mother used to take me to Earle Theater matinées, where in those days they had stage shows and movies It was a real great deal. I remember Cab Calloway's band and, even as a four-year-old in 1944, I can still remember some of the visual images. People think that all this visual stuff happened in the rock 'n' roll era, but it obviously happened before. I remember Cab had all kinds of effects, and Lionel Hampton did something with the lights that felt like the whole room was shaking. All this made an impression on me.

"I got into high school and then things changed. First, I had a next-door neighbor. We lived in a row house, so your neighbor shared the front steps. He was a few years older than me and I thought he was really hip. His family had a stereo hi-fi system and he started to listen to jazz records. The 1950s was a hotbed of West Coast jazz and it was kind of fashionable for college student types to like jazz. It was considered hip. So I was impressed with the whole thing and he let me listen to his records sometimes and I'd even maybe hear a flute player. In school, after orchestra rehearsal, during the five- or ten-minute period between that class and the next class, some of the guys would start jamming a little bit. After school some of them would play and I hung out and decided that I would make an attempt at it. I started to play a little bit and it was a great thrill. I didn't know what the hell I was doing, obviously, but it felt great, whatever it was."

He borrowed a tenor saxaphone and set about teaching himself to play it, applying what he had recently learned in clarinet lessons. "After a couple of hours of fooling around I could actually get a sound. It was not quite like Lester Young but fairly respectable, at least to my ear at that time. I knew that this was for me."

The listening sessions next door were by now encompassing more than just West Coast sounds. For example, Tabackin recalls that his friend was introducing him to "stuff like Milt Jackson's 1954 *Opus De Funk* and Frank Wess and that kind of thing," as well as Sonny Rollins and more of the sounds of cool jazz—for example, trumpeter Shorty Rogers.

"Al Cohn had a big fan club among musicians in Philadelphia; he was like a hero to them, for some reason. I was really attracted to the kind of sound that he got, I really liked it.

"Then I started to listen on my own and I became fascinated. Also, I began to meet some of the local jazz musicians. I was fifteen at the time, and after a couple of weeks of playing the tenor, I was on target and I actually started playing jam sessions. I really did feel that was my instrument from that point because it felt very natural for me. I could always get a good sound, almost from the very first.

All of a sudden I became interested in music. It was like my ears opened up and music became important. Before that, I didn't really care. I'm basically a late developer, so my life began, musically, at fifteen. All those years of fooling around with the flute or the clarinet were totally meaningless. So that's when I started to come alive and realize that I wanted to do something. At first I wanted to be the next Bird or be the next messiah. I think we all have that dream. I tried to make up for lost time and started to practice really hard and concentrate. I basically sublimated all this energy, all this sexual energy and all kinds of energy, and just focused it into playing my saxophone.

"My first jam sessions, when I was fifteen, were mainly with white musicians. When I think back, they were pretty compassionate. The better players, they weren't putting you down because you couldn't play too well in the beginning. There was a certain amount of encouragement and not a lot of 'What're you doin' on the stand?' kind of thing. You'd listen to the better players and then go home and try to figure out what they were doing. I was trying to learn on my own. As I began to develop a little bit I started to play more with black musicians.

"When I was sixteen I would sneak into jazz clubs. I had a phony age card and I would just sit there and try to be inconspicuous and listen to the music. Someone said, 'Hey, you hear about this guy in some club in West Philadelphia?' It wasn't a great neighborhood. I tried to get into the club and there was this big bouncer; he must have weighed three hundred pounds. I mean, he was huge, and I'm tryin' to get in this club. I could do it at Pep's and Showboat—they kind of didn't bother with me—but there I was too conspicuous. I opened the door and I could hear Trane. I didn't know what he was playing but there was some kind of aura that was captivating. I tried to listen as much as I could but the bouncer kicked me out. That was my first awareness of Coltrane.

"I got to hear just about everybody who was active. They'd all come through Philly. If they weren't playing at the Showboat, they'd be at Pep's. Monk played at Pep's, Miles would play at the Showboat, sometimes later on at Pep's. I heard pretty much all of Miles's bands after Coltrane. He had a band with Sonny Stitt, which didn't last very long, and a band with Hank Mobley and one with

J. J. Johnson. Basie came through a couple of times and Quincy Jones brought a band in. Maynard Ferguson's band came to town a couple of times. And a kind of small big band that Slide Hampton had. I don't remember Ellington playing in the clubs at that time, so I didn't get a chance to hear him in person until much later.

"In those days there were two musicians' unions, a black union and a white union. And there were scenes that were more black kinds of scenes and there were white scenes. They were kind of separate, but as far as the jazz audience was concerned, it was much more integrated than it is today; it was much more even. Jazz fans were jazz fans; there was a camaraderie that kind of transcended racial lines. There were more black people who were jazz fans. Today that's not so, for some reason. When I was playing, as a local up-and-coming player, I played in a lot of those more black-oriented establishments. I was like the odd man out. Then, almost overnight, there was the beginning of a revolution. There had come a separation in the black clubs where I was trying to learn. At one point it was really a very happy thing, but then at a certain point it became a problem for a white guy to play in the black clubs.

"I started to think, 'Maybe it's about time for me to find out what I have to say, to find my own voice.' So I talked to some of the older musicians. A trombone player named Leo Vogel had a record collection and was very much interested in earlier jazz. I had never heard some of the things that he had. He introduced me to Lester Young, whom I immediately liked, and Don Byas and Ben Webster. I could immediately feel that passion. But then he played Coleman Hawkins and I couldn't deal with him; I didn't understand it. Even though I'd listened to Sonny Rollins, it still didn't prepare me for Hawkins. His sense of time, it had a certain severity and I wasn't ready for it. It was like giving somebody a 1945 Château Lafitte and they've never had wine before. The Orientals have an expression, 'It's like giving money to a cat.' Totally useless to me. Anyway, I started to listen a little bit more to the tradition.

Lew Tabackin attended the Philadelphia Conservatory on a scholarship on the strength of playing the flute in the all-city orchestra. After graduation in 1963 he was drafted.

"I'll never forget, the week before I had to go in, Sonny Rollins was playing at the Showboat and I had a gig not too far away. After I finished those nights I would go over there to catch his last set. And it was always great; Sonny Rollins was really into the unexpected. I mean, you didn't know what he would do; he was so free in those days, there was so much humor. I think some of the most uplifting music I heard in my youth was Sonny Rollins's. Coltrane's music was very spiritual, and I would go there and listen to him play an hour straight and get mesmerized, hypnotized. After a while I didn't know what was happening; I didn't know if I liked it or not.

"But with Sonny you would laugh; you'd hear these little elements of the giants popping out, and it was that great stream of consciousness happening with him in those days. I'd always feel very upbeat; I'd really feel good after I heard his music. So it was great to be able to listen to him the last set every night. And I met him in a music repair shop one day and we were talking and he was very nice to me. He is a beautiful man and was very helpful to me.

"I wanted to say good-bye to him and tell him that I enjoyed listening to him and talking to him. The last tune, 'Show Me the Way to Go Home,' he played in every conceivable way he could, and at the end of it, he was marching around the stage. He jumped up on the bar—it was one of those stages that was a circular bar with the stage in the middle—playing, jumped down again, marched upstairs still playing, into the hotel that was connected to the club. I waited and waited and he never came down. So I never got a chance to say good-bye! In fact, next time I see him I'm gonna have to tell him that.

"In retrospect, I don't resent being in the army because it got me out of Philadelphia. I probably would still be there playing in some kind of a band or something. To live in Philadelphia was a very limiting thing. In fact, when I was sixteen years old, there was one of the many wonderful musicians in Philly, Buddy Savitt, who played with Woody Herman way back. He told me to move to New York and I said, 'I can't move to New York, I'm just learning how to play.' He said, 'Well, learn how to play there.' And I didn't understand it at the time, but later I realized that that's what you do. You don't come to New York to take the town by storm; it's not a Cannonball Adderley story, where you go to one jam session and then, all of a sudden, you're headlines in the publications. Basically, that's *the* place, it's *the* great school. But that didn't make any sense to me until later.

"I had my flute with me and they gave me some funked-up tenor, and I go for this audition, really feeling as if my life depends on it. There was a black sergeant who was checking me out and he puts a call in to his superior: 'Hey, we got a guy here, man, we want to keep him.' So I get assigned there and was in the band training unit. The commanding officer said, 'Get your chops together and when you feel up to it, then you start rehearsing with the band.' Every time my orders came in to move on he'd change them. He'd say, 'Well, he's changed from tenor, now he's a flute player.'"

Eventually, Lew was transferred to Fort Monmouth, New Jersey, where he moonlighted doing organ trio gigs. "I just stayed around after I got out of the army and after a few months I saved up $400 and moved to New York. I found a place at 93rd between West End and Riverside and I got a telephone. The $400 pretty much went. There were a lot of musicians in that little area. Herbie Hancock was on the block and Jimmy Garrison lived just around the corner. Don Friedman told me about a club on St. Mark's Place. I'm not very agressive but I figured if I'm going to do anything, I'm going to have to just go and play. So I forced myself to go down to this club.

"Tony Scott was there; it was his gig. I said, 'My name is Lew Tabackin. Friedman told me if I came here I could maybe sit in.' He said, 'Well, I can't just let anybody—. Okay, man, lemme see what you can do.' Great welcome! I was nervous and I get up and he sits down at the piano. I look out front and I see all these guys—it's like a jury out there. I recognize Kenny Dorham. Somebody starts talking when I'm playing and I hear someone say, 'He sounds like he practices a lot.' I mean, you're really getting evaluated! I was acquitted and I was allowed to sit in; I passed the test. A guy from my old Philly days who was kind of an underground musician—C. Sharpe, Clarence Sharpe, and a wonderful player, a quintessential saxophone player—was very helpful to younger musicians, white or black; he would be a regular on this gig. I began to meet musicians and then get a little gig here and there and I met Joe Farrell, who started to send me in as his sub in the Thad Jones and Mel Lewis band.

"A lot of interesting things began to happen because New York is where things *do* happen. I got a call to join Cab Calloway's band and I showed up and there are all these old black guys. At least, they seemed to be really old to me—I was twenty-five. And I go into the dressing room and there's one guy on the floor doing push-ups and this is Eddie Barefield. So I'm playing with this band and it was the most fantastic experience because, all of a sudden, I didn't have to hold back. George Dorsey was playing lead alto, Garvin Bushell was the baritone player. They were so nice to me, especially George and Eddie, encouraging and inspirational. I'd hear Eddie practicing all day. He had been through a lot of music, but his attitude was the same as mine. And I realized that that's the way it's supposed to be; you're supposed to maintain your same level. That was kind of a milestone for me.

"I was getting interested a little more in Chu Berry because of that experience, which lasted for a couple of months. Doc Cheatham was in the band. Once in a while we'd play a jam tune and Doc would play the most simple solos, kind of like early Miles, middle Miles—very economic, just playing the essential notes. It was a lot of fun. It was a wonderful experience for me.

"I'd play as much as I could possibly play. It was great because in New York you actually develop faster in one year than you would in five years any other place because you don't know who's going to show up while you're playing. Joe Farrell used to take me around. I think he'd play games with me, in a sense. One night he says, 'Go play with that guy.' It was Howard McGhee. And so I'm playing and then I look up and see Sonny Rollins there. Joe probably noticed it and I didn't. Somebody that you only heard about or knew about, you're on the same bandstand with him, and you really want to maintain a high level; you really feel this need to play like it's the last time you're ever going to play, which is good for a young musician. It forces you to try to be more original because the people you're copying are there. So it's not an abstract thing. If you're living in the middle of nowhere you can live in a fantasy world of being someone else. In New York you have to find your-self really quick.

"After a while I found myself not playing as much. The black rev-olution really hit. When I was with Duke Pearson, we did a package with Nancy Wilson; we played the first set by ourselves and then we'd accompany her. It was a great band and I'm sure she never had any accompaniment that good before or since. Frank Foster was the other tenor player and we divided the solos equally in those days. There wasn't a lot of reaction because a white guy played a solo. Usually, Randy Brecker and I had solos to play, but at the Apollo Theatre they weren't a part of the program. We weren't allowed to play any solos; we weren't allowed to stand up. There was a lot of that kind of pressure. For example, I would get called to do a show and ten minutes later the contractor calls back and says, 'Sorry, I have to hire a black guy.'

"So I began to think, 'Well, it's not working out well for me.' I was playing less and I didn't like it. I felt kind of a resistance. In those days there was still the *Tonight Show* staff orchestra and they snuck me in to do some subs. Clark Terry was in the band and I used to borrow his blazer. He kept the gig but he wanted to play as little as possible; he just wanted to keep his staff status. Then the band moved to California and they asked me to come with them. I said, 'Well, maybe,' but I stayed in New York."

Tabackin did move to the West Coast in 1972. He had finished out the 1960s with a stint as featured soloist with the Danish Radio Orchestra, married Toshiko Akiyoshi, and twice toured Japan with her. The couple settled in Los Angeles and formed the Toshiko Akiyoshi–Lew Tabackin Big Band. Lew also performed in quartet format with her and found himself again playing in the *Tonight Show* orchestra.

"You never know what's gonna set you off," Lew said, looking back over his nearly four decades of making music, "what will be the little trigger. Maybe I wouldn't have gotten a tenor saxophone without being asked to join Frankie Avalon's teenage nightclub band when I was in high school."

"I'm not the first one known as a jazz musician to have played in other types of bands," insisted tenor saxophonist Ron Holloway. We were having a conversation a few days after I had caught him in action at Lewie's in Chevy Chase, Maryland, with singer Marge Calhoun. "Marge and I call it 'urban folk,' and you know I didn't play in that setting the way I would if I was playing in Dizzy's band or in my own group." That evening strengthened my conviction that Holloway is one of the most eclectic musicians I have ever encountered. I had been observing him in varied formats and different genres for more than two decades as a player of awesome strengths.

"For example, if you read John Coltrane's biography, or the story of any musician who's come up in jazz in the last fifty years, somewhere along the line, they've had some experiences with more popular forms. Coming up in the decade that I did in the 1970s, it's like it would have been hard *not* to have played in bands like that," he said, alluding to finding himself in rhythm and blues, soul, folk, blues, and rock contexts over the years. "That was the music of the day for people my age. If you were alive and living in America, you were hearing the Beatles, you were hearing James Brown and Wilson Pickett and Sly Stone and Jimi Hendrix and the Rolling Stones. I'm very glad I had those experiences because in that music you don't really have a lot of time to play a solo; sometimes you just have one chorus. You learn about getting to the point and saying what you have to say and you have to learn the vocabulary of each one of these approaches. And I've learned those lessons as well as I possibly could.

"I have a memory of some very early exposure to music," he continued. "I think my first conscious recollection is being quite aware of the music I was listening to as I was sitting in front of my father's record player with my brother Gerald. We were sitting there playing with blocks and I must have been about three years old. We were living in Washington, D.C., on Jay Street, where I spent the first thirteen years of my life. My father was an avid listener of jazz, particularly saxophone-led groups, and also I guess I heard a lot of records featuring trumpet players. He would come home from work and play music. My mother was also a jazz fan.

"During my pre-teen years I actually began recognizing that different guys had different sounds and different personalities on their instruments. Every now and then I would ask my father, 'Dad, who's that playing?' especially if I heard something I really liked. I got to the point early on that I could say, 'That's Miles Davis, isn't it?' or 'That's Sonny Rollins' or 'That's John Coltrane.'"

Among the artists that Ron's father, Winston T. Holloway, exposed him to were Roy Eldridge, Coleman Hawkins, Lester Young, Stan Getz, Charlie Parker, and Flip Phillips. His mother, Margerie E. Holloway, was especially fond of Billie Holiday and

Ben Webster, "because she liked his very breathy, airy tone and the fact that he was a master of playing ballads.

"It's funny," Ron Holloway reflected, "I'm listening to all this music as I'm growing up and never once did I ever consciously think about learning an instrument. I really didn't have any aspirations to be a musician. I remember very well sitting in the auditorium the first day of school at Carter G. Woodson Junior High School and the music teacher at the school, Arthur Capehart, got up on the stage. He was one of those musicians who could play reed as well as brass instruments very well. He says, 'Little kiddies, I want you all to think about this. If anybody out there wants to learn how to play a musical instrument, please come up to the band room tomorrow, because we don't have enough kids to form a school band this year. I'll show you the instruments and you can pick which ones you want to play.' And I thought it was kind of preposterous. I just could not see myself doing it.

"But the next day came and I went up there, dutifully, to the band room. Mr. Capehart pulled out three wind instruments and one of them happened to be a saxophone. So I said to myself, 'Well, if I'm gonna allow myself to get talked into this I might as well play something I'm familiar with, something I've at least heard all my life.' I said, 'Well, I recognize this instrument here and I know how it sounds, so I want to play it.' He gave me the alto saxophone."

Except for Mr. Capehart's showing him the fingering on the saxophone and teaching him the basics of reading music, Ron has never had any formal training.

In 1966 the Holloway family moved to the Washington, D.C., suburb of Takoma Park, Maryland.

"My parents had told me that there was a large basement and they said, 'If you want to practice down there, that'd be the perfect spot.'" Ron credits his parents with zealously encouraging him in his musical endeavors. "The only thing they used to say was cautionary. They'd say, 'You don't want to *just* be able to play music; you want to have another vocation. You know, have music as a sideline because it can be a very hard life.' But I was pretty much engrossed and obsessed with music from a very young age and that's what I pursued. It was almost as if as soon as that was said, I went off the high diving board as quickly as I possibly could."

During that first year in the new home, Ron switched to tenor saxophone, joined the school band at Takoma Park Junior High School, and secluded himself in his basement studio for hours at a time. His obsession with music paid off when he heard that a band of his peers was rehearsing down the street and he was asked to join them. The band's leader was Skip Jack, a bass player, and the band was called The Speculations.

"That was the first band I ever joined, outside of a school situation. We were playing things by Blood, Sweat and Tears, Chicago, Junior Walker, James Brown, Wilson Pickett, and anything that was catchy on Top 40 radio, the music of those times. We were playing music by black and white artists. One of the things I really liked about this band was the chance it gave me at a very early age to have interaction with people from various nationalities. There was a white guy on keyboards, a Jewish guy playing guitar, a white guy on bass, a Cuban fellow on drums, another black guy on vocals, and then myself. We went through a rehearsal period and enjoyed playing in Skip's basement, but eventually wanted to get out and play.

"I remember the first gig I ever did in my life was at the teen center right near the school, sort of a recreation center. We were very pleased with the reaction we saw at that early age, that girls paid a lot of attention to you if you were in a band. This was something that we were able to surmise from that first gig, and for that reason alone we intended to go on with our careers."

Although Ron Holloway was playing rhythm and blues–type music with this early group, "at the same time all during the week I'd be practicing along with my parents' jazz records." He was also sitting in with other bands. "The mobility of the saxophone allowed me to have a lot of different musical experiences."

One artist who especially appealed to Ron during these teen years was Willis "Gator" Jackson. "There was something rhythmic happening and he would incorporate kind of a gruff, vocal quality in his sound. I also liked a lot of things that Hank Mobley and Lee Morgan did together; they would write these little ditties, these real catchy little melodies based on riffs. So all of these things translated to a guy as young as I was at that time—thirteen, fourteen—and I was trying to get a grasp on these elements in their music."

Continuing to explore his father's collection, Holloway one day encountered John Coltrane. "I realized there was something about his playing that I really liked. I could hear that he was doing something different from most of the saxophone players I had heard. One of his records that made a very early impression on me—I think because it was so atmospheric and so visual—was *Africa/Brass*. Once I had dug that out and absorbed it, I wanted to hear all his recordings. I came to realize that here was a guy who had gone through different periods and different stages in his playing, and his sound and his approach would change every now and then. I also sought out a lot of records by Sonny Rollins because I realized there was something very witty and rhythmic about his playing that I liked."

It was band director Dave Humphrey at Montgomery Blair High School in Silver Spring, Maryland, whom Ron Holloway cites as the first one to truly recognize his promise.

"He was a very hip, cool guy who played several instruments. I remember him playing saxophones and keyboards a lot. He was interested in a lot of the same artists and music that I was interested in and was a big encourager. He even went so far as to let me be exempt from having to go march around the field in the school band on the weekend for various sports. By the time I met him I was further along in my playing and it was evident that I was going to make a career of it. Those were important, formative years."

Out of high school in 1971, Ron began to seek opportunities to play. His first experience sitting in occurred at the Luau Inn and he became a regular at Harold's Rogue and Jar, frequently participating in its jams. Among the musicians he joined in the blowing sessions there were saxophonists Buck Hill and Ritchie Cole, pianist Reuben Brown, bassist Marshall Hawkins, and Dottie Dodgion, the house drummer.

"There were numerous clubs around D.C. where I would sit in with bands that played a wide spectrum of music. I was not only sitting in with jazz combos but with blues and rhythm-and-blues bands, rock 'n' roll groups, and every now and then with some folk musicians. I was very much interested in placing myself in all kinds of music situations. I was starting to gain a lot of recognition around town in the early 1970s because of that. So there was a buzz.

"One group I was in was called the Sounds of Shea, a soul band.

But the next band after that, which probably was around 1974, '75, was called Mad Dog and the Lowlifers. It was the house band at a club over in North East called Jackie Lee's, a black-owned club, one of those neighborhood places where so many young musicians cut their teeth. That was an important time because I was playing in that club four nights a week for a few years, and during that time I learned a lot. And then there was Root Boy Slim, whom I joined in 1977. That was very important. I remember the first formal gig I had with Root Boy Slim was at the Childe Harold. Each week I would sit in with different types of bands in other D.C. clubs, like Desperadoes and the Cellar Door, and also the Psychedelly over in Bethesda.

"I used to play at all the places that were frequented by mostly Caucasians, and I used to also sit in at places where mostly black musicians played. What I would notice during these years, when I would talk to my friends about this, was that they acted like they had some fear of doing what I was doing. I would mention to some of my black friends that I had played at Desperadoes or the Childe Harold or some place like that and they would say, 'Oh, I'm not going over there!' I'd say, 'Why not?' They'd say, 'Well, you know, it's mostly whiteys over there.' So one thing I became *acutely* aware of during these years of playing around was that there were not very many people, black or white, who were crossing over the color line, especially as often as I was. A lot of times there would be some great musician in the black community and somebody I'd know in a white band would need somebody to fill in or somebody to replace another musician they had just lost. I'd say, 'Well, why don't you try so-and-so?' And they'd say, 'Who's that?' I'd say, 'Well, he's just about the best electric bass player in town.' They'd say, 'I never heard of him.' I'd say, 'Well, I can understand that because you never go to any of the black clubs and he never goes to any of the white ones.' But this was a big thing in my mind, the fact that a lot of these people were not getting together. Probably one of the better things about the Washington Area Music Awards here in D.C. is that it makes people a little bit more aware of what's happening in other parts of town. I found early on that not a lot of people were transcending the color line. I realized I was different in that respect and I was very proud that I was."

As much as Ron Holloway enjoyed his ubiquity and that "buzz" throughout his home area, it was becoming apparent to him that he needed challenges that the local scene and area musicians were not providing him.

"Freddie Hubbard was the first internationally famous musician passing through D.C. that I can really remember approaching, in 1974 at the Etcetera. My father and I went over there one night and I nervously went up and introduced myself to Freddie and we talked for a while. I had brought with me a tape recorder and a tape of me playing along with one of his records. Freddie was very courteous and took the time to listen to it; he asked me if I had my horn and I said, 'No, I didn't bring it.' He says, 'Well, bring it back Sunday night.' So I brought it back and played a couple of numbers with him on the last set of the last night. Fortunately, I played very well and the audience went absolutely wild, I'm happy to say. Freddie got on the mike and said, 'Hmmp! You all got any more of these around here?' He told me that any time he was in town I was welcome to come and sit in with him."

Holloway had already met Sonny Rollins backstage at a Smithsonian concert and not long after that he checked him out, also at the Etcetera.

"I walked upstairs to the dressing room and Sonny was shaving, during the break," he recalled. "He saw me in the reflection and we spoke and I reminded him that I had met him the previous year. He says, 'Yeah, so how you doin'?' and I told him what I was up to and said, 'Sonny, I wondered if I could play something for you.' He agreed to listen and then said, 'Oh, yeah, that's good. You got your horn?' And I says, 'No, I didn't bring it, but thanks for asking; maybe sometime I could sit in with you.' And he says, 'Yeah, by all means.'" Leonard Feather quoted Sonny a few years later on up-and-coming saxophonists. After expressing favorable assessments of Branford Marsalis and David Ware, Sonny cited "another kid, Ron Holloway, in Washington, who shows great promise."

"In 1977 I had a chance to approach Dizzy Gillespie for the first time. It was his first night at the Showboat in Silver Spring, Maryland, and I had my usual tape recorder with me and a tape that my father had made. Diz was in the dressing room warming up. He had this ritual of playing long tones, starting from the bottom of the horn, and then he would move his way up the chromatic scale. He looked up while still holding out a note and stopped playing and says—he almost shouted it—'Hey, whatcha got on the tape?' I said, 'Well, Mr. Gillespie, this is a tape of myself sitting in with Sonny Rollins and I just wondered if I could play it for you.' And he says, 'Yeah, yeah, I'd like to hear it.' So I played it and his body language was very easy to read. He just immediately sat forward on the edge of his chair, very attentive, with the enthusiasm of a child. At the end of my solo he had this very noticeable gleam in his eye and he looked at me and said, 'Gotcher horn?' And I said, 'No, sir, I didn't want to appear presumptuous,' and he says, 'Ha, ha, ha! Presumptuous! Now *there's* a word!'" Ron chuckled over the fond memory. "'Well, I tell you what,' Dizzy says, 'bring your horn tomorrow night.'"

The subsequent sit-in resulted in Holloway's being asked to finish out the week with the group and led not only to a standing offer throughout the next dozen years to come on board whenever Dizzy was in the area, but eventually to his becoming a regular member of the trumpeter's group.

"Dizzy was at Blues Alley in June of 1989 when he asked me if I wanted to join. He says, 'When can you start?' and I said, 'I think I already have.' I was in his band from then until his passing in January of '93. Joining Dizzy's quintet was one of the greatest events of my life!" Ron said. "If you are a young aspiring musician, you'd be hard-pressed to improve on standing next to John Birks Gillespie! When I think back on it now, twelve years after the fact, I still have to pinch myself. It's difficult to say whether my life has been enriched more professionally or personally, but I suspect the latter. As great a musician as Dizzy was, he may have been an even more remarkable human being. In some ways I think I'm spoiled for life. We traveled around the world for the most part in first class. I'll probably never work for a more decent, even-tempered individual than Dizzy. When he had a suggestion for me he was always humble and very gracious. I never saw him belittle anyone by lording it over them. He was very much aware of his own historic contribution to jazz, but I remember him getting that childlike gleam in his eyes whenever he would talk about what others had contributed to the music. Once we were appearing at a club in Seattle, Washington, called the New Orleans and Dizzy introduced me to Lucky Thompson. After Lucky walked away, Dizzy whirled around, excited, and proceeded to tell me all about Lucky's prowess on the tenor saxophone.

"The last week I played with Dizzy, in February of 1992, was at a very nice club called Jazz Alley in Seattle," Ron sadly recalled. "It wound up being his last booking. I remember he played so strong and with such precision that week that Ed Cherry and I were pleasantly stunned. We stood dead in our tracks as one set in particular ended, and Ed looked at Diz in amazement and called out Dizzy's name loudly to let Dizzy know how impressive his playing was throughout that entire set. Dizzy just shrugged it off but Ed and I both knew what we had just witnessed. We were both emotionally affected by what we had just heard. It was uncanny, and just a little eerie. It was as if God had smiled down on Dizzy and allowed him to play the way he had twenty years previously. The very next week Dizzy underwent some tests because he hadn't been feeling well. To everyone's shock, the diagnosis was grim—cancer of the pancreas. Dizzy was forced to cancel his engagements until further notice. On January 6, 1993, we lost him. By then he had been off the scene for nine months. It was the end of an era. I will forever treasure the time I was fortunate to spend in his company, before and after joining his band."

With Dizzy's band inactive after that Seattle gig in early 1992, Ron Holloway suddenly found that he had a lot of time on his hands and he started thinking seriously about putting a band together, drumming up some work, and going into the studio and recording.

"Up until this time," he clarified, "performing under my own name was done very sporadically. I had led groups at various festivals around the Washington area, but 1992 would mark the first time I entered the bandleading arena with serious intent. I debuted my new group at the 219 Club in Old Town Alexandria, Virginia, in June. One thing you learn very quickly if you're going to lead a jazz group on a continuous basis: you need to have at least three different players on each of the instruments. This is a must, due to the shortage of steady work necessary to keep a band together and all the free-lancing that goes on."

For the next year Ron's group played the Washington area and in March 1993 they cut the demo that, on Ron's request, Sonny Rollins passed on to his label, Fantasy Records.

"One week after they had received it I got a phone call from the president of Fantasy Records, Ralph Kaffel. He said he'd like to put it out. And I said to myself, 'Wow, it's just been a week! And already he's telling me that!'"

Three more albums followed, establishing Ron Holloway as a major player. Over the years, his group has stabilized itself as Chris Battistone, trumpet; Harry Appelman, piano; Gary Grainger, electric bass; and Lenny Robinson, drums. The wider pool of musicians that Ron draws from includes George Colligan, piano; Paul Bollenback, guitar; Tommy Cecil and Scott Ambush, bass; and Harold Summey and Mike Smith, drums.

"From the very beginning," he sums up, "for me, music has been fun. I have pursued it to the extent that I have because it was exciting, like an adventure. It's also been a serious endeavor because it's how I earn my living, so there's the business side of it. I have been selective about the types of gigs that I play because I want it to continue to be fun and adventurous. I'm forty-five now; I've been playing for about thirty-two years and I've managed to keep it interesting. Every now and then somebody'll say to me, 'How do you manage to play a gig like that when you've played with people like Dizzy Gillespie and Freddie Hubbard and Sonny Rollins? How do you turn around and play with so-and-so?' And I'll say, 'Well, for me, you see, it's not boring and it's not a task, because I'm jumpin' around in so many different situations.' It's never become a job. It's *all* fun."

In the early 1990s, Either/Orchestra was selected for the Saturday night concert on Parents' Weekend at Bard College, a month into my son Sutton's first semester at Bard. That choice was serendipitous as it let me catch the ten-piece band again and to interview its leader, saxophonist and composer Russ Gershon. A listing of some of the program's tunes, along with some titles from its recordings, indicates the eclectic approach of this Boston-based unit. The band's book contains the Duke Ellington/Juan Tizol classic "Caravan," Horace Silver's "Ecaroh," excursions outside like Sun Ra's "Planet Earth" and Roscoe Mitchell's "Odwallah," and some idiosyncratic originals such as the leader's "Born in a Suitcase" and "The Half-Life of Desire." The band's seven CDs include tributes to Benny Moten and John Coltrane and send-ups of John Lennon and Bob Dylan. There are also some odd but effective blends—for example, medleys of Thelonious Monk's "Nutty" and Bobbie Gentry's "Ode to Billie Joe" and of Miles Davis's "Circle in the Round" and Ellington's "I Got It Bad and That Ain't Good."

"We had a gig coming and the band had to have a name," Russ Gershon confided, laughing, as we took our seats in the empty auditorium an hour before the concert was to start. "That was about it, I was forced by necessity to think of something. To name it after myself didn't seem like it was in the spirit of the organization. It's a pun, I guess. It just sounded good, I just liked it. It seemed to have— I mean, the band has always been known for its sense of humor and musical puns."

When I asked about the E/O's musical ethos, Russ said, "It's somewhat democratic." This former Harvard philosphy major and 1982 honors graduate had offered little explanation of the origin of the band's name. He had studiously avoided mentioning its reference to the treatise on aesthetic and ethical choices by Søren Kierkegaard, the Danish philosopher. "We're always looking for balance—balance of styles, balance of personality, a dynamic balance—with sort of a creative tension that allows for a dialogue, whether it's a dialogue between two different styles of music juxtaposed to each other, or whether it's a dialogue between the players. The music—when we're working on it, when we're rehearsing and so on—there's a constant bickering, a bantering back and forth, as to what we're supposed to be doing. That's sort of a vague answer.

"I wanted a band that wouldn't sound like any other bands. I'd never really liked big bands of the Woody Herman–Buddy Rich type, or even, with all due respect, Thad [Jones] and Mel [Lewis], even the later Basie—1950s on. They never did very much for me, although I've learned to enjoy them more since I've been working in the medium. But I always liked Sun Ra and I always liked Ellington and Mingus, and we use some of the ideas of those bands in different ways. Sun Ra had the idea that you can go all the way from total wild anarchy to real clarity and focus in the same set. I've learned a lot from when Sun Ra started playing a lot of Fletcher Henderson tunes in the late '70s. They used to set those tunes up so well by having this build-up of a half an hour of utter wildness, always culminating in John Gilmore's screeching overtones. There was nothing like it; he would always make something go 'pop' in my head. And then they come out, after sledgehammering the audience like that, and roar through five Fletcher Henderson tunes in a row. Whereas if someone just came out and played the Fletcher Henderson tunes, people would say, 'Oh, that's nice, some period swing.'

"But if you contextualize with the opposite, then it has a whole different meaning. I guess that's what the Either/Or idea is—the juxtaposition of opposites or very disparate elements to see what they do to each other. Yeah, we always wanted not to be scared of jamming together things that maybe don't get along, just to see if they have an effect on each other.

"I started playing piano when I was seven, played classical violin from nine 'til about twelve or thirteen pretty seriously, and then after that I played a little guitar. Didn't play too much from maybe thirteen until about seventeen. So I took a few years off actively playing, but I had a basic grounding in music. I was a good student-musician; I was probably the best violin player around town at that point, or one of the best, of that age group. I got to go to all-state orchestras and stuff. I wasn't fanatical about it, but I liked it, I always liked it. I had a teacher, Helen Hauser, who was really into late romantic repertoire—Schumann and Brahms and this sort of thing. I think that gave me a great early taste for playing ballads, which I love to do still, although in Either/Orchestra I don't really do it too much. But when I'm playing outside of the band, I'm a real lover of standard ballads, which brings me to my theory about Coleman Hawkins. He started out on cello and I think his saxophone innovations were his transferring romantic cello music onto the tenor saxophone.

"I've been quite a jazz listener since I was about fifteen," Russ Gershon explained. "I've listened to all different periods, all different styles; I was actually quite a serious listener for years before I started playing. I did a lot of radio shows between the age of fifteen and about twenty-one. I think that might be a big influence on the way this band works. When you're dealing with a radio show you have the whole history of music at your fingertips because you're not limited by your own personal abilities. I would put together these shows on WWPT, at Staples High School in Westport, Connecticut, that went from Art Ensemble to Armstrong, all these different kinds of connections, and I think this band follows that to some degree. I got spoiled, I guess, by having the whole history of jazz as my instrument in years of radio; then, with the band, I sort of thought, okay, we can do that for real. Not that we play all styles equally well, but we certainly play many styles in our own way. We're not limited by thinking, 'Oh, we can't do that, we can't do this.' We try to just do it.

"I started playing when I was seventeen. I was lucky to have a couple of friends who were musicians, who had been playing for a while: Jay Joseph, a great bass player who was studying with Dave Holland at that time, and a trumpet player who later went on to be in Joe Bowie's Defunkt, John Mulkerin. We'd hang out and listen to Coltrane records and stuff and they wanted to jam, man, so they said, 'You better play!' I'd wanted to play the saxophone for a while because I'd gotten really into Coltrane and Rahsaan [Roland Kirk] and various people. And these guys said, 'Let's just play; we're really into free jazz.'

"This was about '77, I guess. We were into Sam Rivers and Dave Holland, and Ornette [Coleman], of course. I barely knew what the names of the notes were on the horn when I first started playing, but these guys tolerated me and we really had some great playing. Then I went to college and was pretty involved with that. I started playing in rock bands, the whole punk thing, where everybody believed you didn't have to know how to play an instrument to be in a band. The beautiful thing about that period is that people were not caught up in thinking you have to have all this technique and all this analytical knowledge. They felt that if you just had a feeling, you could express it. We just said, 'Let's have a band' and started working on music and we sort of learned that way. I was starting to take lessons and study with some people like Bob Mover. I guess he was my main teacher in those years. Then when I got out of college I was playing in rock bands for a couple of years, made records, and learned to be a professional musician.

"When Either/Orchestra first started we used to play pretty regularly at this pretty good club called Ryles in Cambridge. We had many residencies there, when we could go in and experiment on the bandstand, which is absolutely necessary. That started in late '85.

And there was a public library that had a jazz series and there were other clubs we played around Cambridge. We made our first record midway thru '86, and somewhere in mid-87 we started to think about going on tour. We got this idea that we wanted to travel somewhere and go and do something besides play in town. At the beginning of '88 we were lucky enough to be written up in the *Boston Sunday Globe Magazine*. This journalist with the great name Mopsy Strange Kennedy heard me playing with just the rhythm section. We were playing a dance—rock and Motown and dance music. She heard us and loved the small group and I gave her our album. She loved that and put us on the Consumer page as a great band to hire for your party or your wedding. Off that one article we got some huge amount of work, $40,000 worth of work. I saw all this work coming in and I said to the band, 'Listen, if we save 50 percent of this, we'll still be getting paid well and we'll have enough money to start touring.' It's expensive to travel with eleven, twelve people. Everybody said, 'Okay,' and at the end of '88 we did our first tour.

"It was a grassroots booking effort; a lot of the guys in the band were from the Midwest and each guy sort of found a gig in his hometown. I found some other ones to fill it in, and we went out dirt cheap. Everybody thought we were crazy, that the whole idea was preposterous, but I just called up clubs and said, 'Listen, we're coming, we're going to be around, I have a ten-piece band and we can play for "x" amount of money,' and they would hire us. We got about a ten-day tour together and we were able to underwrite it with the money we had saved up. It was so much fun, so good for the band, and it brought the music so much more together that, basically, since then we've just been trying to tour whenever possible. We've been doing about two big tours a year, 'big' meaning three to six weeks, and then little trips here and there. And it does something to the band. I mean, you can see why the Ellington band—and those other road bands—sounds so good, besides the fact that Ellington was a genius and he had a wall of brilliant musicians around him. When you play together every night, the music becomes a different thing. You can listen to Muhal Richard Abrams's albums—which I think are some of the best large-group albums that are made today. You can hear that two weeks of playing every night on the road—or *anywhere*, on the road or not on the road—would make the band sound better. You put on an Ellington record and it's not separate musicians, it's this *sound*. And you can only get that by playing together a lot and you can only play together a lot by getting off your ass and going. We've played all over the country now. We've toured the South, we've toured the Midwest a number of times, we've been out to the West Coast a couple of times, we've been pretty much everywhere in Canada except for Montreal—a lot of college dates, like the one we're sitting in right now, and a fair amount of festivals.

"We met the Willem Breuker band when we were in Texas last year and did a triple bill with them. They're so funny. There was a very brave person in Texas who put our two bands with a large Texas band, the Creative Opportunity Orchestra, and it was quite a show. I think the Breuker band and our band kind of looked at each other and saw a funny mirror effect. They're older than we are and their music's quite a bit different, but we both saw the family vibe in each other, and we had a great old time with them."

Suddenly, as though on cue, the sounds of organ, chimes, clapping, and general pandemonium erupted, terminating our conversation there in the Bard College auditorium.

"How about the bass and drums!" Russ Gershon shouted to the band, which had assembled on stage for a preconcert sound-check. The rhythm section took off, cooking.

"Since late 1992, when you interviewed me at Bard," Russ e-mailed me in the final months of this book's preparation for publication, "I received a Grammy nomination, in '93, for Best Arrangement on an Instrumental, Benny Moten's 'Weird Nightmare.' We got to go to L.A. and party with the stars. I met Charlie Haden; my wife Alessandra Mariano got to smell Mick Jagger's expensive cologne when she was pressed up against him in the crowd; every time I turned around Billy Ray Cyrus of 'Achey Breaky Heart' was standing behind me with his bodyguard; and I ate a lot of nice sushi, which leads me to conclude that *someone* is making a lot of money in the music business.

"We continued touring in the states and in '95 went to Europe for the North Sea Jazz and Pori Jazz Festivals. We also had a ten-year anniversary concert that year and had everybody back for a really big show. Among E/O's releases since the interview is the double CD *Across the Omniverse*, which was an attempt to empty the vaults of good material that had never made it onto CD before.

"In '96 my Alessandra got pregnant and some of my focus was taken away from the band. After Luca was born I decided to give the band a hiatus, so we did no gigs from January until November in 1997. By mid-'97 I was already getting calls for gigs from Portugal, Brooklyn Academy of Music, and Boston and I started getting the itch again. I decided to change things a bit, retire the old material—hundreds of tunes—and start with an empty book.

"I had been frustrated by guys living in New York and not being able to rehearse, so I let the New Yorkers go. I wanted to go beyond the musicians I already knew, so I held some open auditions for six spots. I found some amazing young talent. I wrote a lot of new music for the 'new' E/O and we toured in the United States in early '98 and did a tour of Italy and Portugal. They liked us over there. We did a tour of the Midwest in early '99. We just recorded last week and I think we've got a great album in the can, which should be out in early 2000. The material includes our arrangements of three Ethiopian pop songs of the early '70s, which we call the 'Ethiopian Suite.'

"The band as it stands now has a Latin tinge and the music is more sensual, I would say. Also, the young guys in the band are from a different generation from Charlie Kohlhase, Tom Halter, and me, and that's been an interesting experience. They're from the post-Marsalis era, and although they are open-minded, the whole land-scape of jazz is different from when we were coming up in the '70s. But my music has always had the whole history of jazz in it, and so adapting to the new players has been a pleasant challenge.

"I've also been playing trio gigs under the moniker Russ Gershon's Intimate Ensemble, and I'll probably put out a CD with this group next year sometime. It's a whole different experience, of course, from a ten-piece band with a lot of writing, but a lot of what I've learned from arranging so much music helps me in this context."

"I grew up in Little Falls, New Jersey," Kit McClure told me. The alto and tenor saxophonist, clarinetist, and leader of her seventeen-member all-female Kit McClure Big Band was sitting with me in the empty auditorium of the Mary Harrison Arts Center in Owings, Maryland, on International Women's Day, 1992. The afternoon concert had concluded only minutes before and her band was packing up in preparation for the bus trip back to its home base of New York.

A spirited "Sing Sing Sing" had featured the leader's clarinet on a cooking rendition of the classic Benny Goodman tune; trumpeter Rebecca Coupé Franks was featured on "I Can't Get Started," which she played with a gorgeous Bunny Berigan-like tone. "Stompin' at the Savoy," "Pennsylvania 6-5000," "Jumpin' at the Woodside," and "Take the 'A' Train" were other Swing Era selections the band offered. Many of them were pulled from their album *Some Like It Hot*. The leader hastened to point out that the band's next release would concentrate "on where we can take this idiom" and will have "a more contemporary sound."

"I stayed in the same house from when I was born to when I was eighteen and left for college," continued Kit McClure, who graduated from Yale University in 1973, the first class to have admitted women undergraduates to the institution. "My parents weren't very interested in music. My mother listened to some opera, which I never took a liking to. My father played the fife in the Secaucus Fife and Drum corps when he was a kid. No one else in the family had anything to do with music. They're policemen and so forth. That's about the extent of it. So I learned music in school.

"I started playing piano when I was seven and a brilliant piano teacher, Jean Den Bleyker, taught me a lot of theory, which I think really helped me to be a jazz player. Understanding theory is very important, *I* think, although certainly some great people just play by ear. Then in elementary school they offered band classes. I wanted to play the trombone, but I was told I wasn't allowed to because it wasn't ladylike. I was given the choice between a flute and a clarinet. I think I was thinking about saxophone somewhere in there and so I picked the clarinet.

"Then when I got to high school I went to the band director—I knew he was short on trombone players—and I said, 'Look, I'd love to play the trombone if you just give me a couple of lessons and a practice room for after school and promise that you won't tell my parents and they'll think I'm just playing the clarinet in the band and there won't be any trouble.' So he said, 'Great!' because he really needed trombone players.

"My mother took me to hear Ornette Coleman, Sun Ra, J. J. Johnson. We're talking mid-to-late 1960s, early '70s. That's the first time I remember listening. And I loved that stuff, from Ornette to the more traditional guys.

"So in high school I was a trombone player, and after a couple of years I started entering the county competitions and winning on the trombone. Then it got around to my parents, but by that time it was too late; I was already playing. I got into a couple of rock bands in town and started actually gigging when I was about sixteen." By this time Kit's ears had become her chief learning aid as she began to seriously listen to jazz. She also became somewhat of an autodidact, picking up guitar, bass, and drums.

At Yale, McClure began as a pre-med biology major with a minor in music, but she soon realized that music, not medicine, was to be her future. Also while there she played trombone in brass ensembles and formed the New Haven Women's Liberation Rock Band, in the process teaching many of its members to play their instruments. The nonprofessional off-campus aggregation toured colleges up and down the East Coast and made an album for Rounder Records. Before leaving Yale, Kit became fascinated by the big sound of Sonny Rollins and switched from trombone to tenor saxophone.

Her professional life for the remainder of the 1970s included a stint in the pit band of Bob Fosse's Broadway show *Dancin'*, which had her on stage blowing on "Sing Sing Sing," and membership as a soloist in the all-women Barry White Love Unlimited Orchestra, which performed at Radio City Music Hall. There was work on the rhythm and blues circuit with the Silky Slim band, a nine-piece unit with only two white members, Kit and trumpeter Laurie Frink, and gigs with several New York Latin bands, some of which experiences she recalls not too fondly, albeit with wry humor. For example, there were post-gig departures from drive-by-shooting-scarred neighborhoods with heads ducked below the car windows to avoid potential cross fire. However, she concedes, the music was great.

In 1979, a one-nighter at a women's jazz festival in Rome with a quartet led by drummer Stephanie Chapman turned into an eight-week tour of Italy, with the group opening for the likes of Dexter Gordon at some stops. It was her first experience playing jazz for a living and a memory that she cherishes. She returned to the United States and fell in with soul stars Sam Moore and Dave Prater and once again traveled the chitlin' circuit. This time the group was in parts of the South where, because the venues didn't pay very well, the "chitlins" were in short supply and sometimes they didn't eat well. Also, the band was rife with drug problems.

Before she knew it, she was off, not only to Europe again but to Japan as well, this time with a Sam and Dave package augmented by Eddie Floyd, Carla Thomas, Wilson Pickett, and Chuck Berry. The tour was not without its violent aspects. On one occasion a disgruntled member of its security team suspended the road manager by his heels from a seventh-story hotel window.

Again, she insists, it was a very valuable musical experience. Playing with artists of the stature of Sam and Dave, the other headliners, and the sidemen, she learned much about timing, the interplay between a rhythm section and soloists, and the rhythm and blues idiom in general. Looking back on her time with the tour, she credits the musicians she was with as playing some of the best swing she has ever heard, an element that has become a vital aspect of her own big band.

Back in the States in 1981 after the tour, Kit McClure set about putting together that big band. Once it was formed, five years or so of playing private bashes (among them a Brooke Shields birthday party), weddings, and dances followed. Over the nearly two decades of its history the band has played with—and this is just a representative list—Eartha Kitt, Doc Severinsen, Robert Palmer, Peter Duchin, and last but hardly least, Cab Calloway, who much admired the band. Another admirer was drummer and big band leader Mel Lewis, who often came to the band's rehearsals and who, Kit says, was an important mentor.

The Kit McClure Big Band has done concerts, festivals, and club dates throughout the United States and has released three CDs—the first concentrating on Swing Era fare, the second adding some forays into bebop and later terrain, the third on originals. New York's Red Parrot and the Ice Palace provided the band some of its earliest exposure as did appearances on Joan Rivers's TV show and a comedy special hosted by Jane Curtin and Martin Mull on the Lifetime Network. Engagements at the Bottom Line, the Red Blazer, Tavern on the Green, and Café Society followed, as did participation in the city's summer cultural programs in the parks. The band has also made a number of visits to both Europe and Japan.

There have been other all-women big bands, the most prominent of which were Ina Ray Hutton and her Melodears and the International Sweethearts of Rhythm, both active during the Swing Era. Currently, however, there are only reed player Ann Patterson's Maiden Voyage of the West Coast, drummer Sherrie Maricle's New York-based Diva–No Man's Band, and Kit McClure's Big Band.

The afternoon I caught Kit's band nearly a decade ago left me with a strong impression that they, along with Diva and Maiden Voyage, are well equipped to carry the big band tradition—not just the concept of an exclusively female orchestra—into the third millennium. In fact, these three orchestras, along with all-women small combos and all-male units of all sizes, may well move in the direction of integration of the genders. Of course, this must be initiated by the men, who, as we enter the twenty-first century, maintain a virtual lockout of women instrumentalists from their ranks. Until that takes place, the all-woman band will remain virtually the only source of regular employment for female horn, string, and percussion players.

"I think that women's jazz festivals, magazine issues devoted to women in jazz, all-female bands, and the like are a double-edged sword," observed Washington, D.C.–based multireed player Leigh Pilzer.

She knows the territory, as she has worked in both worlds—the male-dominated general jazz scene and the smaller one of all-female activity. A native of the D.C. area, she had studied piano and cello by the age of ten and played in her junior and high school bands. Her classmate Ron Horton, who has recorded with Jane Ira Bloom and East Down Septet and is very active in the Jazz Composers Collective and the Herbie Nichols Project, introduced her to Bill Potts. She studied orchestration with the great composer and arranger and one night he took her to a performance of the Count Basie band. The concert perked her interest in jazz, and she soon took up saxophone. Later she majored in baritone saxophone and studied arranging with Herb Pomeroy and others at Boston's Berklee College of Music and performed in the college's Dues Band under trombonist Phil Wilson.

Leigh Pilzer graduated from Berklee in 1984 and returned to D.C. Since then she has free-lanced, backing such artists as Mel Tormé, Maureen McGovern, Harry Connick Jr., Steve Allen, and the Four Tops. She has performed with the Duke Ellington Orchestra, the Blues Alley Big Band, and the National Symphony Orchestra and recorded with Chuck Brown and Eva Cassidy, the Bruce Gates Jazz Consortium Big Band, and Lynn Roberts and Reunion Band. Her experience in all-women units includes membership in the combos She-Bop and 2 Funkin' Heavy and performances with the Kit McClure and Diva big bands.

"I think they are of great importance in giving more women exposure," she conceded, alluding to the women's bands, combos, festivals, and publications that she had mentioned in her opening sentence. "But I also think they 'ghettoize' women. There are those who are truly interested in furthering the awareness of women jazz musicians, but there are others who use that type of venue to pay lip service to supporting women players, meanwhile denying them plausibility outside the realm of all-female events. However, even feeling that it would be best if women were not singled out because of their sex, I think the benefits gained by giving women *any* kind of exposure outweigh the detriments, as things currently stand.

"I wonder if it would surprise the women instrumentalists of the 1930s and '40s to hear that some fifty and sixty years after their days as young players facing stereotypes and ignorance, I still hear that I'm the first woman saxophonist someone has ever seen. I still encounter bandleaders who won't hire me and contractors who will only hire me when they've been asked to supply an all-female ensemble. The more often musicians, bandleaders, contractors, record companies, and the public encounter capable women musicians, the more acceptable it will be for women to play jazz. Ideally, the subject of a musician's gender should arise no more often than questions of race or ethnicity. But we are not yet at that point.

"As important as it is for other professionals to be aware of women players, it is as important, or more so, for younger women to have established female musicians as role models and mentors. Young women may play in their high school and college bands and they may enjoy playing jazz, but for many, only after they see a professional female jazz musician can they realize that seriously pursuing jazz is an option for them. I knew of Melba Liston from her days with Quincy Jones's big band, but when she brought a group to Washington in 1980—including herself and Janice Robinson on trombones, saxophonists Erica Linsday and Jean Fineberg, pianist and French horn player Sharon Freeman, bassist Carline Ray, and drummer Dottie Dodgion—it was a momentous occasion for me. I had just begun playing the saxophone and it was the first time I had seen a professional woman saxophonist, let alone that many women playing instruments together.

"Visibility is important, and festivals, magazine articles, and bands all provide opportunities for women to gain publicity. The trick then is to avoid being pigeonholed as 'just' a female musician. Marian McPartland has elegantly managed to remain involved with and supportive of female musicians while still maintaining her identity as a pianist irrespective of gender. Once a woman has become associated with an all-female situation it can be difficult for her later to establish a reputation on her musical merits alone.

"We need to use all the options open to us to meet and exchange ideas," Leigh Pilzer concluded. "Magazine columns, the Kennedy Center's Mary Lou Williams Women in Jazz Festival and other women's jazz festivals, Cobi Narita's International Women in Jazz, and the International Association of Jazz Educators' Sisters in Jazz programs are examples of resources that should be used and shared with other women. With solidarity and increased visibility we can get beyond the stage of being known as women who are musicians and become known as musicians who happen to be women."

Isn't it ironic, and more than a little disappointing, that an art form that helped pioneer desegregation in our land by putting together—on bandstands and in recording sessions—racially mixed musical units as early as the mid-1930s has not caught up with the rest of the country in terms of significantly opening up opportunities for female instrumentalists? In a 1999 *New York Times* profile of her, jazz drummer Susie Ibarra, a Philippine American from Houston now residing in Brooklyn, observed, "People talk about how art reflects life, but if jazz is art, how can it reflect life if there are only men playing it?"

Amen.

3

Pianists

"We speak to each other—it's like a language—and as long as you have the same vocabulary you can speak with any other musicians. The vocabulary consists of rhythm, harmony, melody, form, and all of the riffs and everything in the past of music. When you hear it, you respond to it, you talk to each other."
Mal Waldron

"For all too long this music was known as whorehouse music, smoky barroom music that you only hear in black neighborhoods, or music that you knock three times and say, 'Joe sent me.' I think it's finally beginning to overcome the fact that it was spawned by black people."
Ramsey Lewis

Tomorrow's Sunday, right?" was the first thing Mal Waldron said after we exchanged greetings. He stretched out on the bed, and I settled into a chair in his hotel room a few blocks from the One Step Down, where he and saxophonist Chico Freeman were gigging on a weekend in 1993.

"Let's see, well, it starts when I was six or seven, or maybe even eight. At that time it played a kind of derogatory role in my life because it kept me from going out and playing with the other kids." He chuckled at the memory of two-thirds of a century ago. "I had to stay in and practice for an hour. Practice piano after school, yeah, instead of going right out and play. I had to practice for an hour, then do my homework, and then go out to play. By that time I had to come in the house again and go to sleep. So it didn't leave me too much time to do what I wanted to do.

"It was all classical training and it went on for most of my young years, to about sixteen. I heard Coleman Hawkins some place in there, when I was about sixteen, I think. He played his 'Body and Soul.' I liked it so much I saved my money and went out and bought an alto sax. I couldn't afford a tenor. I had a big mouthpiece, an open mouthpiece, and tried to make like a tenor. I found the music in *Down Beat* and read it. It was fun.

"I didn't give up, never gave up, the piano studies; piano's always gone along with it. But the piano was moving along classical training, and the saxophone's always been jazz. Let's see, I started the saxophone when I was about sixteen and I stayed with it until I was about maybe twenty-three.

"I played saxophone in neighborhood groups for dances, bar mitzvahs, Spanish weddings. The pianist with one of the groups I played with was so weak that I had to play the changes for the guys to solo on. They didn't want to solo before I played the changes from the chord books. They loved it, so they kept me on piano most of the time. So that's why I just forgot about the saxophone. And then also I heard Charlie Parker in there, too, and that discouraged me from the saxophone. Because my technique was not fast enough on the saxophone to keep up with him, but my technique on piano *was* fast enough at least to approach Bud Powell. So the piano took over in the place of the saxophone as far as jazz went. Also, my personality was more introverted, and saxophone called for a more extroverted type of personality. You stand out in front of the audience and take your solos and it was always a big experience for me to do that. But with the piano I could play behind the groups and take my solo quietly, hidden, so to speak. It was much more comfortable for me to play my solos like that.

"The first influence I had on piano was Duke Ellington. I heard Art Tatum and Duke in person about the same time. I heard Tatum down at Café Society and I caught Duke Ellington at the Apollo Theatre. Through Duke I met Thelonious Monk. After that I heard

Bud Powell. I go back and listen to Fats Waller; I listen to Nat King Cole, a fascinating musician; Earl Hines, the boogie woogie pianists. I love that stuff."

Waldron's first recording was in 1950 with saxophonist Ike Quebec. "Ike and I, we did the off-night at Café Society Downtown on Mondays for six or seven months. Kansas Fields was on drums. There was, like, a snowball effect. Other musicians came in the club and used me on other gigs and other musicians used them and it kept snowballing like that. So I had enough work."

A couple of years later he went with Charles Mingus for several years. "It was always in the learning experience area for me; I was just getting my style together, shaping it and perfecting it, and learning from all the musicians around me. I mean, this was very important because Mingus played piano, too. He would show me areas that I hadn't explored and I would explore those and then he would show me *other* areas. He didn't demand, if you were searching. If you were just hanging around, then he would be mad and demand that you be serious about the music. If you were just out there to showboat, then"—Mal broke into laughter—"then he was down on you. Mingus was really out there and we explored free music." Asked who were some of the musicians who influenced him during his Mingus period, Mal named saxophonist George Barrow, drummers Max Roach and Dannie Richmond, and trombonist Eddie Bert

"Jackie McLean, of course, we were very close, and he also opened up the recording area for me, because he got me with Prestige. I became the house piano player for Jackie; he used me on one date and he liked me so he used me for a lot of dates. It was a standard rhythm section, with me, A.T. [Arthur Taylor] on drums, and Doug Watkins on bass. We made many records that way. And every time I'd meet different musicians I'd increase my knowlege of the art, so that I kept going, going, going.

"And then I was writing arrangements for the groups. I was very busy. I would stay up all night long. I lived in St. Albans, out on Long Island, at that time, and I'd write music all night long and then I'd bring it in to the date, go out to Hackensack, and we'd make the recording all day long. Then I'd have some dinner and come back home. I composed making the rides back and forth in the car. I wasn't driving, so I'd write it out when I'd hear it, sitting in the car. I'd work out some of the changes and then when I'd get to the piano I'd finish it off. Then I'd write some more music. The next day, same thing.

"Well, it came about again through a snowball effect," Waldron explained, alluding to his association with Billie Holiday, "because Billie was in Philadelphia and she needed a piano player on short notice. I think the piano player just wasn't functioning. So she asked William Dufty, who had written a book with her, and Bill asked Nellie Monk and Nellie asked Julian Euell and Euell asked me. And the buck stopped with me, of course. I said, yes, and I went to Philadelphia and we hit it off right away.

"Billie was a very, very relaxed person, and very musical, with this naturalness, because she wasn't a studied musician. She didn't tell you the changes, A flat to B flat, nothing like that, but she could *hear* them and she would know when you were doin' it right and when you were doin' it wrong. We went to Europe in 1958. It was easier on *all* the musicians over there. It was like the other side of the coin over there." Waldron added that when Billie returned to the United States, it was "sharp, yeah, *ultra*-sharp for her," alluding to her drug bust and death the next year.

"Well, it's always different," he continued, the context now being his accompaniment of Abbey Lincoln and other singers, "it's always different. Even between soloists it's different, even between musicians it's different; it always changes. That's what's so interesting about the music; it's always changing, never the same. Relationships are never the same; even between the same musicians, relationships change from day to day." He added that going from Billie to Abbey presented no problem because "there's a direct line between them."

In the early 1960s he worked a while with Eric Dolphy. "He had his own area, too, and it was a very interesting area. I learned a lot from him, and I learned a lot from Booker Little.

"I was over there in 1958 with Billie," Mal said about the beginning of a lengthy stay abroad, "but that was to just sample the water, to see if it was better over there. Yeah, it was warmer, so I decided to make the change as soon as I could. Then in 1965 Marcel Carné came to New York City. He had heard the score I did for *The Cool World* and he liked the music. He was going to do a film called *Trois chambres à Manhattan*, a Georges Simenon book, and he wanted me to write the score for it. He asked me if I wanted to do it in New York or Paris. I said, "*Paris, of course!*" So I went back to Paris—and then I stayed. I had to come back at the end of 1965 to finish up the score for *Sweet Love, Bitter* for Herbert Danska; it starred Dick Gregory and was a Charlie Parker–inspired story. Very interesting film.

"It was very free and relaxed in Europe. I could do anything I wanted to do. I didn't have to think about money, I didn't have to think about packaging my art or selling it; I just played and money automatically came in. There was no shortage of work. I had a chance to do composing for films—short films twenty minutes long; I did many of those in Paris. I played on some sound tracks. I also did concerts, many festivals, and clubs, of course. And teaching was an income, from private lessons."

The audiences were "very big, very big. They respected me and they turned out in numbers. I never worked in my back yard. I used a place where I lived as a home base and I got all my mail and contacts there, then I would work *other* places. Always kept traveling. I think the musician has to be a born gypsy because he can't stay in one place. He has to take the music where it's needed, and where it's needed is always shifting. I've been pretty much all over Europe, and all over Japan, too."

Among the musicians whom Waldron hooked up with in Europe were Steve Lacy, Jimmy Woode, Johnny Griffin, Benny Bailey, and Archie Shepp. All except Shepp have settled in Europe for extended stays.

"I had this record that was very popular in Japan in 1969, *Left Alone*. It won a Gold Disc award, and that record has been selling steadily in Japan ever since. I got coverage from it and was invited to come over there in 1970, just to see the country for two weeks, by *Swing Journal*. At that time I made two records, *Tokyo Reverie* and *Tokyo Bound*, two Japanese records. Then they set me up for tours every year after that, '71, '72, '73, '75, '76, '77, '79, like that, and I kept coming back for larger tours. For example, I did two weeks the first time, then one month and two months and three months, practically every year, right up to the present. I'm very well known there.

"Oh, the audiences are fantastic. You feel the air comin' at you and you have to lean forward. Otherwise, if you stand up straight, you go backward! Japan has the best audiences in the world because there most of the people know about jazz and they love jazz. About 90 percent of the people there know about jazz—the largest percentage of *any* country. Well, it's because of the way they're educated. They have coffee shops all over Japan where, for the price of a cup of coffee, you can hear any record that you want to hear. You just fill out a form and tell 'em what you want to hear and they have all the records there; every coffee shop has millions of records and they play them for you. One coffee shop is called the Mingus.

"I think jazz is a mirror on the world today and it has to be spontaneous to keep that relationship. That's why I don't practice; if you do, then you play the thing you practice, and that has nothing to do with what's happening right now. That's what's happening before, when you were practicing. So I try not to practice and I just come out on the stage and respond to what's happening right at that moment, to what's important to me now. That's where the art of jazz is coming from.

"We speak to each other—it's like a language—and as long as you have the same vocabulary you can speak with any other musicians. The vocabulary consists of rhythm, harmony, melody, form, and all of the riffs and everything in the past of music. It's all part of your vocabulary. When you hear it, you respond to it, you talk to each other."

In 1976, I had pianist Terry Waldo and singer Edith Wilson as guests on my radio show *"I Thought I Heard Buddy Bolden say . . ."* They had perfomed in duo for the Folklore Society of Greater Washington the night before. A profile of Edith Wilson, who died in 1981, appears in the Singers chapter.

"I started playing ragtime in the seventh grade and picking up Scott Joplin rags," Terry Waldo began his portion of my show. "At that time there were only a few people in the country who were collecting all that music and you could only get 'em by photocopy, most of them. I did my stint at Shakey's Pizza Parlor—five years of that. I suffered for my art. Maybe it was ten years at Shakey's. There was the red garters and all that sort of thing. And I was going to school for most of that time; I got my master's degree in communications, and I made movies for a while. I discovered that the piano and the music were doing better for me. I even got a grant a couple of years ago to do a radio series for National Public Radio. I continued to play and emerged as kind of an authority. I'm just finishing a book right now that is going to be published in the fall called *This Is Ragtime*.

"I was born in Ironton, Ohio. Lemme explain Ironton. Up until a few years ago, Ironton was in the *Guinness Book of World Records* as having more bars per square block than any other city in the world. That was its main claim to fame and I was raised there. But, fortunately, two doors down from me there was a couple who must have had the only classical records in the city. They had a record collection of 78s. Until I was about four years old I was listening to classical music as well as Spike Jones. And that was really the first influence. Then I heard several people play ragtime, and Dixieland, and different things, and I got ahold of the sheet music for 'Maple Leaf Rag.' That must have been 1957. Everybody used to kid me, decided I was a cornball at the time; they thought I should be gettin' with what was happenin'—Stan Kenton and all that sort of thing. Anyway, I stuck with it and played the stuff and came out playin', I think, pretty well after a while.

"I used to play 'The Entertainer' in Shakey's and people would throw pizzas at you. This was a few years before *The Sting* came out. You'd fight off these little kids. Their parents would send them up with greasy pizza fingers to sit on the piano bench and bother the musician. In fact, I even made a little film about it. You'd be playing with song slides where half of them wouldn't work. I had six notes that did not play at all on a piano one time. And I was tryin' to play classical rags, which just did not go over at that time, in the '60s. Now they go over.

"One of them is called 'Spanish Venus' and it was written by Luckey Roberts. Luckey never wrote it down, but Eubie Blake knew how to play it and he showed me how to play this thing by hand, a measure at a time. So I guess Eubie and I are the only ones that know how to play it."

Terry continued, "When I was in high school and college there was a band working out of Dayton, Ohio, that I used to play with— Gene Mayl's Dixieland Rhythm Kings. Gene had been playing since the '40s; he'd made about twenty albums at different times. There wasn't a whole lot hapening in the late '50s and '60s; there weren't that many bands you could work with, but I had the chance to do that with Gene. Then I spent some time out in California and worked with Turk Murphy, playing intermission piano, and with a couple of other bands out there. I lived in New Orleans for a summer, played with just about all the musicians down there, sat in at Preservation Hall every once in a while, worked with Johnny Wiggs, Frog Joseph.

"Ragtime is a difficult thing to categorize. I maintain that it has to swing and that it's a thoroughly Afro-American tradition. What Scott Joplin was doing was codifying a lot of these improvisations into music, and the European notational system doesn't work very well to do that. I know because I wrote a bunch of Eubie's music for publication in a folio of his rags that I transcribed. I tried to get a real nuance, and you can't do it because the European system does not have the means of putting down, first of all, the subtleties of accents. We don't have any way of doing that or the *very* subtle rhythmic variations. First of all, African music was additive in its rhythmic concepts. Where we think of measures—a quarter note, a half note, an eighth note, that sort of thing, dividing a measure—in an African system, it's adding one beat on top of another rhythm. That's polyrhythm, and when all of this is combined it's pretty hard to write down.

"I was in New York playing at a place and I was approached by RCA and Columbia, both the same day," Waldo went on, commenting on whether the "ragtime fad" had peaked. "For sure it has. This was about a year ago. John Hammond had gotten in touch with me and wanted me to record. I'm very sorry the way this turned out. RCA Classical Division wanted me to do a ten-record set for the bicentennial—a complete history of ragtime, including all of Scott Joplin's things. John Hammond said that Columbia could beat that. And Hammond's word, I guess, was pretty reputable, I thought. So I did not go with RCA. In the meantime, RCA got Dick Hyman to do the thing. Columbia never came through. The Bruce Springsteen furor was coming and suddenly there was a note from the top offices that said, 'We are not hiring anybody with any long-term contracts for more than one album.' Then Hammond was sick for three weeks and di-da-di-da-di-da. By the time we got it straightened up, ragtime was a dead issue.

"I haven't noticed I've been making any money on it," he continued with a sigh as the interview moved into a discussion of whether traditional jazz had made it onto the coattails of the ragtime boom. "They tried to do the same thing with Jelly Roll Morton that they did with Scott Joplin and it didn't work. And in New York they're giving these concerts of Bix Beiderbecke things; they're writing out all of his solos, note for note, and they're gonna put 'em in an archive some place and say, 'This is the correct way to play Bix solos.' They're going to do that with Duke Ellington, too. I can't understand this. It's a different tradition. We're talking about improvisation. Ad lib is a key factor here, and I think they're losing sight of that and missing half of it.

"I have a love/hate relationship with Dixieland audiences. A lot of times they'll say, 'I like Dixieland and I don't care whether it's good or bad as long as you have a banjo and tuba clankin' away, but I don't like roll 'n' roll,' or, 'I don't like anything else.' I like good music wherever it is. There're so many people who seem locked into this nostalgia thing and saying the music in an older time was better. I don't believe that. I like the older stuff and I like ragtime and I've had a lot of fun with it because you can be creative within that medium. Also, an awful lot of things have not been touched. I keep coming into a lot of music that has not been played. There's a wealth of material, so it's challenging to me in that sense.

"I'm anxious to get back into performing but I've been kind of slowed. My band costs so much money to get together, guys from all over the country, that we haven't played in a long time. In fact, my trombone player's up in Toronto right now and my drummer's in Chicago, and I got a banjo player in Youngstown, Ohio. When we get together to play a concert, we usually record the stuff and we'll issue some things, which is what we played here on your show earlier."

Terry Waldo continues to perform into the third millennium as a soloist and with his own Gutbucket Syncopators, Fred Starr's Louisiana Repertory Jazz Ensemble, and other bands.

In the mid-1980s, Oliphant did a caricature of John Eaton at the piano that captures one side of his musical persona, for his demeanor is one of utter seriousness. He is apparently in deep concentration and is totally involved in what he is playing. Turn to the photo section of this volume and you get an indication of the other side, his sense of humor and his wit. This is expressed in both his piano playing and in his verbal asides between—sometimes within—selections.

Graduating cum laude from Yale University in 1956, Eaton dropped out of Georgetown University graduate school in the late 1950s to earn his living as a pianist. And he has done very well at it. There is scarcely a piano bar in Washington, D.C., that has not been graced with his talent. He was a member of the house band of Blues Alley in the 1960s; he has traveled the club, concert, and festival circuit; he has released a number of extremely well-received albums in solo format; and he has recorded and/or appeared live in the combos of many others, including such jazz legends as Wild Bill Davison, Benny Carter, Zoot Sims, and Clark Terry. Among his many honors was his election to the Steinway Concert Artists roster in 1996.

In 1960, he began studying with the renowned classical teacher Alexander Lipsky. For a quarter of a century after that he continued his classical studies and also instructed in the classical idiom. He has performed at the White House and at major performing arts centers, colleges and universities, civic events, and arts festivals. Accolades abound from George Shearing, Nat Hentoff, John S. Wilson, and Marian McPartland—among others.

John Eaton is one of the major scholars on the Great American Songbook and its composers. A series he offered on that subject for a dozen or so seasons at the Smithsonian Institution was always sold out in advance. He is also a leading authority on the stride pianists who were a major influence on Art Tatum, Earl Hines, Thelonious Monk, and others who helped move the jazz idiom into its modern era.

I talked with Eaton in the early 1980s, when he was participating in that year's Kool Jazz Festival in the Kennedy Center. "It's not a question of traditional versus modern," he insisted. He should know, for his repertoire covers the spectrum from Scott Joplin to Bud Powell. "It's a matter of doing what you're comfortable with, and if you do what you're comfortable with, it always sounds fresh. You never run out of ideas. The longer I do it, the more I feel that I have to give my best every night."

An indication of the breadth of John's scholarship was his appearance at Buffalo's Chautauqua a decade ago. *Buffalo News* critic Herman Trotter went on record that he "held Amphitheater audiences spellbound for two days with lecture-recitals exploring the relative importance of music and text in establishing a popular song as an enduring 'classic.'" Trotter wrote that "Eaton's style springs from thorough classical training and is marked by mind-boggling harmonic inventiveness, easy rhythmic freedom, and absolute fidelity to the composer's spirit."

In a wide-ranging discussion in the mid-1980s when he was preparing for a Smithsonian concert on the stride tradition, John Eaton talked with me at length about several of his favorite pianists of that genre.

"Some ticklers would sit sideways," he began, "and go on chatting with friends nearby. It took a lot of practice to play this way. Then without stopping the smart talk or turning back to the piano, they'd *attack* without any warning, smashing right into the regular beat of the piece."

Implicit in that description is the essence of a musical form that derives from ragtime and came into being in the early years of the past century as the entertainment staple of Harlem rent parties and saloons and which, handed down over the decades, remains an element in the playing of all jazz keyboardists. First, there is the showmanship, then the virtuosity, and finally the irresistible momentum of the stride style's seesawing chord-and-single-note rhythms in the left hand and the against-the-beat melodic figures of the right.

"I don't have any idea what John is going to do tonight," the Smithsonian Institution's Martin Williams confessed to me, "but I'm in favor of it. John has such an audience, what you do is open the door and stand back."

John Eaton told me that he planned, at the start, to "give a short demonstration of what stride piano is—and what it is not," citing the then popular piano style of George Winston as a glaring example of the latter.

"I'm going to talk about the indelible influence the whole school of stride players has had on my playing and on my view of popular music and jazz. They were marvelous pianists and they were pianistic players, as opposed to players who sort of made music in spite of the piano. I admire them all as pianists and, second, I admire them as entertainers. They realized that music, to be worth anything, has got to be communicated to the audience. Otherwise, what's the use of it?

"And that's not the same as pandering to the audience; it's recognizing the truth of the old cliché, when the music makes the circuit through the interpreter to the audience and back to the interpreter, that's when it becomes music.

"There was nothing, ever, undignified about what they did. I think that in Fats Waller's case he was a born entertainer, a born clown, so it was spontaneous humor—as Martin Williams says, humor 'in the offhand.' As with all great clowns, there was a hidden serious side of it, too. You don't have to get too analytical about it but obviously the face of the clown always masks a serious issue; with Fats, a lot of it, without getting too sociological, had to do with the plight of the black artist in our culture. When Fats made fun of music, he was making fun of our culture. Also, it was a release for him.

"Willie the Lion Smith was the only one I knew personally; the others were all dead by then, so I'm going to spend some time on him. They're all lumped together as Harlem stride pianists, but they were all utterly different. They obviously learned from one another and there are certain basic similarities in style. Even though Fats owed a tremendous amount to James P. Johnson—and James P. was the first—you put them back to back and you can hear the difference. James P. was more ragtime oriented; he was 'the eastern version of ragtime,' which is Dick Wellstood's statement. And of course Fats was a show-business personality; this is reflected in his playing. His style is more harmonically sophisticated, perhaps, and that's also true of the Lion.

"The Lion was a major influence on Duke Ellington, and in a strange way, he was a major influence on Thelonious Monk. I'm not sure Monk ever heard the Lion, much, but you can hear it in his playing. When I heard the Lion I heard Harlem stride piano for sure, but I also heard somebody who did things that Fats *or* James P. wouldn't do. A lot of what the Lion did was not robust playing, although he was capable of that. A lot was very subtle and harmonically intricate. Not that Fats wasn't that, too, but the Lion had a certain maverick, unconventional quality that doesn't appear in Fats at all, and that sets the Lion apart. Of course, he was also a marvelous entertainer and personality. He did not have the comic genius of Fats Waller, but he had that same old-time show business approach, that love of the audience. Stride is definitely a style, but with James P., Luckey Roberts, Fats, and the Lion, you have four stride pianists, and they're all different. It's not a confining style."

Then Eaton said, "I'm going to touch on all of them as composers. Fats wrote popular songs in the conventional idiom and James P. and the Lion took a crack at that, too. And Luckey Roberts wrote 'Ripple on the Nile,' which became 'Moonlight Cocktail.' They were also composers in the sense that they—and this is not necessarily true of composers today—were *careful* composers; they realized that the substance of what was being communicated had to do with the craftsmanship and thoughtfulness that went into the writing of the piece. It wasn't just a matter of loosely writing some riffs on which to improvise, which is another sort of composing. Their piano compositions have real structure, but they're not stiff or contrived. They wrote as composers. That's what composing music means. It isn't just sort of doing some stream-of-consciousness pseudo-inspirational activity. Even though it was for popular consumption, they were careful.

"Finally, in Fats's work particularly, there was always the implication that whatever he wrote could be used as the basis for jazz improvisation. That isn't true, or even implicitly true, of Jerome Kern or George Gershwin or Irving Berlin. Although their songs are the grist of the jazz performer's mill, they weren't composed for that purpose. With Fats, the stuff was written as sort of quasi-formal composition and yet the chord structure implies that it could immediately be used as the basis for improvisation. And of course he did that himself, he used it for that."

"You ask me how things are going," Ramsey Lewis responded to my opening question as we took seats in the restaurant of the Georgetown Inn; it was less than a block from Blues Alley, where the pianist was that week in residence with his combo. "I'm just excited to think that I've been playing Washington, D.C., since the very early 1960s. First place I played here was Abart's International Jazz Mecca. It was a little place upstairs and they had obviously gutted an apartment and made it just one suite. Maybe they could seat a hundred people in the whole thing. But anyway, here it is almost 1990, and we're selling out shows. I played there at Abart's at least three or four times, then we finally graduated in 1964 to Bohemian Caverns. In fact, that's where *The In Crowd* was recorded.

"Lucille was my older sister," Lewis began the saga that would hold me spellbound for the next two hours. "My father said to her, 'You're going to take piano lessons.' She was six or seven; I was four. And I'm playing on the floor or something. I said, 'She gets to do *what*?' It's as if my father said, 'Well, she's going to go to the circus, she's going to go to a movie.' I said, 'Oh, *I* gotta go, *I* gotta go!' I could care less about piano; it's just she's goin' to get to do something. He says, 'No, I can only afford one person.' Lessons were fifty cents. But in those days fifty cents bought a lot of food. I just cried and cried. He says, 'Okay, okay!' I went to two lessons and I found that you're supposed to practice. So I said, 'Dad, I don't think I want to take piano lessons.' Little did I know that after several lessons the piano teacher said, 'Well, Lucille has a lot of talent. We can't put our finger on it yet but I don't think it's for piano. However, little Ramsey, we think he might have something." He laughed. "That was the worst thing I could have heard! I loved the idea of playing the piano but I hated the idea of practicing. So, from four years old to about eleven years old, it was a hardship.

"I started taking piano lessons from our church organist. She said she'd taught me as much as she could, so it's time she took me down to the conservatory. I started studying with Dorothy Mendelssohn at eleven years old and her approach was a bit different. It was about developing technique but the technique was only a means to reach in. She started talking about things like listening with your inner ear, making the piano tones sing. Make a piano tone *sing*? I mean, you know, eleven, twelve years old, make it *sing*? Yes, more legato; think of a voice. I started getting interested and curious about this thing and by the time I'm thirteen, fourteen, Mom and Dad had to say, at eleven, twelve o'clock at night, 'You got to stop practicing. You go on and get some sleep. You've been practicing all afternoon, and all evening!' I had decided that I would concertize and play Bach, Beethoven, European classical music around the world.

"I started being curious about all kinds of music. My peers were into pop music and so I loved it, too. Pop music of that day was Nat Cole and Dinah Washington—really good stuff. Then I remember Dad coming home with some 78s of the Art Tatum Trio, Teddy Wilson, Dorothy Donegan, Meade Lux Lewis, Maurice Rocco, Erroll Garner, Duke Ellington. And he said, 'Listen to this stuff.' And it really blew me away. I didn't quite know what they were doing but it was enticing.

"I played gospel music from nine years old to fifteen for our church. So in those impressionable years, we're talking European classical music, we're talking really into pop music of that day, we're talking gospel, which is the other side of the blues. By the time I'm fifteen I'm playing at another church and there's not only a piano but there's an organist. He was a college student and he had a band, Cleffs. If I was sixteen, Wallace Burton must have been nineteen. And he said, "We need a piano player; you want to play in our band?' I said, 'Sure.' He says, 'There's no time for rehearsal so just meet us Friday night at Southwest Temple,' where they had week-end dances for high school and college kids. I got there and he says, 'Well, we're just going to play some standards and some blues, you know, just easy stuff." Still didn't faze me. So we got up on the stage, he says, 'Okay, we'll play blues in D flat, about like this.'" Ramsey snapped his fingers in imitation. "'Ramsey, start it off.' I cut out into the meanest boogie woogie you'll ever know! Wallace turns around and says, 'Wait, wait, wait! Lay out!'" Ramsey burst into laughter. "I thought they were going to do a Charlie Parker tune or somethin', based on the blues.

"After the job, Wallace said, 'Those jazz records your dad got you, listen to what they're doing. See what *they* do on the blues, and go get some Oscar Peterson, get some more Erroll Garner, get some Nat Cole, just get some piano players. See what they do on those standards and try to imitate 'em.'

"So at fifteen I started this association with Cleffs, a seven-piece band, and from fifteen until eighteen we played around Chicago. I got better and better at imitating many, many piano players, not specifically, but if you listened to me you might hear the bridge sound like Erroll Garner and the out-chorus sound like Nat Cole and part of the solo be imitating what I could of Oscar Peterson.

But by my late teens, early twenties, I think I must have started coming into my own.

"The Korean War broke the band up 'cause the guys were a bit older than I, but it left the rhythm section—Eldee Young, Redd Holt, myself. We did our first record in 1956.

"And what *really* blew me away was after the record came out, which is maybe a year later, people heard it and they said, 'You really have a style of your own.' Blew me away! I knew how I worked at trying to get all these influences, but what I didn't know, what had emerged, was the classical influence, the gospel influence, and using jazz only as a means to express myself. 'Cause I had *not* studied the bebop vocabulary. Nobody told me to. I *loved* Charlie Parker, but what he was actually doing I just couldn't work it out. I loved Bud Powell, but for some reason the romanticism of Erroll Garner, Oscar Peterson, and George Shearing was more attractive to me. People said, 'I recognize you,' and I said, 'You *can*? You mean, I don't sound like whoever?' 'No! Sounds like *you*.' That was sixty-some-odd albums ago.

"An early influence that I should not leave out was the Modern Jazz Quartet. Because of my classical training they were *very* influential, especially John Lewis, his writing technique and his arrangements, his use of dynamics, and his use of *space*. I was also influenced—you talk about use of space—by Ahmad Jamal. I didn't get the courage to even *try* to figure out what Art Tatum was doing. Although I had had his records for ten years and listened to them, I never sat down and tried to figure it out. But it must have made an indelible impression because now I hear, every now and then, some influences from him in some of the things I do. Especially when I play solo.

"We played the Bohemian Caverns in 1964 for the first time and we recorded there. I think it was our first live recording. The so-called pop tune of the album was a song called 'Something You've Got.' What was neat about it was the people knew the song, and audience participation started happening. We didn't prompt them; we just played the song and they knew it and they started singing along with it. So that's when we started calling those kinds of things 'fun songs.' It was fun to have the audience just chime in.

"A year later we came back to Bohemian Caverns and said, 'Let's record there again!' So we did and we had space for one more song. Neddie Gray, who was here in Washington, D.C., and working at coffee shops, said, 'What're you guys doing?' We said, 'We need one more song!' 'What kind of song?' I said, 'You know, some pop song or rhythm-and-blues.' She says, 'Well, do you have Dobie Gray's "The 'In' Crowd"? It's on the jukebox.' She played it, we listened. So I said, 'Yeah, that'll work.' So I bought the record and wrote out the chord changes. That was on a Monday and we started rehearsing that Thursday. And it felt good. It was simple and we just wanted something simple.

"That night when we got to this song we noticed almost immediately that the audience started clapping. And we looked at each other, like, 'Should we play this thing?' So Friday we played it a little longer, and we did the same thing Saturday, not knowing anything of what would happen in the future regarding this song. It's just that it was fun for people, fun for us. We put the album together. It was the seventeenth album, by the way, with Cleffs. In those days you put out one every six months, almost like clockwork. We released it and went on the road. In July or August, we got a call from Phil Chess, he says—we were in Detroit—he says, 'You guys, it's like we've got a hit.' 'We do?' 'That album.' 'Well, what song? Is it the blues ballad, was it the Charlie Parker song?' He says, 'No, it's "The 'In' Crowd"!' We said, '"The *In* Crowd!" You mean we did all that work on those other songs and—!' He says, 'Yeah! They really buyin' that thing!' It sold a million copies! At the height of it the album was among the top five on the *Billboard* pop chart, holding company with none other than the Beatles, Elvis Presley, and I don't know who else. I mean, it just *totally* blew me away. They're putting out a reissue next year, which will be the twenty-fifth anniversary of its original release.

"The group had broken up now. 'The "In" Crowd' was too much for us. Success, we couldn't handle it. Up until 'The "In" Crowd' we're inseparable, we're more than brothers, one for all, all for one. With that song all the popularity, fame, and fortune, we couldn't live with each other. I mean, I didn't like *his* deodorant, *he* didn't like the color of *my* shoes. 'Why do you wear your hair like that?' You know what I mean? It just got picky, picky, picky. It got to the point that it wasn't fun any more and getting ready to go work at night was, like"—Ramsey made a gagging sound—"'Not *this* again!' Then the nights became long. An hour set seemed like it would go on for da-a-ays and da-a-ays. Finally, I was the first one to say, 'Hey! If it ain't fun why do it?' So we broke up in January '66 and called it quits."

Ramsey Lewis formed another trio with bassist Cleveland Eaton and drummer Maurice White. They worked up "Wade in the Water" and again they found themselves with a hit on their hands. Not long after, an album the former trio had recorded at Howard Rumsey's Lighthouse in L.A. was released and that version of the McCoys' "Hang on Sloopy" also took off.

"So at the end of a twelve-month period we had three really big crossover albums and singles. I mean, it was just great going for a while. It's a fine line you tread between art and commercialism. Commercialism is not a bad word because it's what the American market is all about. It's what *America's* about. And when you sign with a record company *they* expect you to sell some records. You don't sign with them and say, 'Now, don't expect me to sell any records.' They'd think you're crazy. So you're always saying, 'What do I artistically, pianistically want to get across to the audience? What can we arrange in such a way as to maintain our professional and artistic integrity, but the record company can feel that it's something they can get their teeth into and go out and market?' There probably were times when I went too far in either direction. Some albums were a little too artistic, to the point that there was nothing there for radio to play or for the company to market. On the other hand, maybe a couple of times I went totally over to try to get air play and please the company. But out of sixty-some albums, I'd say in well over half I was very gratified in being able to straddle that fence of pleasing both worlds, not losing my sense of integrity in the so-called commercial songs.

"I met Billy Taylor at the very first recording session I ever did. He came by to wish us well. I'd always admired him and he was one of the pianists whose records I bought early on. His technique, his sense of melodic lines and harmony, and his piano tone—he has one of those good piano tones. I'm *always* looking for things to do that I haven't done, or a different way to do something I *have* done. So I'm talking to CBS and they say, 'What about two pianos?' I said, 'Now that's an idea.'

"So I called Billy Taylor and he says, 'Hey, how you been doing? I want you to be on my show.' I said, 'Great!' Came to New York and we were supposed to do enough material for a half hour and of course we did enough for an hour or more. I mean, we just got on so beautifully that, in fact, during the interview on the show we both said maybe we should do an album—sort of jokingly, but honestly. And afterward, we talked about it and we figured that at some point in the future we would do that. But our schedules and what have you just didn't work out. Meanwhile, I signed with CBS Masterworks and I did another album with James Mack with the London Philharmonia called *Classic Encounter*. I could say that album—no work of art is perfect, to the artist—is one of the several of the sixty-odd albums I've done that came close to what I really wanted to say.

"Then CBS Masterworks called me and said, 'What do you want to do for your next album?' Well, by now Billy Taylor and I *have* gotten with each other and we'd started playing some concerts. That was going so well, I said to CBS Masterworks, 'I want to do a two-piano album.' 'You do?' I said, 'Yeah.' They said, 'Who with?' I said, 'Billy Taylor.' 'Great! But we have to have a concept. What's the concept?' I called Billy. He says, 'Well, we sort of already have a concept.' I said, 'What?' He said, 'On our tour we were playing great compositions written by great pianists who also happened to be great composers.' I said, 'You're right! There's the concept!' I called CBS back. I said, 'Here's the concept.' They say, 'I love it!' I called Chick Corea and he says, 'I'll write something for you!' It's called 'We Meet Again.' That's the name of the album. So we ended up doing pieces by Duke Ellington, Bill Evans, Denny Zeitlin, Oscar Peterson, and Chick.

"I feel that it's healthy," Ramsey Lewis said, assessing the state of the jazz scene near the century's final decade. "It's healthy in that the categories and the boundaries are falling. You no longer have to be pigeonholed. The consumer is very open-minded, very sophisticated; listeners feel it's not so much *what* you do, but the sincerity and conviction and commitment with which you do it. And that is a ray of light on the situation. I think it's healthy because more and more young people are studying the music, learning the music, performing the music, being interested in the music. I think it's healthy because smaller jazz labels have proven that you can go out and just do an album, a concept album, and people will buy it. Of course, CDs have helped this a lot, too, and reissues have never been more plentiful. People are goin' in the stores and buying jazz of the '50s, '60s, and '70s like never before! Catalogue is selling—*my* catalogue! They're saying, 'We don't know who you are but you're out there!'

"America is just now beginning to respect and appreciate its own original music, jazz, on the level that it's appreciated at in Europe and Japan. It's *beginning* to get there. The European audience takes jazz seriously; they take the music seriously; they take the performers seriously—and the same with the Japanese audience. There's not as much participation or words of encouragement *during* a performance, but at the end of the performance, all hell breaks loose. I'll never forget the first time we played Japan. In America, you know, you're used to, 'Go on! Yeah, man! Aw*right* !' We open with a blockbuster, hit 'em right in the middle of the nose and chops, knock the shit out of 'em! So we open like that with a high-energy piece and, man, you could hear a pin drop. But at the end of the piece it was, 'Ra-a-a-a-ah!' standing ovation, encores, people lined up outside the stage door with their markers and special autograph cardboard, and they say things like, 'The record you did six years ago with so-and-so and the engineer was so-and-so,' and they name the songs and say, 'I liked the way you played on the bridge.' They're *into* the *music* ! I was just totally blown away! America's just beginning to get to this point.

"For all too long the music was known as whorehouse music, smoky barroom music that you only hear in black neighborhoods, or music that you knock three times and say, 'Joe sent me.' The music has overcome that stigma. I think it's finally beginning to overcome the fact that it was spawned by black people. I think the fact that the music originated from black culture held it back a long time. I mean, America just hasn't been ready to say, 'This music, which is typically American, speaks for and to our country and it came from black people.' I think maybe one of the reasons attitudes are changing is that now there are as many whites, Asians, and Latinos that play jazz as black people.

"It's not only a workshop in rehearsal," Ramsey Lewis said of his current combo, "it's a workshop on stage, and I think that accounts for the electricity in the air. The audience doesn't know—but they feel—that something is happening before their very eyes. Sometimes they see us crack up on stage, because we had been trying it and it came off and it worked and it's fun for us and fun for the audience. And I think that's what it's all about. Being serious about what you're doing, but in the end, was it gratifying?"

A year ago, Sumi Tonooka opened the third evening of the fourth annual Mary Lou Williams Women in Jazz Festival in the Kennedy Center, Washington, D.C., with a discursive romp through her composition "In the Void." On bass was the preeminent Ray Drummond and at the drums, Allison Miller. Drummond I had heard many times in various contexts at the One Step Down, Washington, D.C., and at festivals overseas; I used to catch Miller at D.C.'s Twins with She-Bop, until she relocated in the late 1990s to New York, where she soon began getting many gigs and establishing herself as a drummer to watch.

The next selection, "Susumu," had oriental chime-like effects. Sumi Tonooka then took a few minutes to tell the audience in the packed Terrace Theater how thrilled she was that it was Mary Lou Williams's birthday and went on to recall her lessons, at age eighteen, with the great pianist and composer. "I would take the train from Philly up to New York and then the subway to Harlem. She would say, 'Come on, sit here' on the bench beside her and she would play for me. She didn't say much, just played, showed me things about harmony and so forth." Sumi said her exposure to Mary Lou for those months had "a tremendous impact" on her life and on her music. I went backstage during intermission and complimented her on her brilliant set.

My interview with Sumi Tonooka took place in her room at the State Plaza hotel, Washington, D.C., in 1993. She was in town for a Friday and Saturday gig at the One Step Down. The first order of business, for her, was for me to autograph her copy of my 1991 *The Jazz Scene*. The account of her life that she provided in the interview was supplemented by several later conversations and letters.

"My mother, Emiko Tonooka, was born and raised on Bainbridge Island, Washington State," she began. "I was born in Philadelphia. My mother came to Philly after she got out of the internment camps. My mother is Japanese-American and my grandparents are

Japanese from Japan. And they were all interned—imprisoned—during World War II. She came to Philadelphia with a group of other young women because it was 'this City of Brotherly Love' and they liked the way that sounded.

"Over a hundred thousand Japanese Americans, and Japanese, from up and down the entire West Coast were put behind barbed wire in that period. It was in Manzanar.

"My biggest piece of music uses that as its subject matter. It's called *Out from the Silence*. It's about an hour in length and combines Japanese instruments—shakuhachi and koto—with jazz instruments—clarinet, trombone, trumpet, saxophone, violin, piano, bass, drums, vibes, and percussion—as well as my mother, who's the narrator. Each piece is based on a poem or on prose that was written by a Japanese American who'd been interned, from each generation. I got the idea from accompanying my mother when she testified at the hearings, when Congress did the redress hearings six or seven years ago in New York and in California. That day was really moving because I heard all these people's personal accounts as to what had happened to them and how that experience affected their lives. I was really moved and I wanted to do something. It occurrred to me that day as I was listening to their stories that each generation was represented. They had the Issei like my grandparents, from Japan; and then the Nisei [first-generation American born], and the Sansei [second-generation American born]. The way each generation experienced the internment was very different. The Japanese from Japan were sort of more steadfast about it, and the Nisei were just beginning to talk about it, and their emotions were just starting to surface. Then the Sansei, which is my generation, were very angry and adamant. So I tried to show that in the music and I used their words to get into the music. That's really the biggest thing that I've ever done.

"In the hearing, each person was allowed to speak for no more than five minutes. So my mom had to prepare this speech. She had actually confronted a lot of this earlier on so she was ready to make that speech, because there was a film that was made on my mother and on her life and what had happened to her as a result of the camps. It was a half-hour documentary called *Emi*. The filmmaker took my mother back to Bainbridge Island, where she hadn't been since she'd been taken to the camps, and then he took her to the site of the camps. She told me it was like going through therapy on the film because she had never really confronted her experience before that. It was very emotional. She had had a nervous breakdown when she was in the camps. She was sixteen years old, very idealistic about this country and the Constitution of the United States, and she knew she was an American citizen and here she was imprisoned, put behind barbed wire, for four years. She was aware enough to know what was happening to her but no one was talking about it and she had this very bad reaction that left a scar for the rest of her life. My mom didn't really start to deal with it and we didn't really know what had happened to her until I was in my late teens. It was something she never talked about and I never was aware of until I got older.

"My mother was a real big jazz fan," Tonooka continued. "She liked all kinds of music, and the music that I heard in the house was very eclectic. But she really loved jazz and she had Fats Waller records and I remember listening to boogie woogie, and I really liked that; I liked the motion in the left hand and that rhythm and the feel. And also my mom had—I was really young—a Nina Simone record. My favorite song on it was 'I Want a Little Sugar in My Bowl.'" Sumi chuckled. "I remember hearing Thelonious Monk as a kid and I really liked his music. She exposed me to quite a bit at a young age, as early as I can remember, when I was about five, six, seven.

"When my mother was younger she *really* wanted to take piano lessons, but she came from a very poor home and they never could afford them. My grandfather was a farmer and my grandmother worked in a nursery. So my mother said, when she had kids, she was going to make sure they all got music lessons. So we all got that.

"I started taking lessons at Settlement Music School in Philadelphia. I took a music workshop where they introduced you to all the instruments in the orchestra and they taught a little bit about reading music and made it fun, like a game, so it was really nice. My teacher spotted me as being talented and told me I was ready to take lessons and I had to choose what instrument I wanted and I chose piano. I was seven or eight. My mom had a piano in the house and she sort of took a laid-back approach. She figured if I wanted to do it I would just gravitate toward it, which I did. I remember sitting at the piano and playing and creating sounds for stories that I would be making up—you know, sound effects, as I was telling stories. I would do this with my friends and it was like a way of playing.

"Both of my parents were really encouraging. My father is black American, from Camden, New Jersey, and he and my mother met during the McCarthy Era. They were both very radical and they met writing a leaflet together. I grew up in Powelton Village in Philadelphia, which is considered a Bohemian type of neighborhood—a lot of artists and musicians and people of all races and professions, mixed classes. My parents moved there because they were an interracial couple and they wanted us to grow up in an environment that would be comfortable for us. It was pretty good that way. They were very aware of those kinds of things. My father worked at Campbell Soup Company and he was very active in the unions there.

"It's funny, because at Settlement I was playing completely by ear and I fooled my teacher for a year and a half. She had no idea. One day she said, 'Sumi, where are you in the music?' And I was, like, 'Here? Here?' And she said, 'You're not reading! You've been playing by ear!' And I said, 'I guess I have been.' What would happen is she would play the piece for me and sometimes my mom would play the piece for me, too. So I would be just sort of copying. I didn't really understand how to read, not really; I didn't understand the basics. So the next year I was sent to a much stricter teacher from the old school, and she would probably have been a great teacher for me had I wanted to be a concert pianist. This teacher taught me how to read, but she also almost killed my desire to play the piano because she was *so* strict. And I remember after my first lesson, coming out in tears because she was"—Tonooka raised her voice in simulated harsh delivery—"'*What* are you *doing*? You *can't do* that! You don't know *anything* about music; we have to start you off from the *beginning*!' She didn't hit my hands, but basically, she was just hard, really hard. I was a little too sensitive for her style, I think, and I left her. My mom says she'll never forget this because I brought her a dozen roses to tell her—this is after I'd been studying with this teacher for a couple of years—that I was going to switch to another teacher. And that teacher was this sort of crazy wild musician Gary

Goldschneider, who played classical music but was also improvising a lot; he was into people like Keith Jarrett and he opened up some doors for me by introducing me to other ways of playing and looking at music.

"My parents broke up when I was thirteen. It was tough, really tough; we had some really hard times. My mom was a secretary at the University of Pennsylvania and we just went through some really, really rough times and, basically, we got through it. I finished up high school when I was about fifteen. I went to one of these '6os-type alternative schools that believed you could put your own program together, and I got myself enough credits to get out real early. Also, I think the year I spent with a tutor, Janet Abbey, really helped me, because during that year I got my first job, as a waitress at a Japanese restaurant. I learned about Japanese food and cooking and all that kind of stuff and, basically, how to make a living. Also, Janet was responsible for finding for me my piano teacher Gary Goldschneider.

"I think I was about ten years old when my mother took me to see Susan Starr, who's a very great classical pianist, at the Academy of Music. She must have been in her late teens then, maybe early twenties. Anyway, that impressed me because she was a woman musician. She was this tiny little person and she got up at the piano and she was an *incredible* pianist. I remember hearing her with the Philadelphia Orchestra, too. And I ended up studying with her when I went to college.

"Oh! That was really great," Sumi Tonooka responded when I asked her about seeing Monk at the Aqua Lounge on 52nd Street in Philadelphia when she was thirteen. "My mom took me and that was the night I really decided I wanted to be a jazz player. I just knew that I liked it, I knew that I liked the sounds. That was basically it. Monk was in quite a mood that night; he didn't feel like playing anything, just sat at the piano and kind of poked at it, didn't really do anything. We were waitin' there 'til the last set for him to really get in the mood, and he finally did and played an incredible version of ''Round about Midnight.' It was wonderful, it was real exciting, and his music was just great.

"I was always composing. That was my first love, that's what I started doing from the very beginning; but it wasn't until I got out of high school that I really started learning what I was doing, in terms of chords and the theory behind music and improvisation and whatnot. I knew at that age I really wanted to be a serious musician. I went to Boston and I was thinking about going to Berklee or the New England Conservatory and I decided not to. I decided I'd rather just learn from the source, being around music and musicians. Horace Silver's *Song for My Father*, I wore that record out; I loved it. Horace's playing and Joe Henderson's solo on that, I used to sing to it; I loved it. And Thelonious Monk. Who else? Nina Simone. Tryin' to remember if I was really into Bud Powell at that time. I don't think I was yet. I think that happened a little later.

"I studied with a woman by the name of Madame Chaloff in Boston, Serge Chaloff's mother. She's a great teacher. A lot of pianists studied with her. She taught a special technique. And she helped me. I met her when I went to Boston before I got out of school. She's, like, 'Oh, you must move here and I will help you,' and so I did that. I studied also with a man by the name of Charlie Banacus, who's a great teacher in the Boston area. He was a Lennie Tristano disciple and he really opened up a lot of stuff for me in terms of what to listen to. He's the first person to really introduce me to chords, in the formal sense, and theory—theory behind music and composition and all that kind of stuff. After I studied with him I was able to do a lot of other things, as I was learning a lot.

"When I left Philly I had $50 in my pocket. I went to Boston and I had a lot of different jobs. I worked as a waitress at this Japanese restaurant, and I ended up getting fired from that job; I was trying to organize the waitresses because we weren't getting any salary. I was a grill girl at Sears, I was a janitor at Harvard University, and all little odd jobs. It was ridiculous; I was very young and trying to survive and study music.

"I lived in Boston for about a year and I met some good musicians while I was there. At that time I was just really starting to learn how to play, but not on a professional level. I knew a lot of musicians and sort of immersed myself in the whole scene and I ended up learning a lot that way. My taste was now a lot broader. I liked a lot of Miles Davis, like *Kind of Blue*. I was listening to more Bud Powell and more bebop.

"And then I went to Detroit. I was seventeen and I met Marcus

Belgrave and people like that and that was really great. I started working the 'chitlin' circuit,' as they call it; I did some rhythm-and-blues gigs. Those were my first professional, starting-to-work gigs. I remember sitting in and playing John Coltrane's 'Impressions' and totally getting lost on the form, not understanding when it moved up to the next key and coming back again. Oh, God! I remember being so overwhelmed at how much there was to learn—and it never stops, you know; you just keep going.

"I was in Detroit off and on for about a year and a half. I was very young, I really was. But I was prepared—maybe more so than some people because my parents sort of pushed me to be pretty independent from an early age. But I *was* young. I look at my own children now, and if my daughter was doing what I did at my age, I don't think"—she laughed in a grim sort of way at the thought—"I'd be able to handle it. But the times were different then, too, in the '60s and '70s. It was a whole different environment, what people were doing, the openness. It was just totally different from what it is now.

"When I came back to Philadelphia in the early '70s I actually did my first professional gigs with my own trio. My first gig under my own name was at this place called the Zellerbach Theatre. I think we were doing a women's festival or something and I was playing a lot of my own music. I used a young man from Philadelphia named Larry McRae on bass and his brother Spike on drums. And I did a gig at the University of Pennsylvania where I used Rudy McDaniel, who's now known as Jamaaladeen Tacuma, and a drummer by the name of Newman Baker. That's also when I started working with Philly Joe Jones. I was going to Model Cities, a place that was a music community center. Odean Pope, Eddie Green, Tyrone Brown, and Sherman Ferguson—they were all teaching there. Marcus told me to go check it out. And I went there and they had a big band called the Catalyst that Odean conducted. I would go to the big band rehearsals, and I met some musicians there and that's when I started working around with my own name. I got a call from Philly Joe one night. I was on my way to go hear George Benson with Larry McRae, and Philly Joe called up and Larry says, 'Well! Philly Joe Jones! You gotta go! That's it!' He needed somebody on the spur of the moment. So I did that gig with him at this place called Trays in Philly, a jazz club in Germantown, and then I worked with him for about a year and a half after that. Matter of fact, we played here in Washington, but I can't remember where it was. I don't think, really, musically, that I was quite ready for it. There were a lot of things I didn't really have together, but Philly liked my compositions and I learned a lot from him, in a lot of ways.

"That's when I decided I'd go to college, to the Philadelphia College of Performing Arts. There were quite a few good players there, which was great. I was playing in the big band and writing and arranging for it and it was really pretty driving, as far as some of the students who were there and their professionalism. And I was also studying with Susan Starr. That experience was valuable to me because she got me away from just thinking about jazz; she got me into the piano, to really get as much music out of the piano as I could. I had this whole thing in my head, 'Oh, I'm a jazz musician, I can't play classical music!' But then I realized, 'Wait a minute, I *love* some of this music; why *not* play it?' She'd always say, 'Just approach it like you're approaching jazz; just play!' Once I broke through that I just started going with the classical music.

"I think it's better to learn tunes by ear. I think the tendency is when you *do* know how to read, to save time you'll go to the fake book and you get the chords or something. But I always try to listen to versions done by the masters, in terms of the tune and how it's done. I'm trying to learn more just by hearing them. One of the things I learned from Susan was that it's not about the notes on the paper; it's about the music. Once you get beyond learning the music and learning the piece and memorizing the piece, you still haven't really learned the music; you have to get beyond that.

"After I graduated I moved to New York. It took me a long time to get up the nerve. But that opened a whole new chapter. It's been really an interesting experience because it's through people that you meet people—through musicians and your contacts. I formed a fairly close relationship with Kenny Barron. Some of my first gigs there were at Cobi Narita's place, where a lot of people in my position were able to perform and do gigs under their own name. It's really tough to get work in the major clubs up there. You're competing with people who've been up there and have established themselves over long periods of time, and to work there steadily is very difficult.

"Before I went to college I kind of searched Mary Lou Williams out. Actually, it wasn't that difficult. I called her up on the phone and I told her I wanted to study with her and she was, like, 'Well, come on up and see me and, you know, we'll take it from there.' It was great. I mean, I went for my first lesson, and we sat at the piano together. Comin' into her place was pretty special because she was in the same apartment that she had been in for a long time. That was the place where Bud Powell and Monk and all those guys used to hang out with her and Dizzy and sit at the piano there. She had some kind of spinet, upright piano; there was just a lot of energy in her living space and around her as a person.

"She was very spiritual in her whole approach to music. She wasn't a technical teacher; she was more about tryin' to get you to watch her, or she'd have you listen to her play and you'd kind of get a feeling for what she was doing and then you worked together. At the first lesson, she asked me to play one of my compositions and I played a piece and she really liked it. She thought it was something that Herbie Hancock had written, which was a compliment to me. She changed one thing; it was one little rhythmic thing, and just that one little change made all the difference in the world. It made the lines swing harder than before. Just doing that one little simple thing demonstrated something to me. I studied with her off and on for a year. She was busy a lot of the time and sometimes she was out of town. And she kept pushing me away. She kept telling me that I didn't need to take lessons, that all I needed to do was get out there and play, and I just knew that there was so much she could show me.

"I got a commission this year, through Meet the Composer, to do another large piece that's gonna combine Japanese taiko drums with jazz instruments. I'm gonna be working with a guy from Hawaii who's one of the first Japanese Americans to have a stage name in Japan. He studied taiko drums there for ten years and his name is Kenny Endo. As a matter of fact, I got another grant this year to perform *Out from the Silence* at a major venue in New York. So what I want to do is try to premier the new piece with the other piece, and have just a big splash in the city. I'm also doing some film work right now with Leita Hagemann, doing some composing for her documentary films. That's something I want to get into a lot more, explore that whole aspect."

Last year Sumi Tonooka was a guest soloist with the Philadelphia Orchestra—along with Tyrone Brown, Odean Pope, and Johnathan Blake, Andrea Raphael Smith, conducting—on Duke Ellington's symphonic work *The Three Black Kings*. She has continued her composing for film, scoring for *Daring to Resist*, produced by Martha Lubell and Barbara Attie. Kenny Barron recorded her tune "Secret Places" on his album *Live at Bradley's*.

"I have been in a time of great transition," Sumi recently wrote me. She said that she, her husband, and their two children had left the city and settled in the country near Woodstock, New York, an area where a number of other jazz musicians live. She teaches part time at Rutgers University, has a new CD coming out, and is continuing to grow spiritually, musically, and personally.

"I try to keep the joy of music-making alive in me. Sometimes, with the restlessness of life, it's hard to keep it alive on the same level, and I try to remember that you can't do it all at the same time, in the same way. Life shifts and you have to go with it. There are always new challenges. I feel confident that within the course of my life I'll be able to do most of the things I want to do. Being an artist is a process, a lifelong process of exploration and learning, and sharing the expressing of that through music or whatever it may be."

About a decade ago I interviewed Marcus Roberts in his suite at the Renaissance Hotel, Washington, D.C. Marcus, who lost his sight at the age of four, was appearing at The Barns of Wolf Trap Farm Park for the Perfoming Arts, Vienna, Virginia. As the conversation began, photographer Gene Martin began setting up his equipment in another room for a photo shoot of Marcus that would be part of a cover story in *JazzTimes*.

"I was first exposed to music in church. I was very young and we went to church every Sunday. After church services, I would try to play the piano a little bit. I had an attraction to the instrument even then, when I was maybe four or five years old. My parents bought a piano when I was eight, and immediately, I was very captivated by it and started to practice by myself, playing a lot of gospel tunes, some popular tunes, just whatever I heard.

"I didn't start formal piano lessons until I was twelve. And that's also about the same time I got interested in jazz music. The first time I remember actually thinking that this is something I'm interested in, that I would like to learn more about, I turned on thc radio and I was flipping through the dials and they were playing some Duke Ellington and I thought, 'What the hell was that?'" Marcus laughed. "I had a little tape recorder and I remember recording something and just being very, very enraptured with the complexity and the elegance and just how good it sounded to me. I wanted to learn as much as I could about it.

"I've only had two piano teachers and I was fortunate in my first one, Hubert Foster. I mean, he could not only play classical piano but taught voice and knew a lot of the vocal repertoire. He not only knew classical piano repertoire, but also he knew a lot of jazz standards. I remember one day, I was maybe thirteen or so, he brought in two records. For some reason I wasn't really practicing that much then and he was trying to motivate me. He brought in, first, a record of Vladimir Ashkenazy playing the Chopin Etudes from Opus 10 and Opus 25. He played that for me, let me hear two or three of those, and I said, 'Oh, my God, is that one person doing all that?' He said, 'Yeah, sure is.' And then he put on a record of Art Tatum playing some standards like 'Sweet Lorraine' and when I heard that I decided that I just couldn't accept that one person had that kind of technique or piano could even be played in that way. So it just put me on another whole level of seriousness about what the possibilities were with the piano. Of course, he taught me a lot about harmony and theory and taught me a lot of standards. I was very fortunate in that regard because it was very easy for me to expand once I got interested in the music.

"Oh, they were equal," Roberts said, commenting on the technique displayed by the two pianists, "but I was more astounded by what Art Tatum was doing, just simply because I knew that he was making up what he was doing. For Ashkenazy, who of course was certainly a great interpreter of any classical repertoire, the music was already written for him to play. But when you hear somebody do what Art Tatum is doing at the piano, with that note of clarity, with the type of provocative harmonic concept that he had, the range, and just the power of what he would play, that's what was paramount to me. He could sit down at the piano and create that spontaneously and have it be his own concept. Everything that he did, he did it with complete clarity, total clarity; there was never any point where he was lost. He had a very, very sound and provocative philosophy of piano playing. And also, to me, Art Tatum represents the pianist who consolidated the European technique of playing the piano in jazz. He just completely consolidated everything that everybody had been doing up to that point, from the European perspective.

"Now Thelonious Monk, on the other hand, had a completely different concept of the instrument. To me, this was even more powerful because in addition to being a good pianist, he consolidated a whole philosophy of jazz itself. Art Tatum did this as well because Charlie Parker and John Coltrane and many of the horn players were very influenced by Tatum, just because of the types of chord progressions that he would play. But the thing that puts Thelonious, in my opinion, on even a higher level is just the range of the philosophy he had. You see, he comes directly out of Duke Ellington, who certainly was the most provocative composer we've ever produced. Duke Ellington is like Bach in classical music. And when Charlie Parker came on the jazz scene and completely revolutionized jazz, when everybody was trying to be a carbon copy of Charlie Parker, Thelonious had a completely different philosophy from Charlie Parker. It's a totally different, separate, and *equally* as provocative philosophy from Charlie Parker's.

"You cannot get a degree in physics if you don't know something about algebra. It just doesn't happen. They aren't gonna put people in charge of the space shuttle program who don't know something about the basic fundamental properties of mathematics; it just isn't going to work. So if you're talking about jazz, to me, if you're gonna be a piano player and you don't know about Jelly Roll Morton and Duke Ellington and Monk and Teddy Wilson and Willie the Lion Smith and Erroll Garner, there's no way that you're going to go forward. If the assumption is that the past achievement is old or dated, which is to imply that it's very simple, that it's not really that provocative, that it's considered to be something like addition, then my question is, why don't you have as many people who can walk in space? Why don't you have as many people who can play the piano the way they did in 1945 or 1950, when you could have gone and heard any number of great pianists play? I mean, then there was just any number of people who *truly* could play.

"This is why our generation has suffered a bit, because we couldn't go out and hear Charlic Parker, couldn't go out and hear Louis Armstrong play. I never got a chance to go hear the Duke Ellington orchestra playing live. The best I can do is get the records, and that's what I do. One of the things about the records is that if I want to play a tune, a tune like 'Pannonica,' I can at least hear Monk play his own music the way he heard it, the way he conceptualized it. I can get a lot more clarity out of it when I play it and then I can figure out more clearly what *I* want to do with it. I can't stress too much the importance of knowing your tradition and your past. To me, that's part of moving ahead into the future, and that's the only way you can do it.

"I haven't had a lot of time to study James P. Johnson, but I've listened intensely to a lot of his things. Even though I'm a pianist I listen to a lot of Sidney Bechet and Louis Armstrong. And Fats Waller, Mary Lou Williams. She's one of the first people I heard. Never have been able to find a lot of her work, but that woman could play! Bud Powell and a lot of the cats would go over to her house and learn from her. When you hear records of her playin', I'm tellin' you, it's very clear that she has never gotten the credit and recognition she deserves for her level of artistry.

"Whoo! Yes!" was Marcus's enthusiastic response when I asked whether he listened to the classic boogie woogie pianists. "Not nearly as much as I would want to, because there's so much stuff you have to listen to.

"It's not that big a deal," he explained when asked about his use of the braille notational system. "It's a very logical, consolidated system of notation. If you're gonna play Beethoven piano sonatos, it doesn't make sense not to use it. Put it this way: Beethoven could not go into a recording studio and record the *Appassionata*. The closest we have of knowing what Beethoven wanted, as for the phrasing and dynamic range of the piece, is the score, the manuscript; so if you're gonna play Beethoven sonatas or, especially, music after Haydn, you gotta get the score. So I learned how to read braille music for that reason. Now all the jazz things that I have done, I deal with that strictly by ear because it's an aural-generated music. If I want to study a Charlie Parker solo, then to me it doesn't make sense to get a sheet of paper and write it down when I can get a tape of Bird playing it himself. If I write it out, all I'm gettin' is the notes and most of the rhythms. But if I learn it off the record, then I get all the nuance; I can study the nuance and I can study the soul and the amount of blues feeling and the real, true organic technique that's being displayed.

"It takes a long time and you have to work on it. Certainly I'd have to work on it for at least a week, going over the same material until I felt that it became a *part* of *me*. I practice to the point that it becomes effortless to think of different permutations that I can use for myself. I'm not interested in just regurgitating it. That's the first level; the first level of learning anything is just imitation. The next level is to absorb the information and digest it. At that point it becomes knowledge, which means it's information that you then have at your disposal to do what you prefer, based on your individual concept

"I went to music camps at Florida State University for a couple of years, studied both classical music and jazz. When I was in high school I did that every summer. When I went to college, it was specifically to study piano with the second teacher I had, Leonidas Lipovetsky. I went to Florida State to study his concept of tone production because *I* had never heard anybody play *live* who could get that kind of power and resonance out of a piano. I really didn't do much playing other than that. I played in a jazz band for my scholarship and every now and then I would go out and do trio dates, mainly around Florida, every two to three months. The whole time I was in college I probably did no more than ten engagements. I was in my last year when I went right from there into Wynton Marsalis's group, so really I had no prior professional experience in an organized band.

"I think certainly that that move was the most important stage of my musical development up to that point. I first heard Wynton play in 1981 in Europe at the Montreux Jazz Festival. He was with the Herbie Hancock Quartet. That was even before he got his own group. And I remember when I heard him play, I knew he was the next great trumpet player, I knew it, I could hear it, it was obvious to me. First of all, he just had the power and the range on the instrument. Everybody talks about the technical facility that Wynton plays with and I think, frankly, that's been sort of used against him and he's sort of been reduced to a methodical technical sort of figure, a prodigy. But what really impressed me, even way beyond that, was the leadership capacity that I could hear in his playing. It was very clear to me that he had real passion for playing, and that's what struck me deepest—the fire and the intensity of his playing. He just had somethin' special for the music. I didn't even know his name; I said, 'Whoever that is, that's the ticket, man, who*ever* that is!' So I found out who it was and I went to Chicago to participate in the jazz convention the next year and he was there. That's when his debut record came out, *Wynton Marsalis,* and they played some music from that. And the funny thing is, I didn't know what they were doing. I mean, I didn't know whether I *liked* what they were doin'. But here again, it was just the intensity and energy behind it and I could tell, this is where *our* generation's goin'. I liked that. Any musician you talked to from our generation who heard that, or saw Marsalis's group when they played on the '84 Grammy Awards, when he really started to become a national figure, will tell you that it was just amazing to hear the way that band could play.

"I think the biggest thing that impressed me about Wynton's vision of music was the type of interaction that would go on in the band. When I heard just the complexity and the structure and the whole concept of power that band was dealing with, I knew immediately that I wanted to play with him. And I didn't know how that was possible, because Kenny Kirkland was playin' piano, and he's a *great* pianist, *great* pianist. I just started calling Wynton on the telephone and we would talk exclusively about music. He sent me several Monk records and told me, 'You know, you really need to learn these records.' I didn't really like Monk's playing at that time because I'd never paid attention to it. So Wynton said, 'Well, you don't like it because you don't know nothin' about it.' So I started to check him out. And he told me a lot of philosophical things to deal with in musical development. So I guess that's what led up to it. I just kept in touch with him. One thing led to another and eventually, when his first band broke up, he just called me out to play."

"Each person performs individually, but for this unit collectively, this is only the second night of it." Cyrus Chestnut was talking as we sat in a Washington, D.C., hotel room several blocks from the One

Step Down, where he was performing that night and the next in a quartet format. "It's great fun, yeah.

"Well, I was born January 17, 1963, in Baltimore," he continued. "I guess you could say I come out of a musical family pretty much. My father played piano somewhat—he kind of taught himself to play—and my mother was a natural singer. She tells me that in order to keep me quiet, my father used to put me in the bassinet and start playing and I would get quiet and eventually go to sleep. So I guess between the combination of the two, I was the recipient of a musical gift.

"I remember a piano being in the house and I always had a fascination with the lower register. I would just get up on the piano and start banging away, just doin' something, three or four hours at a time. So I guess music was always a part; it was always there.

"I started actually playing piano at the age of five. I'd be sittin' there, tryin' to create different things, and I guess after a while my father saw that this wasn't just no little phase or nothin'. I remember he bought me a couple of books on piano chords and I just started working out of them. Finally he decided that he'd get me a teacher because I wasn't going to give up this playing at the piano." Cyrus paused and chuckled. "When I was about seven I started studying with a teacher. Her name was Ada Jenkins. Great pianist; she taught me a lot, really did. We had fun. I mean, she was real concerned about me playing music and liking it. I guess she must've seen that there was something about me and the piano. She could always tell when I wouldn't practice or something; she would go in and tell my mother and father, 'He's not practicing enough now, I'm really concerned.'"

At the age of nine Cyrus Chestnut began piano studies at the prestigious Peabody Conservatory in Baltimore. "I went through the prep program, graduated, and was going to go into the conservatory, but things happened. At that time I was primarily playing a lot of classical music, and my mother was singing in churches a lot, so I was always exposed to gospel music. I'll never forget, she had these 45 rpm records hidden in the cupboard. I saw them and I was curious about what they sounded like. She had stuff like King Curtis, Sam Cooke; I think there was even a Jackie Wilson record in there. I had a little teeny record player and I was playing 'em and I liked 'em. I'd just sneak and listen to 'em. My favorite one was a King Curtis instrumental. The singing I always liked, but there was something about King Curtis. I always liked playin' that one record, over and over. One side was 'Twist and Turn' and the other side was called 'Swing and Twist.' Gold record with blue letters on it. Always after doin' this I would sit down and just play a while, just doin' it, nothing really preplanned; it was just whatever idea I had in my head. I just wanted to make up somethin'."

The radio also played a big part in the musical education of the young Cyrus. He listened to "all different types of things," especially recalling a fondness for George Clinton and Funkadelic. "I guess you could say that was the beginnings of my going toward the jazz world.

"My mother would take me to F. W. Woolworth's and one day I asked her to buy me a record. So she says, 'Okay, pick out a record.' I saw this one record that had a real interesting cover on it and I liked the name of it. It was *Thelonious Monk's Greatest Hits*, and I said, 'I want this one. It's neat.' Good price, a dollar ninety-nine, bargain bin. So my mother bought me the record and I took it home and immediately started playing it. I liked what I heard, songs like 'Straight No Chaser,' 'Ruby My Dear,' 'Epistrophy,' 'Blue Monk,' 'Bemsha Swing'—all his popular stuff. I'd sit there and play the record and I just liked it. It was different from everything else that I was listening to and I liked the groove of it; it had a real nice groove.

"I was doin' a lot of playing in local churches around Baltimore and playing some competitions and I was still studying. I guess everybody figured that I was supposed to be a teacher or something. But I always had this Monk record and I guess I played it for a while and then there was a period of time when I didn't play it. I moved to my cousin's house and she had a little 45, Herbie Hancock's 'Chameleon.' It went 'boomp, boomp, boomp, boomp, boomp.'" Cyrus simulated the sound, his voice rising in pitch. "I played it over and over and over and over.

"It wasn't 'til I was about thirteen or fourteen that I took it really seriously, trying to find out what it was about, about eighth grade. I had some money saved up and I saw the Herbie Hancock *Head-hunters* album, so I bought it. My father bought me some Jimmy Smith, 'cause he really liked him. I played it a lot! That and Ohio

Players. I was still practicin' the Beethoven sonatas, Bach preludes and all. You know how you get out of school and run home and do your homework and run outside and play. Well, me, I'd come home and do my homework, sit at the piano and play."

As he approached his mid-teens, radio began to play a bigger and bigger role in his musical life. He began to explore the dial and found a local university station that featured a regular program of Baltimore's Left Bank Jazz Society. "I would wait every day and record the show. It had a little bit of everybody on it."

In the mid-1970s the Chestnut family left their Baltimore home near the old Memorial Stadium and relocated out in Hartford County in Jarrettsville. In the city public school where Cyrus had been, blacks accounted for 90 percent of the student body; the proportion in the county school was just the reverse.

By this time, Cyrus was not only a developing prodigy at the piano but "had played some alto saxophone, just picked it up. I tried to mess with the tenor but that didn't work; I played trombone and baritone horn, also a little guitar. I guess I'm a great enthusiast of many different instruments.

"Oh, boy, the organ story," he said, laughing, when asked if he had had formal instruction on the instrument that he often played in church. "I took lessons at the Hammond Music Company in Baltimore from this phenomenal organ player, Joseph Alterman. O-hoo! When I would sometimes catch him just sittin' there playin,' he really had it goin' on. And there was another guy, the organ salesman—he played a little, too, more modern. Dr. Alterman was strictly classical. He would put me on these organs that had all types of gimmicks and everything on them. I just really dug playin' the organ and even to this day I still enjoy it.

"Jarrettsville was a quiet town, no real serious action there. It was a different time. I started eighth grade there and all of a sudden it's, like, 'Wow!' I didn't know how to take it. A lot of the people I grew up with basically shared a lot of stuff. Now I'm going into this completely new experience. I was sad to be leavin' old friends. First day, I got on the school bus, big ol' yellow school bus. Okay, so I figure all these country hicks goin' to try and give me a hard time. I was ready to fight, had my fist clenched, so if somebody grabbed me, I'm gonna kill 'em, right? Dead on their ass. I'm not even gonna think about it. So I walked up, tryin' to be all cool. Everyone was talkin', right?

"'You want to sit down?' somebody said.

"I said, 'Oh, thank you,' and sat down. And that began the days out there in Hartford County.

"We had a little music class and one day, after doin' the lesson on the piano, I'm calmly just playin'. The teacher kinda exposed me out to everybody and it's, like, 'O-o-o-o-oh! He's playin'!' Out of that little class, one guy could play drums, another clarinet, another electric piano, another was playin' bass. One day we played for assembly, and I guess that's when everybody said, 'Oh, wow! He's a musician. Wow! He can play!' We were playing 'Smoke on the Water,' just playin' all types of rock tunes.

"We played dances, and I thought, 'Yeah, we can really get things going.' I really liked it, the energy and all. It kinda lasted through the eighth grade and then just dissipated. Everyone else wanted to do different things. It came up quick and it died just as quick. The summer before I was to start ninth grade I went to this music camp in Vermont to study theory and really enjoyed it. That was a fun time, that summer. That's when I *really* started getting into jazz real serious. There was a teacher there; his name was Gary and he was studying at Princeton. At that time I was really into playing drums. So Gary would be playing piano—he was into a Keith Jarrett, Chick Corea thing—and I'd be playing drums. He finally exposed me to my first *Real Book*. I started learning some tunes and playing them. And they started seeing that, 'Yeah! this cat plays, he's really starting to become a jazzhead.'

"It was exciting getting into the ninth grade. This one cat comes up to me and says, 'Hey, I saw you in middle school and you play piano, don't you?' I say, 'Yeah.' He says, 'Want to play in our jazz band?' I say, 'Really?' So he took me to the band director, whose name was Michael Pastelak. I think he was the primary introduction, the most significant person in helping me decide this was what I wanted to be. He said, 'Can you read music?' I said, 'Yeah, pretty much.' So he pulled out these charts and I started playing. 'Oh, okay.' So at that time, once again, I was playing in the stage band. There was no bass player, so I was playing the bass line.

"It was really at that point that my interest in classical music just started to dwindle. I was goin' to the Peabody on the weekends and I always loved taking the theory classes because they were showing me a lot of things about harmony and everything. I always liked dealing with composition, just making things up and all. But as far as playin' the actual music, I got tired of it because I wanted to do more things that let me really be creative. I had a lot of sight reading, which was good because there were times when I hadn't practiced in a week. I could come in there and just open the music up and play.

"This one teacher, she said, 'Since you like jazz you could play some ragtime.' So I was playin' some of the Scott Joplin rags. They had repertoire class every week, and I was going to play 'Maple Leaf Rag.' I would sit at home and play it, but not swinging; it didn't feel right. So I started swinging it. 'Yeah, I *like* this!' So I just kept playing it that way, and I got into the repertoire class and just swung the whole thing, had a good time! When I finished, someone asked, 'Is that right, the way he played that?' The teacher said, 'He's just interpreting the eighth note a different way, with a swing factor or something.' She never said anything to me about it. Musically, it was a transition of getting more into jazz and kind of putting down the classical side.

"When I graduated from high school I was thinking about going to Towson State because they had a good jazz program. During the summer they would have a jazz college out in the area where I was living—a little jazz band where people would get together and play the music. I'd meet some cats there and we'd play a lot of Hank Levy's music, ensemble style, and I loved it; it was challenging. I just loved the improvisation. That went on for a while and I knew for sure that I wanted to study some jazz. I looked on the board and I saw this college, Berklee College of Music. They had pictures of Ray Brown, Oscar Peterson. I sent for some information, filled out an application, sent it and all my stuff from Peabody. Next thing I know, I was accepted to go there, 1981. It's like, 'Wow!' Never been to Boston before in my life. Parents figured I was going to go there studyin' to become a teacher. I got up there and said, 'I don't want to teach, I just want to get out there, I want to play!' The first year is real special—so much music and it was so concentrated. Everybody was playing all the time; there was jazz goin' on all the time. There was a big tape library there; you could sit and listen to all the greats—Phineas Newborn, Oscar Peterson, Miles Davis, Charlie Parker, Bud Powell, much more Monk than I had dreamed of, Hank Jones, Red Garland. Red Garland, I tried to buy every record of his, and I got turned on to Wynton Kelly and started collecting a lot of his stuff. I just kind of walked through my four years of school mostly with a walkman on my head, just listening to the music. I grew up in Boston because I was kinda like the little fish in a big pond.

"Finally I started finding out where I stood, seeing what I had to do to get myself to where I wanted to be. I started playing different sessions around. Everybody knew that I was playing and they started to say, 'Yeah, he's the cat! He's the cat! He's bad! He's bad!,' and I started believing that. Yeah. I went there with the attitude that I was going to be top five." One day Cyrus got a call from a friend who asked him to sit in for him in one of the more prestigious bands at Berklee. "So I said, 'Yeah! I'm gonna do this! I'm gonna show 'em who I am!' And I went up there and the teacher asks me, 'You sure you can do it?' I said, 'Yeah, man, I'm cool.' Went up there and made a *fool* of myself. I couldn't even find the seventh chords. It was so wild! It ended up that the teacher had to play.

"The biggest bands were the International Blues Band and Herb Pomeroy's recording band, and then there was the student orchestra. My most influential teacher, as far as the piano is concerned, was Mike Marra. He really got on me; he broke my cockiness, just made me humble, he taught me not just to fluff through. I only had two piano teachers, him and Donald Brown. I learned a *lot* from Donald, too.

"My graduation out of the little pool into the big pool was the day Betty Carter came to Berklee," Cyrus Chestnut continued, laughing. "I was tellin' all my friends, 'I'm gonna go sit in with Betty Carter, show her what I can do!' Went to her master class and went to sleep. Woke up finally and her piano player wasn't there. 'My piano player is gone!' she says. Somebody hollered out in the audience, 'Get Cyrus Chestnut!' Within seconds the whole audience was hollerin' my name. I couldn't believe it. A friend of mine says,

'Man, you said you gonna do it! Here's your chance, go do it!' I was terrified. This lady had a reputation of annihilating people, making them just look like dirt.

"I walked up there and she was, like, 'You like jazz, huh?' 'Ye-e-e-h, yeh.' She looked at me, says, 'Okay, let's do something. Know "Body and Soul"?" Said, 'Yeah.' 'Okay. Fine.' She cues the key on me. I started walking. She says, 'In *G*!' and the 'G' shoots through me from tip to toe like a sword. I felt like I was split in half, I just felt like, 'Oh, no!' *I played the song in the wrong key!* And I *could not* figure out what the first chord was! Terrified! So it got to a point where I just said, 'Well, enough of this!' I'm in this key and I got to try to figure out how to get through it, just get through. She was singin' around me and I was tryin' to follow her.

"We get finished and everybody's on their feet screamin' and I thought for sure that she was just gonna trash me. She gave me a hug and said, 'You're wonderful!' She left and I was in a daze. I was still trying to think what that first chord was. So I'm like the king! Yeah, I could have had anything. I was *the* cat at that point in time. 'Oh, *you* sat in with Betty Carter! *Great*!'

"Tell you one thing, I guess maybe it's just destiny I would be here, because my whole life, there's always been music in it. There's *never* been a time where I have been without music. So much fun. I get up in the morning and I have different things I want to do and all, but as long as I know that the music is there, I feel like I'm on the right track. I can kind of be at peace. I guess, in a sense, it's just having to have it in your guts and having the trust to deal with it."

4
Singers

"The four years that I spent with the Thad Jones–Mel Lewis Orchestra is the basis of my musical training. Basically, I feel like the whole way I approach music came out of those four years."
Dee Dee Bridgewater

"I don't get paid to play—I get paid to travel and for living out of a suitcase. I feel very fortunate that I can do this. How much fun can you have doing what you love to do?"
Diana Krall

That was Edith Wilson singing 'There'll Be Some Changes Made,' accompanied by Eubie Blake," I back-announced on a 1976 Saturday morning of my radio show *"I Thought I Heard Buddy Bolden say..."* "We have Edith here with us in the studio. She performed last night for the Folklore Society of Greater Washington and we're going to be talking with her about her career and playing a few more selections from some of her recordings. Edith, I'd like to get you to do some biography, to tell us where you came from and how you grew up in music and that sort of thing."

"I was born in Louisville, Kentucky, in 1906," she began, "and as a child I started singing—they said I was about two years old. I'd just go through the house singing some song they never heard. So I guess I started writin' too.

111

"Did you at some point have some sort of musical training or was it all just by ear?" I asked.

"Most of it by ear. I used to go visit a girl, and her brothers were in the music business. One was a pianist and the other one put on shows. They used to have rehearsals there and I used to sit outside and listen to what the people were singing. After they'd leave, I'd imitate them. And so a fellow said to me, 'Come in and lemme get you a key. You sound like you doin' pretty good there.' So I went in and started to learn songs, and that's really how I got started singin'. I just kept on singin' from the time I started.

"Did you come from a musical family?"

"I guess I may call it a musical family, in a way, because my father used to play guitar. That had to have some influence, and I had some cousins whose sisters' children, both of the girls sang with the glee club. When I look into it now, we had people who were very good in things like that. I had an uncle who was a singer. So I guess I come by it naturally."

"When did you become professional or semiprofessional? When did you start singing for audiences?"

"I was thirteen years old. They were having some sort of centennial down in Louisville and this boy and his brother were putting on shows and asked me if my mother would let me sing. I was afraid to ask her because I was sure she would say no. So I told them she said yes, and I went to a girlfriend's house where we used to work our school problems. My mother went to bed early and one night she got up to go to the bathroom and found I wasn't in bed. The next morning she said, '*Where* were *you* last night? Don't you stay over there any more that late! You and your girl friend, let her come over here now. And you can't go out no more this week!' And of course that upset me so I went out back and started cryin'. My aunt saw me and took me back in the house and my mother wanted to know, 'What is this? You're not the kind of person who cries for nothin'; what are you cryin' about?' And I said, 'Well, I'm workin'.' She said, '*Workin*? Workin' *where*?' I said, 'Well, the show down to this park.' She said, 'A *show*? You're underage! You have no business workin' *anywhere* without my consent!' And I said, 'Well, if—if—if I don't go back now, *they won't pay me*!'" Edith laughed at the memory.

"So she said, 'Well, you put your clothes on; I'm gonna take you down there.' And she did, and when we got there they wouldn't let her in because she didn't have a pass. Eventually, they called the manager, and he brought her a pass and he told me to go on in and get ready to go on. And he kept my mother pacified and told her, 'Stay here and see what she does.'"

"What type of music were you singing?"

"It wasn't exactly a ballad; it was a straight song, somethin' like, 'Oh, you Georgia rose, in the land where the cotton blossom grows,' that was what I was singin'."

"Did you get into contact with traveling shows, with circus and tent shows that came through town?"

"No, I didn't ever fall in with any of those. I went back to school. I told my mother, 'I'll make money enough to buy my clothes to go back to school this winter and help out my brothers.' So that's why she let me stay, I think. She walked me home and said, 'Is this what you want to do?' And I said, 'Oh, yes, because you're only making seven dollars a week and I'm gonna make thirty-five.'" Edith chuckled at this. "So anyhow, she said, 'Well, will you promise me that you won't pick up the habits or do the talk that the grown people are doin' on the show? Attend to your business, do what you're gonna do, and come on off and come on home.' And I did that for nearly two years. I went on back to school in the fall."

"Until you were fifteen or so."

"Yeah, and by that time, I'd met some people. I was goin' to the theater and would go backstage and meet the people 'n' all. I just started on my own, practically."

"At what point did you leave that local scene and actually go out on the road?"

"I went to Chicago to visit my aunt, and I had already met a girl, Lena Wilson"—also known as Nelly Coleman—"who was with a show and her brother Danny played the piano with the show. I was anxious to go to Chicago because I wanted to sing, but I couldn't do it in Louisville. I used to go to visit my aunt and she would send Danny with me to take me home. He got to likin' me, so he got a job with a band, just a small group, and the show went on somewhere else. He'd gotten used to me, I guess, and he wrote and asked my mother if he could marry me. I guess she was glad to get rid of me 'cause she figured if I was goin' out singin' at night, it would be better if I was married.

"After that, Lena and Danny and I came to Washington. My first job was out with them. We worked at the Thomas Club. I forget what street it was on, but it was a nightclub run by two brothers. 'Course it was the best thing that ever happened to me because my husband made me rehearse every day and learn new songs. Really, he made me the singer that I am because he stuck to it all the time."

"What type of music were you singing then?"

"I was singing ballads, just straight songs. I didn't even sing any blues then, because his sister used to sing all the blues. We had fun. When we left there we went to Atlantic City and worked with quite a number of people, but they were all doin' things cabaret style and I was doin' jumpy things. Then we all got fired. We were fired because the other girls on the show would sing what I call off-color songs. They went out one night to an opening of another cabaret and my sister-in-law and I was left there. When the people came in askin' for these particular songs, I wasn't able to give 'em any. When the other girls heard about it, they told the owners, 'Well, you told us you had two pretty girls, so why didn't they entertain the people until we come back?' So we got fired. The girls said, 'If they can't entertain the people, whacha keep 'em for?'

"As soon as we left there—it was in the spring of '21 that I came to New York—my husband and I were walkin' down the street and met Perry Bradford. He had been in this club and heard me, so he asked if I would like to make a record. And I said, of course. Wasn't workin'; I'd be glad to do anything. We went to his house and got the songs he wanted, and then Danny started rehearsin' me on the songs he wanted me to record. I happened to be the first singer to make a record for a large company at that time, for Columbia.

"'Bout that time there was a show ready to go on called *Put and Take*. A girl named Mamie Smith was supposed to go in the show but somethin' happened to her and Bradford asked me if I would replace her. I wanted to do *anything*, so I was hired to work in that show, and that was my first show on Broadway. Lew Leslie came to see the show and decided that he wanted me to co-star in a show with Florence Mills. We went into what was called the Plantation Room, and that's when I started really to sing all kinds of things, 'cause Florence sang most of the ballads."

"How many shows were you in on Broadway?"

"Well, I was in *Memphis Bound* with Bill Robinson. It was a take-off on *H.M.S. Pinafore*, and I was in *Hot Chocolates*. That's where 'Black and Blue' was written for me. Then Charles B. Cochran came to see the show and he decided that he'd like to take it to London, so I went to London. First trip abroad. And after that I went abroad with Sam Wooding's orchestra and we toured all the big cities in Germany."

"Last night you sang a song in German."

"Uh huh. And then we went to all the big cities in Yugoslavia, Serbia, Austria, Romania, and Turkey."

"So you have really been around, as the saying goes."

"Yes, I have," she replied, chuckling. "I've had a wonderful life in this business, and still goin,' I'm still workin'. So I'm bein' looked after."

"What have you been doing recently? Have you become more active than you've been for a few years?"

"I've never stopped working. I still have different things to do, like workin' club dates and some folk festivals. Now, I don't work as often as I used to because I used to go right from one thing to the other. I'm not gonna work every day. Like one show in Chicago not long ago, there were seven shows a week at night and two matinées, and it just pins you down too much. At my age, I been goin' so long, better take it easy."

"Yes, indeed."

"You know, I worked for eighteen years advertising Aunt Jemima pancakes on radio and TV. Before that I was in California and I worked with the Pasadena Playhouse. I did *Little Foxes*, *Springfield Couple*, and a radio show called *The Prizefight Fix*. I used to do odd things with *Amos and Andy*; I played the old girlfriends. Lil Randolf played Bertie for *The Great Gildersleeve* and I played the girl who worked next door. I worked with Tom Duncan in *Show Boat*. I played Queenie. And I worked in a show called *Lady Godiva's Horse* and I did my show with Dorothy Dandridge called *Sweet and Hot*. So I've been around."

The collective catalogue of professional activities provided during the course of this radio interview is a mere sampling of Wilson's six-decade career. This great performer came up through vaudeville, 1920s music, and the beginnings of African-American musical theater to become a world-class blues and jazz singer, a premiere cabaret artist, and a versatile actress. She appeared as a principal in many stage productions on Broadway and elsewhere, filled regular roles and made many guest appearances on radio and TV, sang with a number of bands here and abroad, and recorded throughout her career. Edith Wilson died in 1981.

In the mid-1990s, singer Dee Dee Bridgewater, who had settled in Paris a decade before, was beginning to increase the frequency of her visits to her native land. I caught her several times in Washington, D.C., during the second half of the decade.

"I'm tired and stressed, extremely stressed," she told me, alluding to an imminent gig, "emotionally *wrung out* because this is such a *bi-i-g-g* deal for me to be back in that club again. It's just very strange. I'm working at the Village Vanguard all next week with my European trio. It's to coincide with the CD release of *Love and Peace*. I did the album with love and tried to do a good job. I'm glad you like it. I just wanted to get Horace Silver's music out to a larger audience. I know that as soon as you put vocals on music it automatically has a larger audience appeal, so I'm really glad it's working.

"There was always music; music was always in my house," she said, talking about her early life, "and so it was just a natural part of my growing up. I always sang. My mother listened to a lot of kind of obscure singers—singers who never had really big careers but have very pretty voices, like Gloria Lynne and Lorez Alexandria. Then we had records of Harry Belafonte and Johnny Mathis. I was in love with Johnny Mathis when I was a little girl and my whole dream was to grow up and meet and marry him. I was also into the Top 50. I turned on the radio and then I watched television and I *loved*"—she giggled—"Elvis Presley and Ricky Nelson when I was a little girl.

"The first singer who made me want to sing professionally and make records was Nancy Wilson. Because she was you-u-u-ng and pret-t-t-ty and she put that album out with Cannonball Adderley and she had that orange dress on the cover and had that nice figure and she was so pretty and I was, 'Uhhhh!'" Dee Dee took a deep breath. "'I want to be a singer like her!' My daddy was always getting me clippings of her wherever she was and interviews and pictures and magazines. I had Nancy Wilson all over my wall. That was the first thing that catapulted me into really wanting to sing and saying to my daddy, 'I want a recording contract.'

"So he took me to Motown and they were ready to sign me, but I was sixteen and they had had so many problems with Stevie Wonder that they decided they weren't going to sign any more child acts and they said, 'Bring her back when she's eighteen and we'll sign her.' And I said, 'I don't want to sign with them, I want to sign with Capitol,' because that's where"—she broke up laughing—"Nancy Wilson was! So that's my first real consciousness about wanting to be in the business and record. I would say the person who influenced me as a young black girl was Nina Simone, because she was so-o-o outspoken. She came out on the stage with her hair natural and I thought that was so daring; and seeing her come out in bare feet and claim her African heritage, that would just blow me away. I remember in college I wrote a term paper for my English class based on her song 'Four Women.' So she was really important to me.

"We left Memphis when I was three, so I don't have any real memory of the first three years of my life. My consciousness starts when we're in Flint, Michigan, where I grew up. My father had stopped teaching music then, he was just taking all kinds of different jobs and playing jazz trumpet on the weekends and in the evenings to make a little extra money. When we were in Memphis, he would play in the bands of Dinah Washington or Rufus Thomas, whoever was putting bands together and going on tours, and he was always first trumpet. He also had a lovely voice, and one of my dreams when I was a little girl was to grow up and have a band with my daddy, Matthew Garrett.

"The idea that he was playing was certainly an influence on me. I *sang* with him on gigs when I was sixteen. He would take me to the clubs in Flint and I would have to sit in the kitchen and then when it was my turn to sing I'd come out. I was little Dee Dee Garrett, who had this big voice and was singing all the Nancy Wilson songs. My favorite was 'Guess Who I Saw Today.' Then he was part of a quintet with a man in Flint who was an alto player named Sherman Mitchell. They would play dances and stuff, and sometimes I would sing with their band on the weekend. I was *always* going to their rehearsals because I just loved being around the music.

"I formed a trio and we called ourselves the Iridescents. We did all the Top 50 black music. Motown had happened by then and a block away from me were some of the girls who were in the Marvellettes. We would do all their stuff and the songs of Martha Reeves and the Vandellas and the Shirelles. That was a period when everybody had a little doo-wop group and sang a cappella on the corners. I would write little songs for us and give us the harmonies. I had a girlfriend who could play a little bit of piano; she would play with us and we'd do talent shows and teen dances and be the backup group for the guys who would sing solo.

"When I chose Michigan State University, it turned out that a very good friend of my father, Andy Goodrich, was working on his doctorate there. My father introduced me to him. Andy had me sing during a rehersal and then he took me into his quintet. We started doing a lot of college festivals and competitions and we won several of them. I won several vocal competitions. One of them was at the University of Illinois, and that's where I met my first husband Cecil Bridgewater, who was with the University of Illinois Jazz Band.

"After we had competed there, I was invited to go on a cultural exchange tour of the Soviet Union with the University of Illinois Jazz Band. I was off and runnin.' The one year I went to college I was going to major in English and I wanted to write. I can't cite a favorite author; I never got that far, because in your freshman year you're just doing general studies, but I liked to write short stories and I used to write a lot of them in high school. I had a couple of them printed. My teachers would send them off to different magazines for teenagers. At Michigan State I wrote a lot of short stories. I want to start it again, but what I have done is write lyrics off and on and I've won some small awards from ASCAP and different places for that. But all the short stories that I wrote the year I was in college, the teacher never gave them back to me. I had some magazines interested and then he just disappeared with all my work. So that just kind of blew me out of the water, and I said, 'Forget it!' By then I'd started singing, doing a lot of gigs around the college and campus.

"Then I got the gig with the University of Illinois Jazz Band and went on the tour and basically dropped out of school. It was 1968 and all the student revolts were going on—Kent State University and a big student revolt in France that year. So I guess it was the

Diana Krall, JVC Newport Jazz Festival, Newport, Rhode Island, August 1999.
Photo by Ken Franckling.

Sumi Tonooka at the Mid Atlantic Arts Jazz Showcase, Baltimore, Maryland, August 2, 1994. Photo by Michael Wilderman.

Glen Moore at Blues Alley, Washington, D.C., 1994. Photo by W. Patrick Hinely Work/Play.

James Morrison, 1989. Photo courtesy Atlantic Records ©1989.

Sue Foley, February 1998. Photo by Robert H. Fitzsimons.

Joyce,
1990s.
Photo by
Marco
Aurelio.

Russ Gershon
at the Boston
Globe Jazz Festi-
val, Boston,
Massachusetts,
June 27, 1999.
Photo by Peter
Halter.

Roy Rogers, Johnny Otis Red Beans and Rice Festival, Luther Burbank Center, Santa Rosa, California, 1994. Photo by David Licht Photography.

The Duke Hampton Band, Indianapolis, Indiana, mid-1940s. The leader is on tenor saxophone (*center*), and Slide Hampton is behind the drums playing trombone. Photo from Collection of Duncan Schiedt.

Jimmy Heath (*left*) and Dizzy Gillespie at Magnolia Gardens, Spoleto U.S.A., Charleston, South Carolina, 1994. Photo by W. Patrick Hinely Work/Play.

The author relating a Joe Venuti anecdote to violinist Regina Carter at the Capital Jazz Fest, Merriweather Post Pavilion, Columbia, Maryland, June 5, 1999. Photo by Jennifer Crescenzo.

Ramsey Lewis at Blues Alley, Washington, D.C., October 2, 1991. Photo by Michael Wilderman.

John Eaton at Jordan Kitts Music Recital Hall, College Park, Maryland, 1987. Photo by Michael Anderson.

Rory Block
at The Barns,
Wolf Trap Farm
Park for the
Performing Arts,
Vienna, Virginia,
January 16, 1999.
Photo by
Joy Chambers.

Dave Hole
at Lewie's,
Bethesda, Maryland,
October 2, 1999.
Photo by
Joy Chambers.

Dave Maxwell with the James Cotton Quartet at Bumbershoot Festival of the Arts, Seattle, Washington, August 31, 1997. Photo by Tom Hunnewell.

Edith Wilson, 1920s. Photo from Collection of Duncan Schiedt.

Monty Alexander (*right*) with Ray Brown (*standing*) and Herb Ellis, Newport
Friends of Jazz, Hotel Viking, Newport, Rhode Island, May 29, 1988. Photo by Ken
Franckling.

Cyrus Chestnut, DeCordova Museum Summer Jazz Series, Lincoln, Massachusetts, August 27, 1995. Photo by Ken Franckling.

Ron Holloway
at Blues Alley,
Washington, D.C.,
May 6, 1998.
Drummer
Lenny Robinson is
in the lower right.
Photo by
Joy Chambers.

Ingrid Jensen with Diva–No Man's Band at the sound check, Mary Lou Williams Women in Jazz Festival, Kennedy Center, Washington, D.C., April 29, 1996. Trombonist Deborah Weisz is at the upper left, trombonist Lolly Bienenfeld is obscured behind Jensen at the top, bass trombonist Lee Hill Kavanaugh is on the far right behind Jensen's trumpet, Carol Chaikin is playing soprano saxophone at the lower right, the blond hair on the far right belongs to alto saxophonist Laura Dreyer, and saxophonist Virginia Mayhew is behind Jensen. Photo by Michael Wilderman.

Debbie Davies,
Twist & Shout,
Bethesda, Maryland,
July 5, 1997.
Photo by Joy Chambers.

Mal Waldron
(*left*) and
Chico Freeman
at the
One Step Down,
Washington, D.C.,
October 14, 1990.
Photo by
MichaelWilderman.

Dee Dee Bridgewater and the author at Coco Loco, Washington, D.C., 1994. Photo © 1994 J. Kliman/Photography You Can Hear.

Cannonball Adderley (*left*) and Nat Adderley at the Monterey Jazz Festival, Monterey, California, 1966. Photo by Ray Avery Photo.

Freddy Cole, Syracuse Jazz Festival, Syracuse, New York, June 30, 1997. Photo by Jack Frisch.

John Stubblefield,
Saratoga Jazz Festival,
Saratoga Springs,
New York, June 1997.
Photo by Ken Franckling.

Lew Tabackin,
Saratoga Jazz Festival,
Saratoga Springs,
New York, June 1997.
Photo by Ken Franckling.

Shirley Horn
at the Benefit Concert
for the D.C. Free Jazz
Festival, Duke Ellington
School for the Arts,
Washington, D.C.,
November 3, 1989.
Electric bassist Charles
Ables is on the left.
Photo by
Michael Wilderman.

Joanne Brackeen
at the D.C. World Jazz
Festival, Freedom Plaza,
Washington, D.C.,
July 3, 1993. Photo
by Michael Wilderman.

Bill Cosby and the author
at Cosby Studios,
Queens, New York, 1990.
Photo by Gene Martin.

year students were saying, 'That's enough; we're not going to take this. *I* was busy singing; I didn't know *what* was going on and was just fluffing my way through university and basically just wanted to sing.

"When we went to Russia that first time in '68, we were followed everywhere. My first impression of Russia was KGB, bugs in my room, getting our luggage and having my clothes just totally in a mess when I'd open my suitcases, and being very, very paranoid. Walking down the street and seeing kids coming to me and waving, Russian kids, and then seeing little old ladies dragging them off the streets into alleys or into doorways and stuff. It was very, very strange.

"And going to jam sessions in the middle of the night, like you see in the movies, and having to get out of the bus with the bus lights off and go two-by-two to some meeting appointment and having special locks on the door and people rushing you in and down some stairs and then ending up in some basement with all these young Russian people, and playing music. It was very strange. I remember that at the end of the six-week tour I was afraid to sleep and really unhappy. That was the time when communism was really strong and the people all wore either navy blue, dark brown, or black. Everywhere you went they sold the same dress, the same suit, the same shoe; they all drove that one make of car. The couple of times I got to go out and was invited into people's homes, I was just amazed at how they lived—a whole family in one room with the toilet down the hall. Poverty, basically—just amazing poverty.

"The second time I went in '72 with the Thad Jones–Mel Lewis Orchestra, things had gotten a little looser. The girls were wearing makeup and there was a huge black market, jeans were the thing and everybody was selling them. There was a lot more variety in the shopping centers. When you'd go to the markets—I liked to go to their open markets—you saw just a little bit of that kind of Western influence coming in. There was this whole craze for the United States and Western culture, and the government was loosening up and letting them have it. On that tour I was pregnant with my first daughter, and they were stunned! It was quite a scandal, seeing a pregnant woman—I was five-and-a-half, six months pregnant—on stage singing. It was a *huge* scandal, and people were always doing caricatures of me in their reviews of the band, with my big belly and my Afro and my funny glasses. That was my second record.

"Lots of stories existed in the band, Thad being the character that he was. I was the person who would go and get him and Roland Hanna when they started acting up in the bars. I was kind of his conscience, like Pinocchio and Jiminy Cricket." She laughed uproariously. "In the middle of the night and wherever the hotel would be, if Thad wouldn't leave the bar—you know, he was quite a lady's man—Mel Lewis would call me up and say, 'Dee Dee, you gotta go down and get Thad out of the bar.' I'd be sleeping—it's two in the morning—and he'd say, 'Dee Dee, *please*, you gotta go down; you're the only one he'll listen to.' And it's true, he would always listen to me. So I'd go down and say, 'Come on, Thad, we gotta go,' and he'd leave.

"The four years that I spent with the Thad Jones–Mel Lewis Orchestra is the basis of my musical training. Basically, I feel like the whole way I approach music came out of those four years with that band. It was unusual because it was a big band but at the same time it was like a combo. Thad was always improvising the arrangements. It was the most amazing stuff. Now I realize it because since then I've always been looking for that Thad Jones–Mel Lewis band. For me, it was basically Thad Jones; he was really the creative aspect of it. Mel was the business end, and I was always arguing with Mel because I couldn't stand the way he played. I *hated* his Chinese cymbals—I *hated* those doggone studs all the way around the cymbals and that sound that he'd always be making." She simulated it with a hissing sound and laughed, "*I hated that sound!* So I didn't get along with Mel. And they always knocked you down for your salary. They tell you one price and they knock five dollars and ten dollars off. The biggest salary was fifty dollars, and as I was married to Cecil, we were a bargain; so I was working for twenty bucks and shit. It was very strange. But it was my musical upbringing and, like I said, the way I hear and think and even my approach to this album *Love and Peace*, it all comes out of what I was doing with Thad and Mel. Like the riffs—Thad used to always give riffs to the horn sections behind somebody's solo. So I'd say, 'I want riffs, I want to sound like a big band and I want the horns to play the same thing as the voice, but I want it to be a little bit under so it has a kind of big band feeling to it, and then I want some specials.' And what was going on with Thad's band is basically what I'm doing. It's like a small group version of what I *learned*.

"I also became the darling of the jazz scene in the '70s. I was, like, *the* singer and so I did guest appearances on just about everybody's album. If I didn't sing with them on their album, I played with them in concerts, so I worked with everybody—from Rahsaan Roland Kirk to Pharoah Sanders to the lesser known musicians like Cecil McBee and Stanley Cowell. The Collective Black Artists Ensemble—I sang with that band; I did gigs with Dizzy Gillespie and Clark Terry. I always was kind of taken under the wing of and felt most comfortable with trumpet players—probably because my father was a trumpet player and my first husband was a trumpet player. It was always a trumpet. I think a lot of the time when I listen to the way I sing I sound like a trumpet. You have a trumpet play along with me, and a lot of times I really blend in with it to the point that now I feel like I should maybe not have a trumpet any more; maybe I should have a 'bone, so that we can have different colors. I can blend *so well* with a trumpet now that it sounds like one horn. So trumpet is, I guess, my instrument because of my daddy and Thad.

"I did *The Wiz* 1974 to '76 because I wasn't making enough money working with the band and they just kept cutting me back. I was singing less and less and there was a lot more tension. If I didn't sing on Monday nights, people would leave the club, and Thad and Mel started complaining that I was stealing their big public. They started cutting back on how much singing I was doing on Monday nights, and sometimes I would go off on a tour with them and they would say, 'Oh, we forgot!' I wouldn't sing!" She guffawed. "They forget to call me up on stage! So I got a little funky. It was like love-hate the last year and a half that I was with the band.

"I heard about this play because I had become good friends with Stanley Cowell and his girl friend and she says, 'You ought to go audition.' So I auditioned and then went on that second tour in Europe with Thad Jones and Mel Lewis. When I came back I got the role of Glenda the Good Witch. And I just said, 'See you!' to the band and I said, 'See you!' to Cecil. We did a six-month tour out of town, try-outs, and then we came in to New York.

"I always loved theater. I used to always look at the musical movies from the '30s and '40s. I used to lo-o-v-ve that nice dream about coming downstairs. I always wanted to come down those huge spiral staircases with men on both sides, wearing those flowing gowns, and being picked up and all that kind of stuff. That's exactly what happened in *The Wiz*. I came down the stairs, which weren't spiral, but I came out of a kind of gorgeous teepee and there're men on either side of me. I've got this huge train on my dress, and I'm picked up, and I sing, and they're carrying me across. It was just like living my dream

"I moved to Los Angeles in the later '70s and lived there for seven years. Then I went to France with the first national touring company of *Sophisticated Ladies*. We did a six-month tour in the states and then we went to Japan for six weeks and on to Paris. That was in January of '84, and I stayed until September. In '86 I was offered the role of Billie Holiday in a play called *Lady Day*, a one-woman show *in* French *in* Paris, and that is when I went back definitively. In September I met my present husband, whose name is Jean Marie Durand.

"I am very settled there. But I don't look at myself as an expatriate. I don't know why I feel really sensitive about that word, but I feel when someone says 'expatriate' it means that she's given up her history. I'm very happy living in France. I decided to stay there for personal reasons because I was in the midst of a *very* ugly divorce with my second husband and I decided I better stay over there. Also, I liked it and I felt respected. It was a place for me to find myself. I found that they have this incredible love and respect for jazz music. I was able to start back singing jazz—not in clubs but doing concerts. Everything that I had ever wanted to do in the States I found myself *doing* in France. The better my French got, the better the offers got, until I had my own jazz TV show and I had my own radio show, which was the number one show on the second biggest radio station in France for four months. I did a kind of jazzy version of the opera *Carmen*, which was a very big hit. I was the first black actress to do the role of Sally Bowles in the musical *Cabaret*, which was also a big hit. You know, I've been able to do just about everything I've ever wanted to do, including being my own producer, which is great.

"Yeah, I kind of am," Dee Dee Bridgewater said, responding to my observation that she was recently described as "the darling of Europe" in the press. "It's true, it's really true. In France now they call me 'Josephine Baker the Second.'

"I noticed something when I was here in August doing a promotional tour for the album, and now since I've been here for three days: these people say, 'Where are you from?' And I go, 'What do you mean, where am I from?' They say, 'What country are you from? You're not American.' And I go, 'I *am* American.' And they go, 'But you don't *act* American.' And I go, 'What do you mean? What does that mean?' They say, 'We don't know, you just don't act American and you don't dress American, and you just don't look American.' And I say, 'Well, I am.' People say that I just *look* and *act* European.

"In the '70s when I got that exposure to Europe, I always wanted to get back there. I always felt really good when I got to Europe because I never felt my color. I always felt like people just accepted me for who I am. Now I feel like there's a heavy racial tension going on here in the States at this time; I really feel like there's kind of a polarization between blacks and whites. I just kind of walk around and I go, 'Hey! How ya doin'?' to white people, and they go, 'Hi, how are you?' And then they're, like, 'Where're you from?' 'Cause they don't get it. And I don't understand what the problem is. I'm just treating people like people, because that's what it is in Europe.

"I get a lot of static having these European players with me and the fact that they're white. When the black musicians come to Paris or when they come to France or when I run into them at jazz festivals, it's always, 'Sister, whacha doin'? You gotta come back home. When you gonna come back and start playin' with your brothers?' And, 'Whadaya doin'? They can't play for you; they can't give you that rhythm.' But they *do*, and I *like* it and we *do* have a good musical communication. It's *not* about color. There's no difference, no difference at all.

"It depends on the song I'm singing," Dee Dee said, answering my question about how she interprets a song. "Like doing the Horace Silver repertoire, some of the lyrics he wrote are really funny. So, with the funnier lyrics, I just kind of clown and it's more acting. It's a combination, because at the same time his songs are not easy to sing, so you have to stay disciplined and really concentrate. Now that I've been doing it for a year and a half, I've got it well enough that I can play with it. I can also, through the comedy and the acting and the theatrics of it, and with the moving and the gestures, pull the public into what I'm doing and really make them feel like they're a connection between the song and myself. It's really basically a combination of everything. I'm not sad, so a song like 'Lonely Woman' does not necessarily touch me, but I've been there so it becomes more of an acting thing than a personal thing. And I think Horace's lyrics are about his life, so it's like I'm telling stories. So I'm a storyteller, basically. That's what's happening now."

"I built this room for that Steinway Grand D, that big one there," began singer and pianist Shirley Horn, pointing to the massive instrument. It was a very hot July evening in 1995 and we were talking in her home in her native city of Washington, D.C. "And the day they brought it in I told the men they'd have to bring it in through the wall.

"I used to always want to pick at the piano when I was a kid," continued Shirley. "My grandmother had what people now don't know about. It was called a parlor. Parlor was for company, you know, and it was always closed down with the French doors. My grandmother had an old upright piano in there and I wouldn't want to do anything but just play on that piano. And my grandmother told my mother, 'Give her lessons; she's interested in the piano.' So I had my first lessons when I was four. In fact, at the end of my fourth year I had a concert with my piano teacher at that time, Mr. Fletcher."

Shirley Horn studied from then until she was eighteen. She does not remember specific music that she heard during these early years, but affirms that "my people loved music. I didn't get the Mickey Mouse music. I didn't hear that at home, growing up. I don't know what I was playing, but my grandmother used to say, 'Well, this sounds like *something*, what she's playing.' I just know that I would go into the parlor, and the parlor was cold, all the time, summer and winter, 'cause it was always closed off, and I remember in the winter playing on the piano, sitting on this little round, wind-up seat, with my coat on.

"At four years I was playing by ear. My mother took me to Mr.

Fletcher, who was interested in me and he took me as a student. Before I could read and write I was playing the piano, playing little things, whatever he taught me at that time. I remember always *wanting* to go to piano lessons. I remember hearing kids yelling and screaming because they didn't want to go. But I *wanted* to go; I wanted music like a passion. And that's what I remember first in my life—music. I was about six, I guess, when I learned to read music.

"My people loved the good singers. My mother went to school with Billy Eckstine, and he was kind of a star even at that time. I remember Dinah Washington's voice, I remember Joe Williams, Louis Armstrong; I remember *plenty* of Billie Holiday, and all the great singers. I remember the voices, not that I knew what they were singing about. And about the playing, I really can't remember.

"My first teacher told my mother, 'I can't teach her any more— got to move her on.' Then I went with Dr. Gladys Hughes, who's still living. At twelve, thirteen, I loved Debussy and Rachmaninoff, but it was Erroll Garner who was really strong in my life. Mother would buy his records. I listened to his music and I'd play everything note-for-note. I loved his music.

"Around twelve years old, I played for Sunday school and church. I remember when I was in junior high school, I was taken out of class a lot because I played for *all* the classes and the musicales and things they used to have at those times. I could read music and I could play like Erroll Garner. You see, I was famous," she said, laughing at the memory. "You know, sometime I'll see somebody from school days I haven't seen in years and he'll say, 'You still play like Erroll Garner?'

"I was very shy and I remember that I sang in the choir at school. In fact, I played for the choir. But singing? Hmmm, not really, until I was almost eighteen and I took a job in a dining room that was very famous at the time. I played from five to seven, and I remember an old man who used to come in every evening and have dinner. It was getting close to Christmas time and my parents knew nothing about this because I was supposed to be in school. So he came in one night and brought a teddy bear, a beautiful great big turquoise teddy bear. He sent a note up to me, 'If you sing "Melancholy Baby" the teddy bear is yours.' Well, I'd heard all these songs at home, so I remembered the lyric and I sang the song. I was scared to death.

"I wanted to play in clubs because my mother and father took me to see Erroll Garner. I wasn't quite eighteen; I was in the junior school of music at Howard University at the time. I don't know if you remember Clara Bow from Washington, D.C. She was a great pianist and singer, an older woman. Clara Bow took an interest in me after she found out I could sing. She went to the club owners and said, 'She can sing; she can get more money.' I went to audition for this job and the woman hired me, because I put my age up two years. I got more money, I got paid $175 for five days. Then she went to—can I call a name that you remember?—Olivia Davis. Olivia Davis at that time owned the Maryland Club on L Street, which was a fine dining room. Later, I worked a lot at Olivia's Patio Lounge.

"The last part of my eighteenth year I had a trio and I remember their names. It was Louis Powers and Harold Minor. I didn't know what I was doing; I knew absolutely nothing about jazz. I'd go around and want to sit in with the guys and Buck Hill was the only person who was nice to me. He said, 'Here comes this pest again.' I wanted to learn. He let me sit in a little bit on the jobs he played. At one time the Howard Theater was going great guns and I remember this place called the 7th and T Cocktail Lounge. All the musicians who came to the Howard Theater came to the 7th and T, and I used to go there. Eventually, I worked that job. There was so much music coming out of there! Oh, wow! It was great! Things were different then. I had a convertible at one time and I'd park right in front of the place, top down, nobody bothered it. But it's all different now.

"Olivia Davis knew me because I worked at the other dining room; and when she opened that Patio Lounge, I got really known then because I worked there as opening band for all the big artists. Everybody came through there. When Oscar Peterson came through, I thought I was going to die; I couldn't play. And I met George Shearing there and Ahmad Jamal; I met everyone there.

"Then I got a call from John Levy in 1960 to do a record and I went to New York and made *Embers and Ashes*. And things started happening. Quincy Jones heard me and recorded me and I met Miles. I was in Virginia with my husband's mother, having breakfast. It was early in the morning. I got this call. I said, 'Who's calling me?' My mother was the only person who knew where I was. 'This is Miles Davis.'" She simulated a Miles-like croak. "I said, 'Who?' ''S Miles Davis; I want you to come to New York. Some people I think you should meet.' And I laughed; I said, 'Who *is* this?' I'm thinking this is a friend playing a joke, right? Anyway, he sounded serious and I went back and finished all that good food I was eatin'.

"It got on my mind, something he said to me, and I said, 'Shep, you know, I got a feeling I should go to New York.' So I called a friend's family to meet me at the train station and we went directly to Miles Davis's house. We got there, I heard his kids—a lot o' kids—and each one of those kids was singing a song from my new album. So I knew Miles knew about my music. I met Gil Evans, I met Teo Macero—they were all there to meet me. I mean, I really didn't know who these people were. Miles insisted that I open for him at the Village Vanguard. He told Max Gordon, 'If she doesn't open, I don't play.' So that's the way we got started.

There was a period of national inactivity for Shirley Horn in the 1960s and '70s. "Well, I got married and then I had a baby, my daughter. I have no regrets. I was a mother and my daughter needed me and I needed her. I decided I'm just going to stay home and see about her. And I'm happy I did. She's a wonderful, wonderful lady. I have two grandboys, one ten and one fourteen."

An observation of mine that in the late 1970s she made a comeback elicited laughter. "Well, I was still out there performing. I was doing everything. I played all the concerts and everything, I even played at a funeral home one time. I didn't do a lot of traveling. I'd go a little bit and come home. Percy Heath said, 'You got the strongest rubber in the world because you're always bouncing back to Washington.' Well, I had my baby here and I was fortunate that I had two grandmothers at that time living.

"I remember one time I was working in New York at a place called Carlo's Circle Bar and I was so disgusted. Number one, it rained every night and I've got a foot that bothers me. Everything was all wrong—the piano was wrong, the sound system, everything was just horrible. But I said, 'I got to finish out this week.'

"In the meantime, this man comes in, gives me a card, and he's from Polygram Records. I said, 'What is this Polygram?' I was in a very bad mood that night." She chuckled. "I had some friends sittin' at the bar. They said, 'Polygram is—.' But I never heard of it. The man who came in was Richard Seidel.

"So we recorded, and recorded. I had no idea it would balloon like it did. I'm a home person. I don't like to be away too much. But I've learned. Like, I'm in love with Paris and Paris is in love with me. There're a few places I like to go to, like in California there's a place—San Francisco.

A fateful occasion for Shirley was her meeting North Sea Jazz Festival founder and producer Paul Ackett at the 1981 *JazzTimes* convention at Washington, D.C.'s, Shoreham Hotel.

"I was at the beach and I got a call to come there, and I thought, 'I don't want to go.' Anyway, it rained like crazy; it was a bad storm, and there was a family reunion. But I told my cousin, 'I think I better go.' So I went home and changed clothes and went to the Shoreham and I met Paul Ackett there. I want to say, he was one of the most wonderful men I ever met in my life. I respect him. He invited me and I went. He treated me like a loving uncle would; he was just so wonderful. He was almost like family. He was just great. I did a lot of those North Sea festivals. Steeplechase recorded me every night at that first one.

"Then this woman calls and she set up a concert in Paris at the beautiful Theatre du Chatelet, and the Parisians just loved me. However, I didn't realize that they knew more about my music than I knew. It was a beautiful concert. Then I did another one and I did another one. I eventually recorded one about five years ago. I'm looking forward to doing it again.

"This year July was crazy. I was in Japan, I was in Holland, I was at five dates in Canada. It was too much. Even though I kind of miss it, and travel kind of gets in your blood, the blood gets weak.

"Let's talk about the new record," Shirley Horn suggested. "Who was here? Elvin Jones was here, Billy Hart with my Steve Williams, Charles Ables, Steve Novosel, Buck Hill, and Joe Henderson. So we were all here in this house; we recorded everything right here. I cooked all four days. Name of the album is *The Main Ingredient*—which is the music. It was quite a job for me, but I enjoyed it. They sent a truck, I mean the longest truck, tallest truck I've ever seen in my life. They had to get a special permit to park out there. Well, here's what I'm thinking, 'Oh, here's the truck. Only thing I'm looking to get is those big wires coming through here.' But, baby, let me tell you. I came downstairs, it was so quiet; everything was done. They had these big black boxes, machines, all this stuff, stacked up to the ceiling in here. They had to move my drapes and my plants. I was worried about my plants. Then the second day the video cameras were in there, and I said, 'What am I going to do?'" Shirley burst into laughter. "Only thing I could think of, 'It Don't Mean a Thing If It Ain't Got That Swing.' But it was quite something. It was a big thing for me."

The resurgence of her career the past decade and a half has reestablished Shirley Horn as an uncompromising jazz artist of the first rank. It has also taken her to major jazz festivals here and abroad, to Lincoln Center, the Blue Note in Tokyo, Paris, and other far-flung locales. Shirley's *Here's to Life* was declared *Billboard's* 1992 Jazz Album of the Year. In 1990 she made her movie debut, with Peter Falk and Barbara Hershey in *Tune in Tomorrow*; backed by Wynton Marsalis and his band, she sings "I Can't Get Started" in a nightclub scene. Last year Shirley Horn was awarded the fifth annual Phineas Newborn Jr. Award for her lifelong contributions to jazz. Among those performing at the award ceremony in New York's Merkin Hall were singers Carol Sloane, Vanessa Rubin, Teri Thornton, Carrie Smith, and Andy Bey.

The first time I planned to catch Diana Krall at Blues Alley in Washington, D.C., I couldn't get in the door, even with my press credentials. It was a one-nighter, and I had waited until the eleventh hour to call the club; by then not even a bar stool was unspoken for. A year later I applied early through her management in Vancouver. They not only put me on her guest list for opening night of her four-night engagement but also arranged for me to meet her that evening.

Already familiar with her strong showing on her several CDs, I was transfixed throughout the hour-long set by her thoroughly comfortable way both with standards from the Great American Songbook and with later materials, by her keyboard skills, and by her tremendous swing. The interplay between her, guitarist Russell Malone, and bassist Ben Wolfe was also something to behold, coming out of the tradition of piano trio established better than a half century ago by Art Tatum and Nat King Cole and perpetuated by Oscar Peterson. I also found her to be a charming and warm personality when we spoke later in the evening. A few weeks later, I had an opportunity for a real interview with the Vancouver-area, British Columbia native.

"I don't remember not being aware of music," Diana Krall responded to my opening question; "It's something that I probably just heard as a baby. My dad played music at home and I took piano lessons from the age of five. My teacher, Audrie Thomas, used to play Albert Ammons after our lesson. I liked the rhythm of boogie woogie. And church, my mother singing in the choir." Those piano lessons were classical and Diana, too, sang in that choir.

That music was a family tradition going back three generations became clear as Diana Krall recounted her family's history.

"Every Sunday since I was a baby, we'd go over to my grandmother Jean Krall's and everybody would sing music. It was 'Oh, by Jingo' and 'Hard-Hearted Hannah.' It was from old songbooks. I remember 'Ebb Tide' being on the piano. It's very complicated, because my grandmother's aunt, Jean Krall, was in vaudeville in New York. So *she* taught my grandmother. She did comedy and song. And my grandmother's brother, my uncle Johnny, was very musical and used to sing in Nanaimo pubs.

Diana's father, Steven James ("he's known as Jim") Krall, played stride piano ("and still does"). Her uncle, Randy Krall, "plays totally by ear and didn't play jazz so much; he plays music from the '50s, like Buddy Holly, just these gigs around my hometown. Later on, when I was fifteen years old or so, I started playing at my grandparents'. I would go over there and hang out with them and go through stacks of music books and play the piano.

"I remember when I was in fourth grade we had talent shows and I played 'Baby Elephant Walk,' a Henry Mancini tune, and when I couldn't figure out the rest of the piece I made it up." Krall had learned to read music when she was five but she was soon picking up tunes by ear from records. "I was playing Elton John and Billy Joel and Clean—I loved Clean—and pop music. In elementary school, in the seventh grade, the stage band from the high school came to visit in performance for the school, and I wanted to be in that band. But I had to play in the concert band, too, and they didn't have piano in the concert band so I played clarinet. They used to give me the Dixieland solo feature. But I wasn't studying clarinet, just playing it. I was improvising already without really knowing what I was doing." She also "checked out saxophone and trombone," adding in an ingenuous understatement, "but piano is my favorite instrument."

High School was Nanaimo District Senior Secondary School, which trumpeter Ingrid Jensen attended a couple of years later.

"In the eleventh grade I was playing piano with a trio at school. We were doing a jam session and my band teacher Brian Stovall heard us and said it was great and called my mother. My mother said, 'What has she done now?' and he said, 'She hasn't done anything wrong.' He told her that he thought I had talent. So I found a teacher in Victoria whom I studied with. I had had a teacher earlier, in the summer, who taught me 2-5-1 progressions and gave me the basis of jazz harmony. On my own I studied with another pianist through junior high school. I had all that preparation I'd done on my own before I entered high school." In addition to Stovall, her instructors were Dave Strong, Chris Donison, and Louise Rose, the last of whom had studied in the 1960s at the Oscar Peterson School in Toronto. "In the stage band I was playing Cannonball Adderley things like 'Work Song.' And I was playing all over the place. I'd go to bars and just sit in at jazz sessions."

After high school Diana Krall won a New Westminster Jazz Festival scholarship for outstanding soloist and for three semesters attended Boston's Berklee College of Music, where she studied with Ray Santisi.

"I was only seventeen and I think I got more out of being in the big city and going to the art galleries and going to the symphony and hearing live musicians and meeting people at school there. I met wonderful people because there are people in the city from all over the world. Culturally, it was a really great experience for me. And musically, as well—all those musicians in one place. That had a big impact on me. I got together with a lot of people and played and it was a great experience. There were a lot of musicians and we were all passionate about jazz music."

After a visit home she intended to return to Boston to study at the New England Conservatory. However, her plans were altered when she met drummer Jeff Hamilton at the Port Townsend jazz camp.

"I told him that I loved the records he did with Ray Brown and John Clayton and said it was kind of my dream to play with them. He was playing in my home town with the L.A. 4 the following month and I'd found out that I'd got the scholarship, a government grant, to go to the New England Conservatory. Instead I went to L.A., and with the help of Jeff and Ray Brown I studied with Alan Broadbent initially. I wanted to study with Jimmy Rowles but they told me he was not teaching. And I loved my studies with Alan. I think he is brilliant. But I wanted to study with Jimmy because he accompanied Billie Holiday. John Clayton came back to town and he said that he had just played with Jimmy the other day. So I called Jimmy up and went over, and I ended up spending about four years with him. I went over to his house every day, pretty much, and he played the piano for me and he'd write out things for me, write out solos. He taught me about Duke Ellington and, mostly, about beauty in music. I was too young to understand that fully, because I was trying to play fast. But he was different; he was unique. I first heard him when I was sixteen years old, playing 'My Buddy.' That was something my grandfather liked. I felt like he was very modern in his approach to standards. And I liked his writing as well. He hasn't an equal, you know; he was very open-minded. He'd give me this chord from *Daphnis and Chloë* one minute and then play something by Wayne Shorter for me, and then something by Teddy Wilson or Art Tatum or Billie Holiday. It sort of hit me that Jimmy had a very unique voice, although it wasn't a pretty voice. He was a very complete musician. He was somebody as a person I seemed to relate to. His way of teaching was a very musical way; it wasn't a theoretical sort of approach. It was, 'Here, borrow these records, listen to Ben Webster.' He was very passionate. I was nineteen and I'm still very close friends with his daughter Stacy. She's a great musician.

"In L.A. I worked at Dick Berk's Jazz Adoption Agency. I was always playing with the best musicians I could find. Usually they were duos in L.A., mostly piano bar gigs. They were jazz, and making-a-living gigs, too. But there weren't a lot of jazz gigs in L.A.—or Toronto either."

After L.A. there was a stay in Toronto and, when she was twenty-four, a move back to Boston. There she worked with bassist Whit

Brown, whose day job was teaching at Berklee. She had discovered that she could get steady work in piano bars and hotels.

"I didn't start singing until 1990. I sang at home privately but I never sang in public. I liked to sing, but I was listening to people like Ernestine Anderson and Sarah Vaughan and Ella Fitzgerald and I didn't think I had that kind of voice. So I guess when I started playing with the trio, with guitar, bass, and piano, I found that I could sing very quietly, and I liked the intimacy of that. It's a growth thing. You learn what works for you. It's just finding yourself."

There was a period when she was commuting back and forth from Boston to New York. "I'd work in Boston Thursday, Friday, Saturday and go back to New York on Sunday, come back on Thursday. I was playing solo piano for three hours and trio—we were using drums—for four. Eventually I worked with guitarist Gray Sargent in a guitar/bass/piano trio. I did that for four years, 1990 to 1994." Of her current musical companions, guitarist Russell Malone and bassist Ben Wolfe, Diana said, "I'm really enjoying working with them.

"I already had a record out"—the 1993 *Stepping Out*, with Ray Brown and Jeff Hamilton—"that I'd done on my own on a Canadian label, and a woman by the name of Barbara Rose gave me my first club gig with John Clayton and Jeff Hamilton. A bunch of record companies were interested in signing me—one of them being GRP—and Carl Griffin was at the time the A & R [Artist and Repertoire] person there. I sent a demo tape to Mary Ann Topper, and she, along with her assistant at the time, Anna Sala, set up a showcase for me at the Blue Note for a Monday night and started booking me with my trio. I was playing and doing things, not tours so much, but U.S. things in clubs, from the time I was twenty-four. I was really busy.

"But I didn't start doing festivals until I was about twenty-nine. Mary Ann and André Menard from the Montreal Jazz Festival put together a package where we'd do the Canadian festivals. I did a week at the Montreal Jazz Festival with Russell Malone on guitar and Paul Keller on bass, a double duo with Benny Green, and a tribute to Nat Cole. That was Mary Ann and André's baby. The real turning point came when we did *All of You*"—produced by Tommy LiPuma—"in 1996. Then we started going to Europe and Japan.

Basically, the Jazz Tree"—Topper's management firm—"really put us out there. And it was Christian McBride's band or the Clayton/Hamilton band, different bands. We just got back again from Paris and England last month. I haven't stopped in, basically, two and a half years. We've been touring very hard to Europe, back and forth, I don't know, fifteen times, maybe, and six trips to Japan. Nagasaki, all over the place. Just this last summer we went from Tunisia to Malta to Ireland. We've really covered a lot of ground. I just got back yesterday. I went to L.A., did the strings with Johnny Mandel"—for her 1999 *When I Look in Your Eyes*—"went to Knoxville, then Utah, San Diego, Atlanta."

Reflecting on her musical education via recorded sounds, Diana Krall said, "It wasn't a conscious thing, something I thought about. I'd just go through my Dad's record collection. Later on I bought my own records. I'd grown up with Fats Waller and Louis Armstrong so I was familiar with all that, had that history already. I'd listened to early American dance bands, like Jean Goldkette. I had exposure to that without really knowing it. I'd sit and listen to records with my dad. Outside of that, in high school it was Bill Evans and Miles Davis—and Cannonball Adderley, of course. Anything I could get my hands on. I just took records from my band director's collection, and other teachers would turn me on to different musicians. I listened to Al Haig, Bob Brookmeyer's Concert Jazz Band, the Pianoless Quartet with Gerry Mulligan and Chet Baker, a *lot* of Bill Evans. The first two Bill Evans records I got were *Waltz for Debby* and *Live at Village Vanguard*. And Oscar Peterson, of course. Nat Cole and Teddy Wilson. Everything. I listened to Art Tatum, but it was too much for me to comprehend; it scared me. I didn't pick up Art Tatum until later. I had one Art Tatum record but he was playing with a band and a guitar. Art Tatum scared me. I was listening to Jimmy Rowles, too." She also cited Ahmad Jamal, Hank Jones, George Shearing, Cedar Walton, and Dave McKenna as others she has paid careful attention to, the last named in live performances frequently while she was at Berklee College of Music. Singers she acknowledges as influences include Connie Boswell, Bing Crosby, Frank Sinatra, Nat King Cole, Rosemary Clooney, Sarah Vaughan, Ella Fitzgerald, Carmen McRae, Lorez Alexandria, and Annette Hanshaw. "And Billie Holiday, of course. Everybody. I just listen to so much. My dad has thousands of records."

Indeed, her listening tastes are eclectic. In addition to those named so far, she has expressed affinity for and interest in everything from opera to Willie Nelson to Dusty Springfield to Joni Mitchell to Dave Frishberg to Alanis Morissette to Sting. Her performance book draws from George Gershwin, Irving Berlin, Duke Ellington, Cole Porter, Harry Warren, Jerome Kern, Nat Cole, Dave Frishberg, Stevie Wonder, Canadian songwriter Shirley Eikhard, the blues—you name it. Stanley Turrentine, Ray Brown, Christian McBride, Lewis Nash, and Jeff Hamilton have been some of her musical associates on recordings and/or in performance.

In a schedule that reflects her broad tastes and varied talents, Diana Krall has done cameo appearances on the albums of performers of different genres, for example, the 1999 CD of the traditional Irish group, the Chieftains, *Tears of Stone*, on which she sings "Danny Boy." She performed in as unlikely a setting as the Lilith Fair, at which the 17,000-strong rock-oriented audience paid enthralled attention to her trio's rendition of Cole Porter's "I've Got You Under My Skin." Her singing has been praised by, among others, Tony Bennett, Abbey Lincoln, Nancy Wilson, and the late Betty Carter. She sings three new Benny Carter songs on the venerable saxophonist/trumpeter/composer's *Songbook*, Volumes 1 and 2. Her albums reach—and remain for weeks at—the top of the hit lists and she wins awards right and left. In New York, it's no longer piano bars; it's the Oak Room of the Algonquin Hotel. She was featured as a soloist at the 1996 all-star Carnegie Hall tribute to Ella Fitzgerald and was a judge for the 1998 Thelonious Monk Institute's vocal competition. For her Japan tours her itinerary is the Blue Note clubs. Cover stories on her regularly appear in jazz magazines, perhaps most notably the one last year in *JazzTimes* by author Gene Lees, who was unstinting in his praise of both her singing and her pianistic craft. She even appeared in an episode of Melrose Place, performing at a club where the show's principals hang out, and she had a cameo appearance performing in the 1998 film *At First Sight*.

"The most important thing for me is my family and my friends, of course, but my passion is playing the music. There are many things that music is and it's my passion and I feel very lucky. Jeff

Hamilton always told me, 'You *get* to do this.' And, you know, I don't get paid to play—I get paid to travel and for that 'living-out-of-a-suitcase' thing." She chuckled, having quoted a phrase I had earlier employed. "But I don't get paid to play. I feel very fortunate that I can do this, that I have the opportunities that I never thought I'd have—for instance, working with Johnny Mandel, Ray Brown. And to just learn and grow. My experiences sometimes overwhelm me, you know? How much fun can you have," she said, laughing, "doing what you love to do? I'm so lucky that I do something that I love."

5

Composers

"I'm anti-composition. We like to think of keeping the taxi waiting while we make the record, as opposed to spending three months in the studio."   Paul Bley

"I have no method, other than I sit down at the piano and do this."   Joanne Brackeen

"When you're trying to create something that's a little different and you really have the time, I think that's better than having to create on demand."   Jimmy Heath

What with the extemporaneous nature of jazz and the ease with which its performers create without paper in front of them, the discipline and labor that go into jazz composition is often lost sight of. Composing in jazz is sometimes thought of as players just mounting the bandstand and blowing whatever comes into their heads. Well, that is certainly one aspect of the process, for any performer in this improvisatory art form must be able to think ahead for a few bars while playing and, ideally, come up with something different from the last time he or she performed the tune at hand. Sometimes the player creates anew a melody, a set of chord changes, or a rhythm, and sometimes a combination, thereby literally composing on his or her feet. However, unless this musician soon makes

some sort of a record of that moment, the creative act may well van-
ish into thin air. Still, many jazz artists do compose in the quiet of
the study and, as we shall learn from those profiled in this chapter,
their methodologies are both diverse and similar.

I have caught saxophonist Jimmy Heath so many times in so
many contexts and formats that it would be fruitless to try to recall
more than a few of them. Some of the highlights would be the times
I saw him with big bands or combos led by Dizzy Gillespie; the
unforgettable times when he was in the company of his brothers
Percy, on bass, and Tootie, at the drums; and the many weekends
during the 1980s when he was in residence with his own group at
Washington, D.C.'s, One Step Down. In 1983 he brought that
quartet—with regular members guitarist Tony Perowne, bassist
Stafford James, and drummer Akira Tana—to Woodie's Hilltop Pub
across the street from Howard University for a two-nighter. Jimmy
and I got together during his brief visit to D.C. and talked.

Jimmy had by then already been a professional musician for more
than four decades. His early history put him in contact with the very
roots of the idiom. He had toured in the mid-1940s with the
Nebraska-based territory band of bassist Nat Towles, who had
played with such pioneer New Orleans jazzmen as cornetist Buddy
Petit and Jack Carey, the latter of whom is said to have originated
the feline roar on "Tiger Rag" with his trombone.

An even earlier experience gave Jimmy a taste of the tent show
life.

"I was just out of high school," the Philadelphia native told me,
"and I and another saxophone player, a trumpet player, and a piano
player who played boogie woogie style used to go over to Jersey and
work in this carnival. We were known as the Dixie Red Hots."

Heath's father played clarinet, his mother sang in the church
choir, and his two brothers became major jazz players. Jam sessions
often happened in the Heath home or nearby at trumpeter Johnny
Cole's house "because both our mothers were receptive to the
music. The people who would come to those things were Philly Joe
Jones, John Coltrane, Ray Bryant, Benny Golson, Dolo Coker—
people like that—and Percy and myself. We would get together and
have sessions and people would stand around at the windows and
listen from the street. At times I'd have a whole rehearsal of a big

band in the living room. We were trying to get familiar with the repertoire that was being played in the clubs. Those jam sessions were a place for education because of the commonness of the repertoire and what you can learn from everybody else. Today you can get so much from records now that we didn't get, but there's a personal thing about being able to communicate that you miss, I think, without that immediate contact. When there's a so-called jam session today, most of the young people don't know the same repertoire. They all try to be composers.

"It was very valuable in the sense of who was there," Jimmy said with conviction, "the camaraderie, the way everyone wanted the same thing, to develop their music, and nobody was thinking about being famous or being rich or nothing. It was just everybody wanted their music to be right.

"I was the first professional in the Heath family because Percy was in the air force and I was already out in Omaha in the Nat Towles band. I met Billy Mitchell and Ray Brown and Neal Hefti and a lot of other people who were from around there."

After leaving the Towles band, Jimmy Heath returned to Philadelphia and formed his own combo, which trumpeter Howard McGhee soon took over as leader "because he had a bigger name in the jazz business than I did." In 1947 Jimmy and Percy went to New York with that band. Jimmy joined the big band of Dizzy Gillespie in 1949. "John Coltrane and I got in Dizzy's band a month apart and we would watch Paul Gonsalves play the tenor saxophone and get all the girls, while we were playing alto and didn't have near the appeal that Paul had." He laughed out loud at the memory.

In 1959 Heath did a stint in Miles Davis's combo and in the 1960s he and Art Farmer worked together. Other associations include Kenny Dorham, Gil Evans, Clark Terry, Billy Higgins, Stanley Cowell, and Curtis Fuller. Since the 1970s Jimmy has led his own combo and devoted much of his time to composing. About eighty of his songs had been recorded, he said, and added that his "Gingerbread Boy" had been covered on albums by about ten groups and that he had published two books of his tunes.

"I stay in a room with scores and piano and saxophones and stay at it," Jimmy began his account of how he writes music. "It's a matter of experience now. I've been doing it a long time. I started it, I would say, at the time I was with Nat Towles's band. That's when I first got interested in writing for big band—not necessarily composition, but orchestration at that time, and *then* composition. It all came together and I studied later when I was about to write the *Afro-American Suite of Evolution*." To work on this he received a New York State of the Arts grant in 1974. "I studied to get some string writing and other techniques I needed to continue composition. It's a personal thing; you just have to work hard on it, and then when you get it, you have to realize that somebody already got that song and then"—he chuckled at this admission—"you have to change it! It's like Duke Ellington says, 'All the songs have been written and it's just rearranging it now.' It's almost true, you know, because there are very little differences. Once in a while you find something, but after we've been out here so long we hear the same thing again."

Jimmy Heath said that he gets ideas at any time, "but they usually flash and go away. So recently I keep a tape recorder handy, a Walkman type. I think that's the only way to keep the stuff. The ideas come and go.

"Some of them take longer to write than others; some of them I mess around with for a long time. When you're trying to create something that's a little different and you really have the time, I think that's better than having to create on demand, as I'm doing now—which is to complete four big band arrangements by next Wednesday! I can't spend as much time mulling over ideas. I have to settle sooner.

"I've been doing quite a bit of big band work and doing college band work where I perform with the bands. And I've written a lot of big band arrangements on some of my compositions."

Our talk then turned to the status of jazz.

"New York is a place where you have a lot of opportunities for creative musicians to do just about their own thing, and Europe maybe, too. In America every city has its jazz fans, but the masses of people are still going for pop music around the world. The level of awareness of jazz is still kind of low. I think there's a little bit of movement in the colleges. But there should be movement *before* that. That's the problem. By the time young people get in college they've gotten their favorite people. The education system doesn't allow them to like more than one thing at a time; that's what I can't understand. Why can't you like pop music and like jazz and like classical music? What *is* it? It's very difficult; it's still a fight. We're still left out of the books.

"I'm sure there will be some people playing jazz in another twenty years—I don't know how many. I heard one guy when I was in Aspen, Colorado, doing a workshop—a kid who's a saxophone player in a big band; he's fourteen and from Columbia, South Carolina. His name is Chris Potter, and he's a great jazz saxophonist. Slide Hampton tells me he saw a girl in Sweden who's nine who played the trombone and she could play Jack Teagarden and had a concept of J. J. Johnson. She knew all this stuff already. So with a few young people here and there, it's going to be here forever. But we should stop trying to compare it with pop music and just consider that jazz and classical music are not commercial. They should be supported."

"I cry a lot," baritone saxophonist Gerry Mulligan confessed, chuckling, when I questioned him in the mid-1980s about his compositional methods, "and when I'm not doing that I roll around under the piano." Gerry was in Washington, D.C., for a week at Charlie's Georgetown with his quartet—pianist Bill Mays, bassist Michael Formenak, and drummer Richie DeRosa.

"It just requires time concentration, continuity of time," he continued in a more serious vein, "so that you can follow through on ideas. It's good to work at the piano and then, at various times, to get away from the piano for a while to try to avoid the trap of the keyboard. Even so, I've been thinking for horns on the piano for so many years that I've been kind of able to get beyond my own limited piano technique." Mulligan explained that the piano has limitations as a composing tool in that "a lot of times you find yourself restricting yourself to what your fingers can do and what they fall into naturally, and when you're dealing with orchestration and specific instruments, there are things that are particular to an instrument and to a section that, away from the keyboard, you're more likely to think about." He clarified that he also composed with the aid of his baritone saxophone.

Assuming, correctly, that the composition was written down as it came into being, I asked if he ever simply played, whether at the piano or on his horn, with a tape recorder going.

"In the manner of Bach, who would improvise a piece on the organ and go home and write it down? No, I have no luck at all with tape recorders. They've been absolutely no help to me in a compositional way. What I'm curious to look into are some of the new computer possibilities, the kinds of things that you write directly on a computer and then when you want to make changes you can change a note here and a note there without having to rewrite a whole section. If I ever get around to it, it *will* have some effect in terms of ease, in the sense that, like a word processor, you can write a paragraph and move it around where you want it, and I'm fascinated with the possibilities of that, because now when I want to do that it means that I have to write pages all over again. So far, I'm only at the curious stage. I read a couple of books on computers a couple of years ago and that put me off for at least five years.

"I've been doing a lot of writing the last couple of years," said Gerry, who was already arranging for big band when he joined the Gene Krupa orchestra as a nineteen-year-old in 1946. He also wrote arrangements for the bands of Claude Thornhill and Elliot Lawrence and tunes for Miles Davis's 1950 *Birth of the Cool* album, on which he played. After a brief association with the Stan Kenton band, he formed and began writing for his own pianoless quartet and his tenette in the 1950s. From the 1960s into the 1990s he wrote for his own part-time big bands.

"The big band is sixteen pieces," Gerry pointed out, "and we only do concerts with it. It's made up of musicians who are based in New York. Some years we work a lot with the band and some years very little, but because of the continuity of the personnel it's never a problem to get a full complement of people who've played the book. So if we go out and play one or two concerts somewhere, it's an organized band. We did a world tour five years ago and last year we did just a handful of concerts, mostly around the New York area. This year we've done two concerts, also here in the area. And, you know, with the dollar in the condition it's in overseas, it's very difficult for them to plan ahead in Europe. They're having a terrible time this year.

"I do a lot more with the quartet, actually. I always think of the quartet, even when we're playing in a concert hall, as more of a recital than a big show and I like to do that very much. Most of the members of the quartet have been with me a long time and in almost every instance in both the big band and the quartet there are at least two players in each chair that've played with me long enough and in different situations that we can take a group out and not have to start from the beginning.

"What I'm working on now is new material," he elaborated, "more things to play for the symphony. Last year I took off from playing for the whole winter and wrote a piece for the symphony, a solo piece. We did quite a bit of symphony performing last year, about a dozen concerts. We had some very nice ones. The first playing of my new piece was in Italy with a small orchestra in a little town twenty minutes north of Venice. It was wonderful. We had three days to rehearse the piece and went out and played it four times around the area. Since then we've done it with the Los Angeles Symphony in the Hollywood Bowl for two days and with the London Symphony at Festival Hall. At the same time, I'm writing new things for my big band and trying to come up with some new things for the quartet as well.

"We live in Italy part time, in Milan," Gerry Mulligan informed me. "It's a very special place for me. I think here in the United States, it seems like maybe people are getting a little more enthusiastic about going out to a concert. There for a while it seemed like they were all nailed to their television sets and didn't like to go out to any place of entertainment, where they couldn't go to the refrigerator during the commericals. If that is indeed a new trend, that people are going out, like for an occasion you have to get yourself together for, that's a very promising sign for everyone."

Gerry Mulligan died in 1996 of complications resulting from surgery. He was sixty-eight.

It has been nearly two decades since *Down Beat* ran a feature entitled "Leading Lady Pianist." No little irony resided in the circumstance that the same issue of the magazine carried the results of its Thirtieth International Critics Poll, in which that "Lady Pianist," Joanne Brackeen, headed the otherwise all-male listing of pianistic "Talent

Deserving Wider Recognition." It was at about that same time that some *Down Beat* readers wrote to the publication objecting to their outmoded use of the term "Jazzman of the Year." Future polls employed the term "Jazz Musician of the Year."

In the next year's poll, Joanne Brackeen made it into fifth place in the "Established Talent" category, treading on the heels of four major male pianists. She has been awarded grants by the National Endowment for the Arts and has received commissions from a number of universities, was recruited by the U.S. State Department to tour Europe and the Middle East, has been a faculty member of New York's New School for more than a decade and of the Berklee College of Music since the mid-1990s, and has recorded more than twenty albums as leader. Her itinerary since the late 1970s has taken her all over this continent and on many tours overseas.

"We've gotten an excellent reception in Europe," Brackeen observed when we talked two decades ago. She had recently returned from abroad and added, "They have jazz all over, in tiny, tiny cities that the U.S. would *never* have a jazz club in. Usually, they're quite full, packed, halls, festivals, or clubs."

Last year her trio of Ira Coleman on bass and Horacio Hernandez on drums was augmented by saxophonist Ravi Coltrane for a week at New York's Jazz Standard in celebration of the release of her debut album on the Arkadia label, *Pink Elephant Magic.* Saxophonist Greg Osby joined the trio for a follow-up trip to Europe with stops in Scotland, Austria, and Germany. Joanne also recently did a solo concert at the Kennedy Center, was booked at the Smithsonian Institution with her quartet, toured Switzerland and Germany with Pharoah Sanders, joined the 100 Gold Fingers Tour of Japan (with the likes of Hank Jones and Kenny Barron), and was featured in the Legends of the '70s at Town Hall.

Of course, it was and is pointless to think of this outstanding performer, leader, and composer in terms of gender. She is simply one of our major contemporary keyboard artists.

In the late '70s and early '80s, I made it a point to hear Joanne Brackeen at Washington, D.C.'s, One Step Down whenever she was there. On one of those occasions, when she had brought along the extraordinary bassist Clint Houston, we sat in a booth between sets and talked into a tape recorder.

"If I want a bass player," she explained when I asked if she ever used women in her combos, "I want a player at Clint's or Eddie Gomez's level." She said that she did not know of any women who could match the craft and creativity of these two artists or of other male bassists she had worked with. She believed this had nothing to do with their gender but was simply because no women players had developed to that level, to the best of her knowledge.

Of course, that was a view she gave expression to two decades ago. As an indication of her increased respect for the level of playing by women instrumentalists, she participated in 1996 in the first Mary Lou Williams Women in Jazz Festival in Washington, D.C.'s, Kennedy Center. Leading an all-star ensemble of trumpeter/flugelhornist Ingrid Jensen, trombonist Lolly Bienenfeld, saxophonist Fostina Dixon, flutist Dottie Anita Taylor, bassist Miriam Sullivan, and drummer Cindy Blackman, Joanne made a point before departing the stage of commending her band members for their performing of the arrangements that she had especially prepared for the evening, as well as expressing high praise for the festival itself and the many women participating in it. Joanne also headlined at the 1999 Women in Jazz series at the Ossining Library in Ossining, New York.

This Ventura, California, native has an unlikely early history for a jazz musician. Her hometown, she says, was "like living in a cave; there didn't seem to be anybody that I ever ran into who knew what was going on." Her first piano teacher "gave up" on her after six months or so.

"I thought she was going to teach me what I heard on the radio," Joanne recalled, but once she learned to read music, what her teacher gave her "would be these ridiculous tunes, so there was no way I could deal with it and she couldn't deal with me. She told my mother to forget it."

Her parents' few records got no closer to the jazz idiom than pianists Carmen Cavallaro and Frankie Carle. The stride element in the latter's playing appealed to her, so the eleven-year-old put to work her extraordinary ear and the rudimentary reading and notational skills she had acquired in those several months of piano lessons and transcribed, note for note, six or eight Carle solos.

"Those records were not cocktail music," she hastened to point out, "they weren't what he did later on. These were with the stride bass; that's what he was playing.

"I wasn't thinking of becoming a piano player," she insisted. "I just wanted to learn the tunes so I could play them." Before she knew it, music had taken hold of her and she was playing those Carle numbers in school assemblies.

By her mid-teens she had moved to Los Angeles. "I learned how to play, I can't remember how—took a few lessons here and there just to learn the tunes." She began hanging out at clubs to check out saxophonists Dexter Gordon and Ornette Coleman and others. She learned solos of Charlie Parker and John Coltrane from recordings, "putting them in every key, just for fun," and she was listening to the albums of Bud Powell and McCoy Tyner. Eventually she began working with Dexter and saxophonists Harold Land, Teddy Edwards, Charles Lloyd, and others.

Married with several children and relocated in New York by the mid-1960s, Joanne Brackeen spent the next decade in, successively, the groups of Art Blakey, Joe Henderson, and Stan Getz. Often, she played alongside players of the stature of Woody Shaw and Freddie Hubbard. This took her to the threshold of her career as a leader in duo and trio formats with musicians such as bassists Houston, Gomez, and Cecil McBee and drummers Billy Hart and Jack DeJohnette.

Inevitably, I asked what performers she was currently listening to.

"I never listen to any music. I don't have time," she insisted, then qualified the statement. "Charlie Parker sounds very good to me right now; John Coltrane sounds good to me. I listen to Trane and I can hear exactly what he was thinking, not just what he was playing, but why he was playing what he was and what there was at that time that he wanted to play that he wasn't playing. I can hear what elements in the rhythm section were causing him not to be able to play what he wanted to play. I can hear a lot now that I didn't used to hear when I was copying his solos. But you ask me that question a year from now I'll give a different answer, because I keep hearing things different; they don't sound the same. I know how Art Tatum sounds to me now; he sounds fantastic. He was a very pianistic piano player.

"We had the same manager," she revealed when I brought up the name of Bill Evans. "In fact, he's the one who told her to manage me. I can't say that I ever knew him, but he came to hear me somewhere and told her that. Very musical pianist. The most important thing about Bill Evans, he knew about the magic, and that's what he attempted to portray. Some of that was never really captured on his records, those last two years. He was at the Vanguard all the time. A lot of us heard those moments."

To my surprise, when I returned to the One Step Down for a second evening and broached the subject of composition, inquiring what her methodology was, she said that she had never been asked that before in an interview.

"I can't remember how I started doing it," she began, "except that I always felt that there were a lot of tunes that I heard in my head and nowhere else. So that's probably why I started writing. It seems as though I had a lot of tunes inside my head and I kept waiting for someone to write them and no one ever did. I hear music inside, and when I compose I try the best I can to get an accurate picture on the outside, on the piano, of what I'm hearing. As we play the tune six, eight months, a year or so later, then the possibilities of the tune start to come out. It seems as though I was always listening to something, but it wasn't necessarily from this planet. It's like a silence, like a very vast black colorful silence, and that's what I used to hear. Tunes would be fragments of that and it's remained that way all throughout my life.

"I don't have any method of composition," she insisted. "It's like after you're on the planet for a while you begin to feel there are forces and energies coming through, and it could be that there're other beings, not human beings, perhaps a little past the point of a human being, that inspire us. That's what it feels like to me. Or you could just call it energy, but there're things that come through all the time.

"And so I just keep writing and it keeps changing and evolving. But I have no method, other than I sit down at the piano and do this. I don't write away from the piano. As a matter of fact, my hands very often create something that I could never have thought of. Then afterwards, I look at it and try to figure out what that was, try to capture that.

"Actually, I put them on tape," she explained. "That's how I capture it, and then later on, of course, you have to write it out. Like now, I had some tunes I wanted to play here, so I had to write them down. I wish I had someone else to do it, but I can do it and I do do it, one way or another."

Intrigued by her account of the passage of a composition from her creative imagination to piano to tape to paper to performance and perhaps again to tape, I asked if a piece she might play later that evening and which had been taped on other evenings would vary a great deal, a little bit, or not much at all from those earlier renditions.

"As far as playing the actual melody of the composition, which lasts from a few seconds to maybe a minute or two, that's pretty much the same. But as far as playing *on* the composition, anything goes. It might sound similar, it might sound totally different and you wouldn't be able to relate it one night to the other. So it's anything goes. Just like our conversation.

"Some of the tunes are kind of short, some are a little longer. I have to learn it. Very often I can't even play what I have composed. That's why I put it on the tape. It might take a week to learn how to play it—different combinations of things that you can hear or things that come out of your hands that you can't quite play. Oh, yeah, I have a tune that I just composed called 'African Aztec' and that took about a week to learn how to play. I knew what it was, but the notes and everything, I couldn't play it.

"It's not like a memory," Joanne Brackeen went on, trying to put into words what she experiences as she improvises on one of her creations. "See, memory of music is not a memory. The memory of music is like the memory of 'I am,' in a sense. You can't forget what you are. It's not quite that but it's into that sort of thing. The memory of music is like remembering who you are. Or the memory of how to drive. It's not like an intellectual memory like you went to school and studied history and had to take a test and then four months goes by and you take the test again and you forgot everything. It's more like a long-term type of thing.

"If you write your own tunes, you write from the nature of the sound that's in you, so that even makes it closer. It's like the way a poet remembers his own poetry, as opposed to almost anyone else's. There might be someone else's he would feel close to, but his own is a living thing to him. That's how the memory of music ought to be for everyone, because that gives them freedom of playing. It gives you a freedom in your improvisation that you wouldn't otherwise have.

"You evolve your own music by working and by performing it," she said, preparing to do just that as she glanced at the clock above the bar. "There's no other way, really, to evolve it totally. It's because I'm working as a leader and I'm working in a context that's comfortable. I feel fortunate to be in the position that I am. Perhaps I can give the same inspiration that I received from innovators like Monk and Bird and Trane and Ornette Coleman. I received that at an early age and I feel indebted to give at least what I received before I make my termination on the planet."

We conclude our selected survey of jazz composers with some remarks from an artist whose attitude might almost seem to disqualify him for inclusion in a section dealing with composition. Actually, though, his approach partakes of the very essence of the creative act of composition in terms of the jazz idiom.

"Well, I'm anticomposition," was pianist Paul Bley's immediate response to my query as to his compositional methods. I had picked that tack as the main focus for my essay that would be on the back of his and Paul Motian's already recorded LP *Notes* on the Milan-based Soul Note label. "Having lived with two composers and having studied composition at Juilliard for a number of years, I guess I was overtrained at composition."

The Montreal native Paul Bley, whose first instrument was violin, began studying piano when he was eight. A soundtrack of a 1953 Canadian TV show catches him playing with Charlie Parker. By his early twenties he was performing in New York in Jackie McLean's quintet, and in the mid-1950s he relocated to Los Angeles, where he formed a combo that included Ornette Coleman and Don Cherry. The '60s found him back in New York leading trios and performing or recording with his first wife Carla Bley, Charles Mingus, Sonny Rollins, and his second wife Annette Peacock. His associations since the mid-1960s in performance and on his many albums have included such artists as Jimmy Giuffre, Gary Peacock, Steve Swallow, Milford Graves, John Gilmore, Evan Parker, Jesper

Lundgaard, and Adam Nussbaum. Paul Bley played a major role in 1960s avant-garde jazz and has been cited as a sort of transition figure who created a link between Bill Evans and some of the free-form pianists who came later.

"What I envision," he continued, "is an ensemble where there is no written material. Most of the album *Notes* is, in fact, improvised. Any relating back to a song and so forth is more like a courtesy to the past. Improvising is real-time composition and I think that only North Americans could have perhaps begun with free jazz, whereas Europeans are more concerned with the history and the structures of composition and seriousness and so forth, and that's very inhibiting to people.

"I think today world-class players can get together and compose pieces of different material, each following another's lead, and do it in real time. Even though all my pieces on the album are titled as compositions, in fact, other than the ones that were prerecorded, they are all made up at the record date. My goal is to do the record date in one fell swoop. We like to think of keeping the taxi waiting while we make the record, as opposed to spending three months in the studio. The album was done in one take, so to speak. We sat down one afternoon and almost recorded it in the sequence it appears on the album.

"I find that the larger the unit, as you add players, each player makes the project more difficult and complex. So solos and duos are the thing to do preliminarily, and since the last two years I've been working again with quartets. One of the things about working with a fixed ensemble is that you're sort of a prisoner of the history. In the case of the piano, bass, drum group, there's so much history to that instrumentation that, by leaving out the bass, you avoid the history and the problems of dealing with it. Also, you make everybody the bass player when there's no bass player because they're always thinking of the bottom of the music as well. They're taking on the added responsibility, so to speak, of a different range of music.

"One thing happened in the 1960s when Albert Ayler and Sunny Murray and Gary Peacock and Paul Motian began playing music where the rhythm was free. That allowed the musicians to choose players based on their ability as opposed to the instrument they play. It was only when you had the time proceeding in a metric manner that the fixed instrumentation—the big band instrumentation, the trio instrumentation, the trumpet, sax, and rhythm instrumentation—was necessary. But in free music, of course, you can let an oboe and a clarinet be the ensemble. In other words, just pick the player based on his ability to compose to suitable instrumentation. Having mastered the various trios and duos and so forth, it seemed to me that part of the problem of finding spontaneity and originality was in the fact that the instrumentation was too fixed."

I had to ask two questions before I felt I could let Paul go. First, how did he explain his long association with Paul Motian, and second, who were his chief influences? To begin, I noted that the tape of the duo album for which I was preparing a liner note left me with the sense that I had been "listening to a kind of conversation."

"Correct, yes," Paul Bley agreed without hesitation. "As a matter of fact, to a conversation that has one or two interesting points. In the case of Paul Motian, he's one of the few free players who very often will create a part that's *not* related to the person he's playing with. In the beginning this might seem off-putting, but on the other hand, if you're playing with someone like that who's not accompanying you, so to speak, but playing a parallel part, if you decide to change direction or do something other than what you're doing, you don't have to worry about having the drummer relate to you and catch it because he wasn't relating to you in the beginning. If you make a left turn, you don't have to worry about whether he's going to follow you." Paul laughed at this revelation. "It's very liberating to have a player like that.

"Influences are *dan-ger-ous things*," he said with deliberately exaggerated emphasis. "I'd be happy to talk about this subject, as opposed to listing six names—which I may do as well. But influences are a dangerous thing. They're not like personal relationships. When you're in love with someone, you can consummate a relationship. In the jazz world, if you're in love with another jazz player who's a major player, especially if he plays the instrument that you play, there's a danger of being overwhelmed by the records of that person, making it difficult for you to find your own voice. So you have to be very careful about your passions.

"If I go to a saxophone player's house and I see nothing but Sonny Rollins records, if I'd never heard the saxophone player play,

I pretty much have a handle on what he's going to do when I finally get to hear him. In other words, you are limited by your enthusiasms. Therefore I would say that, in terms of influences and so forth, what I've tried to do in most of the listening I do is to find things to *avoid*, so to speak.

"To begin with, it's necessary to avoid the work of almost *all* your peers on your instrument because the audience is sitting there almost with a laugh meter, judging whether you sound like this pianist or that pianist, since they've heard all the records. So the first thing to do is to steer clear of an obvious influence, for that's what ruins most players.

"So, on the one hand," Paul Bley continued, chuckling, "when you say who your influences are, I must admit to taking a very hard stance on influences on myself and everyone else. I think we've all had enough of Coltrane saxophonists. *There's* a case of somebody ruining a generation of saxophonists, as Louis Armstrong may have ruined a generation or two of trumpet players.

"But given all that, I think it's healthy, if you're going to have influences, to take them at least from someone who doesn't play the instrument you play. In other words, confine your enthusiasms to those people who play instruments unlike yours so that not only will you take in their material but their tone, take in their phrasing.

"I would say the most crucial thing is not how a player practices or who he plays with, but his or her attitude toward their influences. It's necessary to *avoid* your influences, so to speak. For instance, how could an avant-garde pianist be influenced by Art Tatum, who in fact wasn't a great improviser but a great pianist? He was disjointed in his playing, where one thing would be an improvised line, here an arpeggio, there some large movement over the piano followed by some very short improvised line. It was almost an ornamental piano style as opposed to an improvised kind of style.

"Now *my* influences have usually been horn players," Bley concluded, "which gives me a little room. I'd say my greatest influence is Don Cherry, trumpet player with Ornette Coleman."

6

Strings

"Flaginzie atflagat flagoot flagoozie magwatnie."

Slam Stewart

"A lot of people say they don't like violin and they don't think it fits in jazz, when actually it was one of the instruments in the big band era. Those cats used to double on horn and violin."

Regina Carter

"The audiences I was trying to reach were not interested in harp, period. They were certainly not interested in seeing a black woman playing the harp. I think I had to pave my own way in terms of that area."

Dorothy Ashby

In the 1970s, Slam Stewart began a long-lasting duo collaboration with guitarist Bucky Pizzarelli. A week-long engagement of the pair at the King of France Tavern in Annapolis, Maryland, provided an opportunity for me to interview both artists on my radio show *"I Thought I Heard Buddy Bolden Say . . ."* on Washington, D.C.'s, now long-defunct WGTB-FM. (Excerpts from the Bucky Pizzarelli portion of the program appear in the Musical Families chapter.)

"I was listening to music when I was around seven years old," Slam Stewart told me, "listening to a few of the big bands on radio.

My parents put a little violin in my hands and I actually started out on that. I didn't care much for it. I've always called the violin a 'little squeak box.' Finally, I went to the Boston Conservatory of Music to study the violin further and at that time I chose the bass fiddle. There was something about that depth of sound that really fascinated me and I made a quick switch."

Now, anyone who has heard Slam Stewart perform knows that his approach to the bass is unique. Here is his account of how that approach came about.

"When I started out in the early years playing the bass fiddle I was working with a group around Boston in a couple of night clubs. The group had a youngster playing alto sax in it and he also doubled on violin. When he took a chorus on this fiddle he used to sing along with it. Every note that he played on his fiddle, he used to sing the same note in the same register. And I didn't know how in the world he did that because the violin is very high in tone. So I was playing the bass in this group and I got the idea of humming and singing along with my bass, right? *I* tried it and I found that I couldn't hum or sing the same notes in the same register that I was playing on the bass. So I raised my voice one octave, which was a little easier for me. And that's actually how I started humming and singing along with my bass. So I've kept it in all these years. I originated it."

"Flaginzie atflagat flagoot flagoozie magwatnie" and "Heginzianie hagonie sagukle ragose" are not newly unearthed inscriptions from a lost civilization. They are simply the way Slam introduced "Flat Foot Floogie" and "Honeysuckle Rose" from the bandstand back in the 1930s and '40s. He attributed the origin of this jive argot to his "former partner Slim Gaillard, who had quite a way of messin' up the English language.

"That goes back to 1936," Stewart said. "Slim and I met at a little jam session up in Harlem and somehow we got together. At that time he had a radio program on WNEW, the station where Martin Block was quite a figure. Martin was a famous disc jockey and he became our manager and we decided on my name to be Slam. Slim and Slam sounded a little better than Slim and Leroy, which is my real name."

The duo had several hit records, including "Cement Mixer" and

"Flaginzie Atflagat"—oops!, I mean, "Flat Foot Floogie." I asked Slam how the lyrics (e.g., "Who wants a bucket of cement?") of the former had come together, and he said that he and Slim Gaillard were out in the parking lot taking a smoke break from recording and were eyeballing a cement mixer when they were informed that another 78 rpm side was needed. So, inspired by the rhythm of the huge machine and the clatter of its motion, they made up a tune and put words to it on the way back in to the studio.

"I joined Benny Goodman my first time back in 1945," Slam Stewart recalled, citing the initial tour that he did with the great leader and clarinetist. "Lionel Hampton had left, so on vibes was Red Norvo, on piano Teddy Wilson, on guitar Mike Bryan, and on drums Morey Feld. That was a wonderful experience, playing with the Benny Goodman Sextet and we recorded quite a bit. I was with Benny for about two years. I'll never forget one recording I made with Benny and his big band, 'It's Gotta Be This or That.' If anyone remembers the solo I took with my bass fiddle, on the very end of the solo I said"—Slam abruptly dropped his voice to a descending bass line for me—"'It's gotta be this or that.'"

Still another of his musical personae was as a member—along with four-string guitarist Tiny Grimes—of Art Tatum's 1940s trio. I asked him how much preparation was done for the seemingly tightly prearranged performances that, number after number, the trio brought off without a hitch. As a fledgling jazz fan better than a half century ago during the several years of the combo's activity, I was bowled over by the intricate interplay of these three musicians on their recordings.

"The answer is very simple," he insisted. "As a matter of fact, we didn't rehearse very much. We actually made things up as we went along. Say, for instance, we were playing an engagement, we were learning as we went along. And Art, the piano that man played! It was fascinating! Of course, Tiny and myself, we were blessed with the capability of being good listeners and keeping our ears open to what Art was playing at the time. And that *is* a blessing, that communication, when you can hear what's going on, and you can sort of blend in with what is being played. It was quite an experience, playing with Art Tatum. He was so great."

Slam Stewart proved to be a master accompanist and sideman

from the 1930s to his death in 1987, working with such other nota-
bles as trumpeters Roy Eldridge and Dizzy Gillespie, singer Rose
Murphy, and pianist Beryl Booker. "I Got Rhythm," one of the duo
selections he recorded in 1945 with saxophonist Don Byas, was cho-
sen by Martin Williams for inclusion in the Smithsonian Institution
collection *Classic Jazz*. His disciple, the late Major Holley, carried
on the bowing-cum-voice style of Slam, but with one departure
from his mentor's approach: he sang in unison with his instrument.

The category of "miscellaneous instruments" employed in jazz has
so burgeoned over the past several decades that it now includes virtually all members of the brass, woodwind, string, and percussion
families. Before, some of these were rarely, if ever, heard in jazz. In
addition, a vast array of exotic instruments has been added—from
Asia, Africa, and other parts of the world.

Still, the harp remains a virtual stepchild of jazz, although its use
in the idiom dates from the 1930s when Casper Reardon recorded
on it with Jack Teagarden and Benny Goodman, and Adele Girard
played it in her husband Joe Marsala's combo. The only other jazz
harpists of note until the 1990s were Corky Hale, who led her own
group and accompanied singers Anita O'Day and Kitty White in
the 1950s, and Dorothy Ashby. Dorothy, who came up in Detroit in
the 1950s and died in 1986, believed that special reasons account for
the small number of harpists throughout the history of jazz.

"I think it is probably the most difficult instrument to improvise
on," she explained to me in 1983 when she made a rare visit to
Washington, D.C., for a weekend gig in the Great Hall of the Fol-
ger Shakespeare Library. She was in the company of saxophonist
Orrington Hall the first evening, saxophonist/flutist Frank Wess the
second, and bassist Benny Nelson and drummer Steve Williams
both nights. "In creating things spontaneously you have to be thinking in several directions because the harp doesn't have any way to
make chromatics, and jazz is a rather chromatic way of playing. The
problem comes when you're trying to design chords that have acci-
dentals in the changes—wanting one thing in the melodic line and
being unable to get it because you're using particular intervals in
your chordal structure, if you know what I mean. Like wanting middle C in your melody and needing C sharp in your chord."

Outlining why the harpist must think ahead, she continued, "Your pedals have to be set before you get there. It's similar to having a piano minus the black keys. On the harp, all that the black keys represent tonally are made with foot pedals. Each pedal has three positions and you have seven pedals. The number of possible combinations goes into several thousand."

Dorothy Ashby had received extensive instruction in harmony and melodic construction from her father Wiley Thompson, a self-taught jazz guitarist, and she would sit in on piano when he and his friends rehearsed. She said that she learned more from him than she did from years of private lessons and instruction in public school and at Wayne State University. She took advantage of the opportunity to train on one of the five school-owned harps at Detroit's Cass Technical High School, where she also played saxophone in the marching band with trumpeter Donald Byrd.

"I took up harp in high school, but my main sources of inspiration were my father and my brother and my piano teacher. They were all interested in seeing me get all that I could musically. All I was doing was transferring to the harp what I heard all around me. Nobody told me these things were not done on the harp. I had no real plan; it wasn't that I intentionally planned to do jazz on the harp. I was just doing what I knew I liked."

Dorothy Ashby is to be admired for overcoming a mountain of obstacles in order to make her way in the profession of jazz musician. She did this with musicality and virtuosity on an instrument that seems quite unsuitable to jazz expression. In her hands, however, it produced sounds as swinging as those from a piano played by one of the greats.

"In the old days, when I first started playing," Ashby expanded on the theme, "it was more of a surprise because little was being done with the harp in popular music. But it's being used a good bit more now, at least in the places where I've found myself—Detroit, Chicago, New York, and Los Angeles. In other cities where I've gone I suppose it's still more of a surprise to an audience. They're prepared for it if they've had some preliminary promo, but I think they equate the harp with classical music and that's generally the place for it—chamber settings, small classical orchestras, classical things.

"It's been maybe a triple burden in that not a lot of women are becoming known as jazz players. There is also the connection with black women. The audiences I was trying to reach were not interested in harp, period—classical or otherwise—and they were certainly not interested in seeing a black woman playing the harp. I think I had to pave my own way in terms of that area.

"The next area is that there are not many things written for the harp and you do most of your work in terms of transcribing. A lot of piano things transfer very easily to the harp; but in jazz, you have to create and design your own solos because nobody out there is playing solos that you can just pick up in sheet music and read for the harp. A few harpists are doing things but they are not particularly jazzy. They've transcribed a few things for popular music but it's not what jazz players would call jazz.

"It still hasn't made a lot of ground because there aren't a lot of people doing it and writers often do not experience playing with or writing for harp. The guys I've been fortunate enough to work with are using the harp in their arrangements, but they are still limiting it to what they have heard others do, and very often no one pioneers to make the harp a solo voice. I guess in that area I can claim to have been the pioneer."

She went on to perform with artists across the jazz spectrum from Louis Armstrong and Woody Herman to Sonny Criss and Stanley Turrentine. She eventually developed a fluency in bebop that no other harpist has come close to matching. In addition to club appearances over the years with her trio, in which her husband John Ashby played drums, Dorothy did much studio work. Her harp can be heard on the albums and singles of hundreds of performers, including Stevie Wonder, Aretha Franklin, the Manhattans, Helen Reddy, Barry Manilow, Freddie Hubbard, Natalie Cole, Diana Ross, Dionne Warwick, Nancy Wilson, and Earth Wind & Fire.

"There is quite a bit of work out in Los Angeles," she said in conclusion to our talk. "There are maybe as many as two hundred in the L.A. Harp Chapter, the professional organization of harpists, but I haven't run into any who really do what jazz musicians call spontaneous improvisation. There are some who play what we might call cocktail music—I hate labeling—but there are really no harpists out there who are improvising."

The picture has not changed much in the decade and a half since

I interviewed Dorothy Ashby. Casper Reardon died at the age of thirty-three in 1941. Adele Girard was not much heard of after the 1950s until a year before her death in 1993; at eighty, she made a fine album with clarinetist Bobby Gordon on the Arbors label. Corky Hale has been only sporadically active in recent years as a harpist and actually considers the piano her principal instrument. Pianist Alice Coltrane played the harp on several of her 1960s albums. In the 1990s three harpists have emerged to continue the tradition of jazz harp and have proved themselves creative improvisors. Deborah Henson-Conant has toured the world, while Lori Andrews has established herself in Los Angeles, the very locale that Dorothy Ashby, back in 1983, lamented had no jazz harpists other than herself. Both have documented their playing on their self-produced labels. Susan Allen has performed at jazz festivals and in concert here and abroad and recorded with Anthony Braxton, Vinny Golia, Dave Brubeck, and other jazz artists.

"I grew up on the outskirts of Portland, Oregon," bassist Glen Moore began when I talked with him in 1992. He and singer Nancy King were in town for a weekend gig at One Step Down in Washington, D.C. "My parents got a piano for my sister when I was nine years old because she expressed an interest in studying it. I immediately glommed onto it and they agreed to give me lessons. They got me a really good teacher who taught me a couple of Bach pieces and a little bit of Rachmaninoff and Chopin. And then the high school band teacher recruited me to play the bass because I was the largest kid in the music department. They didn't need any more piano players, but I loved the piano and would sit and play it in the dark and hold down the sustaining pedal. I would improvise, mostly, and play my classical pieces. I was in love with Rachmaninoff and with piano concertos and with George Gershwin's *Rhapsody in Blue*. I listened to jazz music on the radio. This was 1951. From a recital that I did a little later I found a judge writing about me—and it was something that very appropriately, totally still stamps me—that on the slower pieces you could tell that there was some missing technique but the more robust things were very spirited and really emotional, that I really had the feeling properly but I maybe needed more discipline. I can always hark back to that.

"I made up little songs, bits and pieces of things. And of course back then there were a lot of great examples. I was listening to Frank Sinatra and Nat King Cole and Erroll Garner. Then, when they talked me into doing the bass and told my parents that I would always work if I played the bass—that bass players are always needed—I began imitating walking bass lines. By the time I was fourteen, I had a girlfriend in high school who played the accordion and the bass in the orchestra. She asked me to come and join her because she had won a contest the local newspaper sponsored. In the contest, you'd go on television and if you won three times you could become part of the Oregonians, a troupe that traveled around the state and did fairs and other events. She played 'Lady of Spain' and a boogie woogie and something else and I played the bass for this. It was terrible, but after it I was asked to do a tour in the spring term of my freshman year. In that group was Jim Pepper, who played tenor saxophone and did an Indian dance and a tap dance in tuxedo. Then he put on a zoot suit and played the tenor in the band. We played behind fifteen little vaudeville acts. We did a school concert in the afternoon and radio things and then we'd drive into another town and play an evening concert. After a week of this I was hooked, I loved it. I thought this was a great way to spend my time, to be treated like a little celebrity and to get to play music and in the middle of the day get to talk on the radio and then play at night. And then be given a place to stay and treated to a meal. I liked this. I'm still doing it. I still like it. So, from age fourteen, that was the beginning.

"Then I went to the University of Oregon, in Eugene. I took music courses and studied history and literature. I had several teachers who were just brilliant; they just took me away. I was content to just read and read.

"By this time I was playing with Ralph Towner quite a bit. We had gone through, first of all, Oscar Peterson and Ray Brown's repertoires and then discovered Bill Evans and Scott LaFaro, Clare Fischer, Gary Peacock, a lot of piano and bass duets. We were playing that music and Ralph was beginning to write original pieces of his own. Ralph and I had met in 1960 and played together in Eugene and we won a little combo contest. I met Nancy King at that point, too, and after I left the university Nancy and Ralph and I worked together a bit. She was the first really great singer I heard. She was incredible. Ralph and I kept playing in duo. I went to Copenhagen to live, to listen to Niels-Henning Ørsted Pedersen, who was just an astonishing bassist, and to be able to play with Dexter Gordon and Stuff Smith and Ben Webster and these great people who were there. And I met Paul Bley at that time.

"Ralph and I played together in Seattle and then in 1967, when I moved to Europe, he went back to Vienna for another year with Karl Scheit. I played with Jeremy Steig and Tim Hardin and worked with Zoot Sims for several months and with Jake Hanna. Did some bebop things for Nick Grignola, Ted Curson, and Dick Berk. We had a quartet, we did some recording; some of my first recordings were with that group.

"And then Ralph came back from Europe and to New York and we started doing duo things around Manhattan, all kinds of, at first, just silly little things. Eventually, Tim Hardin asked me to come and play at the Woodstock festival with him. I had worked with him a number of times, but it was always kind of disappointing; he was sort of an unreliable character, thoroughly wonderful, but strange. I said I would work at Woodstock if Ralph could come along and play guitar, so we joined a large group that Tim put together for Woodstock, and in that group were a couple of people from the Paul Winter Consort who were just leaving.

"Right after the Woodstock festival—which is a whole long interview in itself—we went into the recording studio and did an album called *Bird on a Wire* for CBS with Tim. Tim had a lot of trouble finding a drummer who was really proper for this thing—the drummer who had been with Paul Winter didn't even show up. These are the days of LSD trips; people would take a drug and decide to change their life and just not appear. Interesting times. I had met Collin Walcott that summer. He was playing tabla and sitar, and when a drummer couldn't be found that suited Tim, I got Collin to come. There in the hallways in Columbia Studios in New York City, Collin played the sitar with Ralph Towner playing guitar and they played their first duet. It was incredible, the sound of these two instruments together. And Paul Winter came and heard this in the course of these recordings. It was in the fall of 1969, and by the end of the year he hired Ralph and myself and Collin to join the Consort. And we came very near here; actually, we started in Virginia and did a nine-concert tour in Virginia for the Virginia Museum Society. We did a total of fifty concerts on that tour in ten weeks, five concerts a week.

"We drove 25,000 miles, mostly through the South, and by about two weeks into that tour Ralph and Collin and myself, along with Paul McCandless, gravitated into one of the vehicles. We traveled together and we started playing after the concerts and before the concerts and by June we were determined that we were going to set off on our own. We did the *Road* album with the Paul Winter Consort, but then right after that, friends of Collin's in Los Angeles hired us to play, to make an album for them, an independent production company. The record didn't come out until Vanguard released it in 1979, many years later.

"So our group Oregon was born in 1970 as a result of the work with Paul Winter. He was into different things and having a group with a guitar rather than a piano, in a non-jazz situation, really. It wasn't a jazz music feeling. We played a lot of early Elizabethan music and it was based on that concept, Elizabethan house band sort of music. So it was our first experience, really, getting up on a stage. We'd been in bars all this time. For ten years we played in bars and been kind of ignored, which had made us very strong and able to assert ourselves and develop what we had to do. So when we started working with Paul Winter, it made us realize that there was an audience for music that was not just the barroom—where everybody got just drunk enough and the music would be okay—but there could be a different way. So that was really the inspiration for Oregon happening and combining these odd instruments. It was originally Paul's idea but we'd already been working for ten years with guitar and bass, so it was a good encouraging move for us and led us to set off and finally get the Vanguard record contract. And now here we are eighteen records later.

"Ralph and I had come to New York to eventually play with Miles; that was why we were there. We'd listened to and learned Wayne Shorter's music and to that whole period up past the mid-1960s, to Tony Williams and Herbie Hancock. That was really a *high ideal* at that time. And when Dave Holland and Chick Corea left Miles, Ralph and I were at the point of going and being at

Miles's door and saying, 'We're the next white guys that you need.' But he decided to go completely electric at that point and his focus became more the street. There were very few white players involved with that and we weren't prepared to play electronic. That was a kind of sobering thing to realize, that we weren't going to get to play with Miles.

"Ralph and I had a band, a rehearsal band, with John Abercrombie, John McLaughlin, David Holland, and the Brecker brothers. We'd get together and play music that we'd written. We were never a working group; it was a once-a-week get together and we played old tunes and new things that we'd written. So there were a lot of associations during this time. I worked a lot with Jeremy Steig and with Jan Hammer. In fact, Jan and I worked at Bradley's the week the first Mahavishnu Orchestra record was made. Jan talked every night about what it was like to have to kind of unlearn his jazz things and focus on this music that was more like Indian music than anything else because of the odd meters and the duple feeling rather than a triplet thing. When Return to Forever formed, we were there for the first gigs.

"It was the beginning of the times when the jazz musicians were going from the corner of the barroom into the arena. Oregon was formed at the same time as Weather Report and started playing on the same show with Ravi Shankar. Many things were being put together. Musicians were playing together who had not played together. A lot of the jazz walls were being broken down, people were sharing, there were bass choirs, people with like instruments were getting together and sharing all their stuff. Before that it had been all kinda"—Glen adopted a sneering tone—"'I have this little thing I can do, but I'm not going to show you or you'll do it and I'll lose my gig.'

"The '60s really helped break those walls down. From what I can tell about the way a lot of the young jazz players are now, they didn't experience that; they've kinda climbed back into a black and white, much more racially conscious time now. It's kind of sad. I read liner notes and realize that people missed that whole time. I don't want to go back to that time, but it's something that's *been* missed. The players from that time, though, are still some of the most attractive players to me—the Jan Hammers, the Miroslav Vitouses, the Joe

Zawinuls, the people from that time. They were incredibly strong players who had all this acoustic bebop experience, and then all kinds of electronic experience, but without forgetting about their real acoustic upbringing. If you sit down now in front of Miroslav Vitous, you just forget every bass player, ever. The young, wonderful, technically magnificent players go right out of your mind if you listen to Dave Holland or Miroslav or these players who came up through the gut-string school on the bass and through playing with Miles and all that. I was really fortunate to be in New York at that time and to experience all those things.

"Oregon was the real beacon through that whole thing; Oregon really stayed in existence because of Manfred Eicher at ECM. He invited us to record. ECM organized tours for us in Europe. We went from playing in these little bars where we had to clean the floor and put down the lines of baking soda to keep the cockroaches off our instruments to going to Europe and playing in the radio houses and beautiful halls and in Vienna where Beethoven conducted and where Mozart had played. ECM really gave us the opportunity to feel like adult musicians, away from America, where there'd always been a lot more pop emphasis and all this electric kind of superstar feeling. Because of ECM, we were able to hang in there.

"Then we had a nine-record contract with Vanguard Records, which was so long that we just did five quartet records for them and then started inviting guests in. Elvin Jones heard us play and said, 'Gee, we didn't have a drummer, we didn't have a trap drummer, why couldn't he record with us?' So we did a record with him that was quite wonderful. We did a record with Zbigniew Seifert, a great Polish violinist with whom I later did a recording of my own. And then we did another one with Benny Wallace; David Earl Johnson, a great conga player; and Larry Carrish, one of the fine pianists with whom Miles did a record on ECM.

"Collin Walcott died in an accident in 1984. He had told us when he started playing with Oregon, when he first met Trilok Gurto, 'Guys, I've found the guy that when I get tired of you and this shit, you get Trilok. He's a great jazz player and he'll be able to do even more jazz things than I can do with you.' So after Collin died we did a tribute show for him in New York and a tremendous number of musicians came and Trilok came and played with us. We loved playing with him; he's just a marvelous player. So we began playing with him and most of our work with him is in Europe now. He lives there. He's very busy there. And so we do thirty or forty nights a year in Europe and we work pretty much as a trio in the States.

"That's some of what I've been up to—for this life."

I had seen David Eyges (pronounced EE-jus) perform fifteen or so years ago at D.C. Space, a haven for two decades from the mid-1970s for avant-garde jazz and rock. I caught up with him again when the trio Synergy turned up at Blues Alley last year in Washington, D.C. Arthur Blythe was on alto saxophone and Abe Speller on drums.

"I heard about the instrument in the late 1980s," recalled David, who holds the distinction of being the pioneer of electric cello in jazz, "and I met the maker, Tucker Barrett, who designed it. I was very impressed with it and bought it immediately. I just said, 'This is the way to go.'

"I actually sold my old acoustic cello because I didn't really need it anymore, and since then I've been very happy with the electric. There're two main attributes to it. One is that you can play it from a volume perspective—with a drummer—much more successfully. And the other one is traveling. You can put it in the baggage department of planes or trains.

"I grew up in Belmont, Massachusetts, which is next to Cambridge," he said, "and I started playing piano when I was five. My mother was my first teacher, as a matter of fact. It was sort of neither here nor there, really; it was just something you did as a kid. I started playing the cello when I was eleven, and it was an instrument just kind of selected for me."

David Eyges doesn't think the home situation provided much of an influence on his musical tastes. His mother, he says, "was a pretty good pianist" and his father, now a retired physicist, "really enjoys music, but has more of a scientific nature." He reflects for a moment and then adds, "I would like to say that my father has been a tremendous influence on my life—just his approach to life and people and his generosity and his kindness. All that has really influenced me considerably."

It was "mostly classical music that my parents listened to," he explained, "and that really wasn't much of an influence. I didn't start listening until I was a teenager and then I started listening exten-

sively. I was very influenced by what was called the British Invasion—the Beatles and the Stones—not so much by those particular
rock-and-roll groups but by their sources. That's when I discovered
the old bluesmen, like Lightnin' Hopkins and John Lee Hooker and
Muddy Waters. This is about 1964. I really went directly to the
source and I started buying a lot of blues records. I remember very
distinctly buying that Robert Johnson record called *Crossroads*. I
even named one of my own records *Crossroads*." For the album session he used multiwoodwind player Byard Lancaster and drummer
Sunny Murray.

"There used to be a club in Cambridge called Club 47. It was a
great club for me to go to as a young man just becoming involved
with the music. I remember very distinctly seeing Muddy Waters
there and I also heard John Lee Hooker there. I did meet Lightnin'
Hopkins much later at Tramps, just once in my life." Listening to
records of these and other classic bluesmen, David learned to play
blues guitar.

"This was when I was around fifteen years old, and I continued to
play the cello. I went to a private school for two years, Cambridge
School of Weston, and from there I went to Boston University for a
year and studied cello. The following year I went to New York and
was at the Manhattan School of Music for three years. I graduated
there with a bachelor of music degree in 1972.

"But going back to jazz, I was introduced to jazz by friends at the
Cambridge School. As a matter of fact, I remember the first jazz
record that I listened to was Jim Hall and Bill Evans, *Undercurrent*.
And I just went on from there. I listened to Miles and various peo-
ple, including Duke Ellington, Thelonious Monk, Charles Mingus,
and Ornette Coleman. And then when I was at the Manhattan
School I became friendly with the people in the band Circle, Dave
Holland and Chick Corea. Those were the two main people that I
knew. Dave was very helpful in furthering my knowledge of music.
Immediately after graduating, I joined a European band led by
Gunter Hampel and I toured with him and made several records
with him. We traveled pretty extensively through Germany and
went to Austria, Belgium, Holland, and Luxembourg. The singer
Jeanne Lee and saxophonist Mark Whitecage were in the band.
That was the early 1970s.

"Then I'm back in New York and it's about 1975. I decided that I wanted to be a leader myself and I started writing quite a bit. I have over a hundred tunes in my catalogue, which is all with BMI. I made my first record as a leader in 1977. It was called *The Captain* and it was on Chiaroscuro Records. It's a quartet date with Mark Whitecage on alto sax, Ronnie Boykins on bass, and Jeff Williams on drums. I also did a record with the drummer Bob Moses. As a matter of fact, I'm on his first record. It's called *Bittersuite in the Ozone.* And I did a record with a Latin musician, which is kind of an interesting record. His name is Bobby Paunetto. He's kind of disappeared. I had a duo with the saxophonist Byard Lancaster for a couple of years, which was quite successful. We did residencies and workshops at North Country Community College, in schools, and several in prisons. We got grants, including one co-sponsored by Painted Bride Arts Center and TV station WHYY and another called a Michael Paul Residency Grant. We did some radio programs and some TV shows.

"In the '80s I did some work with the Metropolitan Opera Guild as a music consultant. They have a musical theater program and they send a team, a theater consultant and a music consultant—which was myself—into the schools and we do a program. Actually, the kids do it from scratch, a whole production, and we advise them how to do it. It was quite successful.

"I also co-produced a radio series called *Another Face of Jazz,* funded by the National Endowment for the Arts. It was a program focusing on solo and duo performances and we only managed to get three programs out. One was a duet with Gil Evans and Lee Konitz, the second was Jaki Byard solo, and the third was myself and a synthesizer player named Greg Kramer. But I did manage to get funding for that series and it was aired on about 180 stations.

"Also, in 1986, I produced a couple of records for a now defunct label, Aspen Records—more pop-oriented stuff. I produced an Oliver Lake and Jump Up record—that was his kind of reggae fusion band—and I also produced a band called Kelvynator, which was led by a guitarist named Kelvyn Bell.

"Then things were kind of quiet for several years. My son Eric was born in 1984 and I guess I became very involved with raising him. I also did a lot of sailing at the time. We were fortunate, my ex-wife and I, and cashed in on the co-op boom in the late '80s in New York. Our apartment became co-op and we sold it, what was called 'flipped' it, and moved up to Nyack, New York, and lived there for several years until we went our separate ways.

"I was somewhat disenchanted with the music business and kind of took a breather for a while. I never stopped playing, but I wasn't performing very much. Then for some reason my *Lightnin' Strikes* record, which was my first compact disc release"—and the first recording on which he used the electric cello—"was held up several years. It was recorded in '88 and it wasn't released until '92. I feel I'm in the second stage of my career now, basically, and I think there will probably be three or four stages of it. The first was, I would say, from 1972 to '86, something like that, and then there was a breather of a few years. In '92 I started up again with this *Lightnin' Strikes* release, and since then I've had a few more out—one with Jeanne Lee, one with Paul Bley called *Modern Chant*." During this "second phase" David has also recorded *Synergy* with Arthur Blythe and Bruce Ditmas on drums and *Night Leaves* with Jaki Byard.

He has also long had one foot in the classical camp. I asked him about the application of the electric instrument to that idiom.

"Well, there really is none. My chamber music is kind of a separate venture. Basically, I haven't been performing it very much. It's more of a compositional endeavor. I've written a couple of string quartets and I wrote a piece for alto sax plus string quartet, which I'd like Arthur Blythe to play, and I wrote a piece for flute and string quartet. I'm not performing classical and at this time the chamber music is kind of on the shelf. I mean it's a secondary endeavor, something that I did because I wanted to grow musically. I had some time on my hands and I said, 'What the hell am I going to do?' I wanted to combine some of the musical influences I've had in jazz and blues with some of my classical training and see what I could come up with for some string quartet pieces, a form of music I've always enjoyed. But I have not introduced the electric cello into classical performance. It's an interesting thought, but I don't think it's gonna fly. So I think I'm going to let that one go."

I first heard—I had never even heard *of* her—violinist Regina Carter at a mid-1990s one-night engagement of the Detroit-based all-women's group Straight Ahead. It wasn't very far into her first solo that evening that I recognized her as a major performing artist.

Although she began on the violin at the age of four, Regina Carter's first instrument was piano—she started lessons at two. "My two older brothers were taking piano lessons and my mom says that one day I walked up to the piano and started playing one of their pieces by ear. And their piano teacher was over that day and said, 'Who taught her that?' And my mom said, 'Nobody, she just started playing it.' So my mom enrolled me at a place called Your Heritage House and I studied with a woman named Mrs. Love. But Mrs. Love said that I was too young to take lessons and was very stubborn. I never really would practice my lessons. I would come in and say, 'This is my tune I wrote this week' and play her something that I composed. She didn't want to take away the creativity and she thought that formal lessons would do that, so she suggested to my mother to just let me play on the piano like I was doing until I was a little bit older. When I turned four Mrs. Love called up my mother and told her there was a place called the Detroit Music School that was teaching Suzuki on violin and she thought that would be good for me since I was already picking up things by ear. So my mom enrolled me there. The teacher would play melodies and then we'd play them back to her and she also did a thing where she would make up a melody—we had private lessons once a week and then a group lesson on Saturday—and when she would finish with the line she was playing that she'd made up, she'd tap somebody on the shoulder and that person had to pick up where she left off and create a line until the next person was tapped. So it was improvisation, in European classical sense. I think that really got me started on being free from the paper, making up things."

Her parents didn't play any musical instruments, but her grandmother was the pianist for one of the churches in Detroit. So Regina grew up hearing church music when her grandmother visited. Her mother did not listen to the radio, but her father liked easy listening radio stations. "He would hear Simon and Garfunkle and groups like that. Then, of course, Motown was here in Detroit at the time, so I listened to popular radio stations that would play Smokey Robinson and Aretha Franklin."

Also, her teacher would send home classical records for her to listen to during the week, "everything from Bach to Beethoven, Mozart to Debussy, maybe five records. And next week you'd trade with one of the other students. So you just got a mixture of every-thing. Then, as part of our lessons, we had to attend concerts of the Detroit Symphony Orchestra. We'd get free tickets and go see cer-tain soloists play with them. In fact, whenever Itzhak Perlman was in town, he would come to the school where we studied and give us master classes. So I had a chance to do that, and also with Yehudi Menuhin. My first eight years was basically music on the radio or going to the symphony.

"My mother was a school teacher and she wanted us to have a really well-rounded education so that when we got older we could pick from many things for a career—and to keep us off the streets. So we had something to do every day after school and on Saturdays. The only free day we had was Sunday, unless we went to church. So we were pretty busy. I studied at the Community Music School all through elementary school and they had an orchestra. For a while I played in that. At Cass Tech you had to take orchestra and another string instrument besides the one you played, and you also had to take a woodwind instrument. So I took oboe and viola. I was in a chamber group, the choir, and also in madrigal.

Cass Technical High School, she explained, "is basically a school of arts and sciences and you have to know what you're gonna major in in college before you get in and you have to have a B average and maintain it throughout. You take your basic state requirements, but then the rest of the time you take the courses that would help to get you into college. A lot of people once they got into college, they were able to test out of their first-year courses, whatever they were majoring in, because we'd already had them at Cass Tech."

By the age of twelve, Regina Carter had made up her mind to become a professional violinist. Still playing only classical com-posers, she nevertheless had been improvising for several years. "I wasn't doing it on a conscious level, but sometimes, if I were prac-ticing my pieces, I would deviate from the music and just start play-ing something. My mother would always hear me from the other room and say, 'Regina, that doesn't sound like your lesson to me.'" She chuckled at the memory. "She would always kinda stop me and get me back on track, 'cause I guess I was always trying to do that."

In addition to the music that was spilling over into her conscious-ness from Detroit's Latin, Greek, Chaldean, and other ethnic communities, a strong jazz influence was about to appear. By the time she had entered her teens, the family had relocated to within a mile of Baker's Keyboard Lounge, a club founded in the mid-1930s. Here the likes of Tommy Flanagan, Kirk Lightsey, Eddie Jefferson, and many other jazz greats appeared regularly.

"In fact, that's where Eddie Jefferson was actually killed," she pointed out. "Noel Pointer used to play there and my mother would take me and one of my girlfriends who also played violin—she still does—and we'd sit there for all three sets. So he got to know us, we'd come every time he was there and we'd go every night. He was just really, really nice. He had to borrow a bow of mine one night and I was just too elated. He had played through both of his. I ran home and got it and he played on it and at the end of the weekend he gave me money to have it rehaired. And I never did. I just didn't even want to touch that bow any more. In fact, to this day I've never had the thing rehaired. He was a big influence. I didn't get to know him that well then, but later I did a little bit in New York. He was just a super nice person. After he died a few years ago I got to know his family really well and they're just great, really great people."

In high school, Regina Carter joined classmates in a band that did all the latest Motown tunes, upon which they would improvise. Not until her second year did she begin to be at all aware of jazz. One day the band's other violinist played records of Noel Pointer and Jean-Luc Ponty for her and, despite wondering, "What is jazz?", she immediately decided, "'This is what I'm gonna do now!' 'Cause the music was just so free. The improvising side of it really attracted me."

In the eleventh grade she went out on the road with Brainstorm, a popular funk/rock group that had made some records, touring with them Thursday through Sunday and attending school the rest of the week. She says that to fit into their idiom, she had to do a lot of improvising. The larger world of jazz did not really open up for her until college. "All I knew was those few records. I had no idea what was ahead of me."

Attending Boston's New England Conservatory of Music for two years and majoring in European classical music and African-American Studies, she joined the school's symphony orchestra and its jazz band.

"It was really difficult because at that time they hadn't had any jazz violinist before me that I know of, so they didn't have a program set up for me. Basically, I was in the big band with Jimmy Giuffre and he was teaching about improvisation, so I got a lot out of that. Then I tried studying with Jaki Byard, but he was just way too advanced, because I didn't know anything about jazz. I knew absolutely nothing. Most of these people coming in had some kind of a background in jazz. I tried to study with Fred Hersch and he became more like my"—she laughed—"therapist than a teacher. I mean, I couldn't understand anything, it was like every time somebody tried to help me to understand anything about improvising and to tell me about chords and scales and stuff, it was like they were speaking a foreign language. I just could not get it. But I could do things by ear. If they didn't play behind me, though, I couldn't understand. So that really frustrated me. And then I hated being in the orchestra, because the music just seemed so rigid, in the way you had to play. And it was really difficult there, too, because at that time it just seemed like there was such a division between the jazz department and the classical department and there was a little animosity.

"After two years I left and came back home to Michigan and went to school at Oakland University. There was a big band there led by a saxophonist, Doc Marvin Holiday. And a lot of the cats who were in the band had already graduated but they would come back and just play. Actually, a lot of those cats played in a band led by J. C. Heard. That was a good thing for me. I read the first alto book because, of course, there were no violin charts, and that helped me with the phrasing and the breathing. That's basically what Doc taught me, and playing in the middle of a horn section definitely helped me to understand how to play. Being a string player, I would just play and play and play a whole lot of notes and not breathe, so that was a good experience for me.

"Then I started to work with Marcus Belgrave, the trumpet player here in Detroit. He had a group that included the bassist Bob Hurst. Every day, all day long, we would read through tunes and Marcus would teach us about soloing, how to make the band follow you, about dynamics, about comping behind a soloist. I was also in a jazz orchestra led by a saxophonist named Donald Walden. He would write out charts, string charts, for us to play, and then he'd have guest artists come in in the summer, like Barry Harris or Wendell Harrison, and we'd back them up. We'd have string arrangements and play behind them, actual string jazz charts. That was a good experience. Then I started working with a lot of people around Detroit—for example, with Lawrence Williams and Lyman Woodard and in an organ quintet for a while."

At Oakland University she was assigned a paper on jazz violinists. "So I started listening to some Stephane Grappelli and someone told me about Stuff Smith, so I went and got ahold of him. But my teacher, Doc Holiday, said, 'Don't listen to the violin players too much because you're so new at this you'll start to sound like them. Only listen for pleasure. Listen to some horn players, so that you get the breathing and the whole phrasing thing down.' So I would just go to the store and pick stuff out, some Charlie Parker, and tell my mother, 'Get me some jazz records for Christmas.' She came home one year with Eric Dolphy's *Out to Lunch* and some John Coltrane but I was wa-a-ay too young for them. It took me a while to grow into those records."

Following her teacher's advice, Regina Carter sought out records by horn players, especially those of Johnny Hodges, Ben Webster, and Paul Gonsalves. She picked the last named because she had played in a band with his drummer son Renell Gonsalves, who would talk about his father. Then she took the logical next step and began to check out Duke Ellington. For her current listening, "That could be an array of everybody. A lo-o-t-t of Johnny Hodges." She also named Kenny Barron, Arthur Blythe, and Billie Holiday, whose vibrato and phrasing appeal to her.

Before leaving Oakland University she taught there for one semester. After graduating she taught in the public schools. This included a stint with the Detroit Symphony Orchestra in the String Specialists Program, in which orchestra members went to the schools to work with students. Carter would go twice a week for two hours and tutor the students who were taking violin.

"When that was over I'd saved up enough money and I wanted to take a trip out of the country. I had already decided I was going to Germany, and I was only supposed to stay for three months. I just kind of needed to clear my head because it seemed like I'd been in school forever and I just wanted to get away from everything. I have no idea why I picked Germany. It was just a very strange thing. It called me. I don't know if it had to do with me being a kid seeing *The Sound of Music* and thinking that was Germany and that's what I wanted to see. That could be very possible. I have no idea though. I wanted to go to Munich. Fred Hersch had given me the name of this guy Stefan Winter, who used to own JMT Records, and told me, 'When you get there, call him up.' So I took the trip to Munich and checked into a youth hostel and that night I went to a club and asked them could I sit in and play a tune. The audience responded really, really well and when I came off stage I met this Yugoslavian trumpet player Dusko Goykovich and he said, 'Where are you from?' and I said, 'I'm from Detroit,' and he goes, 'Detroit! Oh, one of my good friends lives there named Marcus Belgrave. You know Marcus?' So it was like an instant hook-up and we just started talking and he asked what I was doing here and I told him I wanted to live in Munich, I wanted to move there, and he says, 'Well, my son Michael lives here and he may be needing a roommate and he may be coming into the club tonight, but if not I'll give you his number.' And about half an hour later Michael walked in and we decided we'd hook up the next day—it was a Sunday—and just get together and talk.

"Then I got a chance to meet Stefan Winter and hang out with his family and he gave me tickets to go see Geri Allen. I'd never seen her play even though she's from Detroit. I went to see her perform and I met another guy who is a critic over there for one of the papers, and also a woman who's a translator; they became really good friends. To this day we're still good friends. So I had an instant little support team over there. I ended up moving into that apartment a couple of months later. It just all seemed to work out. I just felt like when you're where you're supposed to be, things work out the way they're supposed to. Of course, I wasn't sure why I was even there."

Regina took a trip one day to Frankfurt to see fellow Detroiter and old friend Carol McKinney, a saxophonist and member of a musical family, who was living in Giesen and teaching there.

"She was playing with a band and had a gig that night, more like a pop kind of funk thing, and she took me there and I sat in with them. So whenever they were playing anywhere I could get, I would go and play with them."

After the first year in Munich, Regina Carter lived in Kassel, a small town in the north. It was here that she applied herself to a strict routine of practicing all day. "I would transcribe Charlie Parker solos every day, just put it on until I got it and was able to play it. So I just did that every day because I really still didn't have a foundation of how to learn jazz and how to practice it. I said, 'Well, my ear is really good. I'll just learn these solos.' And from doing that I started to understand a little bit of what people were trying to tell me. I did that for a year and then I decided to come back home. It just felt like I was living in a fairy-tale land and I needed to get it together.

"I moved back home and I joined a band here, an all-women's band called Miche Braden and Straight Ahead. Miche is a vocalist. She had done all these fabulous jazz arrangements of different tunes and we would play around the city and had a big following. When Miche moved to New York to further her career, the band stayed together and we actually got an opportunity to go to Montreux, Switzerland, one year and open up for Nina Simone. That was a great push-off for us because we did three tunes and they video-taped it. Oh, we got such a great response! Atlantic Records ended up signing the group. I recorded two records with Straight Ahead on that label before taking off on my own."

It was also during her first year back in the United States that Regina Carter received an NEA grant to study with violinist John Blake. "I would fly to New York, maybe once a month, and take lessons with him. And it was really funny because at the first lesson he said, 'Well play for me.' So I played something for him, and he says, 'Well, what do you want me to show you?' And I said, 'I want you to help me understand what jazz is about' And he says, 'Well, you already know,' and I said, 'No, I don't.' After I studied with him for a while he said, 'Just do what you're doin'. Don't worry about anything else.' So I was really frustrated because I thought, 'No, I have to know what everyone knows.' I felt like it was this big secret."

When she moved to New York in the mid-'90s she continued to do gigs with Straight Ahead and was asked to join the String Trio of New York. Calls started coming in from other musicians—for example, Oliver Lake and Mark Helias.

"And then it got to be a little bit too much. My schedule was clashing with Straight Ahead because people in New York would call me for a gig and then Straight Ahead might call me afterward and it was getting to be more and more that I couldn't do dates with them because I was working with other people. So after the second record I left Straight Ahead. Atlantic had first option on me, so they picked it up and I recorded two records on the Atlantic label that were more like smooth jazz" (the 1995 *Regina Carter* and the 1997 *Something For Grace*, which was named for and dedicated to her mother). "Meantime, I was getting calls from Muhal Richard Abrams, I subbed in the Uptown String Quartet at the Blue Note for a week, I was working with the Soldier String Quartet, I got calls to work with Steve Turre's band and then from his wife's string group Quartette Indigo. I got calls to do TV dates with Dolly Parton, Tanya Tucker, and Billy Joel on the *Rosie O'Donnell Show*, playing country/western and pop. And doing record dates as well. I just started to get calls from a lot of people and my schedule started getting busy. It was great because then I could stop calling home and asking for money!"

Last year Regina Carter released her first CD under a new contract with Verve—*Rhythms of the Heart*, an acoustic jazz session. It is a distinct change in approach from the electronic funk that dominated her two releases on Atlantic.

In addition to the recordings cited earlier, she has recorded or performed with a diverse array of artists, including Dizzy Gillespie, Tom Harrell, Kenny Barron, Dionne Warwick, Smokey Robinson, Lauryn Hill, and Elliott Sharpe. A week at New York's Sweet Basil, solos on Wynton Marsalis's *Blood on the Fields* tour and in Cassandra Wilson's *Travelin' Miles* concert at Lincoln Center, and coast-to-coast club and festival appearances have consistently garnered strong praise for her virtuosity, passion, improvisational flair, and wide-ranging knowledge of the jazz and blues traditions. She has frequently been cited as one of the most outstandingly gifted jazz artists to emerge in the 1990s and was in first place in the violin category in last year's *Down Beat* International Critics Poll. As one of "25 for the Future, a Cast of Rising Jazz Stars," Regina Carter shared the May 1999 cover of *Down Beat* with pianist Brad Mehldau. *Entertainment Weekly* picked her just released CD *Rhythms of the Heart* as the lone jazz album reviewed in its initial issue of that same month. I caught her most recently at the summer 1999 Capital Jazz Fest at the Merriweather Post Pavilion, Columbia, Maryland. With her on the outdoor Symphony Woods Stage were pianist Werner "Vana" Gierig, guitarist Rodney Jones, and drummer Alvester Garnett. After the set, about two hundred people lined up at a nearby vendor's tent for her autograph on CDs, festival posters or programs, and T-shirts.

Considering the listening habits she has alluded to, it is not surprising to hear Regina Carter say, "I don't approach the violin as a violin; I approach it as a jazz instrument. The minute you approach it as a violin, it has a stereotype about it and ways that you're supposed to play it. I've gotten rid of all of those ideas and because I'm so drawn to percussion I tend to approach the improvisation from a rhythmic point of view. Just to be able to play lines or rhythmic lines like a percussion player or like a bass player would, but more so, really takes people's stereotypes away. A lot of people say they don't like violin and they don't think it fits in jazz, when actually it was one of the instruments in the big band era. Those cats used to double on horn and violin. Once they hear it, though, and they don't hear it in a syrupy kind of manner, then they say, 'Okay, this instrument can do what anyone else can do on an instrument, and that's my thing.' It's like, don't look at it as a violin; just let it speak to you first and then make a judgment. So that's how I'm trying to get rid of people's prejudices."

7

Other Climes

"I'm a cross-cultural kind of guy. I was hangin' out with the common folk, I enjoyed that. The local musicians took a liking to me, they saw my sincerity, and I was able to fit in because I had the ears."   Monty Alexander

"Once you start putting the air through the horn or putting your fingers on the piano, you can't fool anybody. People are going to know what you're about."   Ingrid Jensen

Multi-instrumentalist James Morrison came to Washington, D.C., several times in the 1980s and early '90s. On his very last visit, while he was in residence at Cates for a week, I picked him up at his hotel one spring morning and drove him to my Silver Spring, Maryland, home. I made sandwiches for us and interviewed him in my backyard. Several months later I caught up with him and his brother John at the North Sea Jazz Festival, and we talked some more.

"I was born in 1962 on November 11 in a town called Boorowa. I'm using the term 'town' loosely. It was a collection of houses and a church and a pub, a very small place, on the edge of what Australians refer to as 'the outback.' It was sort of the last frontier, and we lived there until I was about four or five. Then we moved to another country town, slightly bigger but still very much a small

179

country town. You go west from Sydney and keep going west"—he laughed—"until you've passed most of civilization. And we moved to another country town just a little bit closer to the city but still, in those days, a ten-hour drive away. We never went to Sydney. My father was a Methodist minister and every couple of years, every three or four years, ministers get moved to a new church.

"My earliest recollection of music of any sort was that my mother used to play the organ in church and I'd sit on the stool beside her and watch her and listen to the hymns. I would have been three or four. And it's funny, because years later some of the things—jazz harmonies—I could sort of hear where they'd come from in some ways; those movements of the chords in a lot of those old hymns are really almost like a foundation for the movements of chord changes in jazz pieces. I guess they'd be the standard Methodist hymnbooks, a lot of Wesleyan hymns. Just the basic movement of a 2-5-1, which is so prevalent in jazz, and of course that's just about all a hymn does.

"And then Dad left the ministry. He started out as an air force mechanic, working on jets, and then became a minister. It's a colorful career. He got involved in television as a preacher, just doing a Sunday service on the air sort of thing. When he decided he didn't want to be a preacher full time, he got interested in the other side of television and became a cameraman; he ended up being a producer of the nightly news and current affairs.

"We moved to Sydney when I was six, just turning seven; to that point, the only music I'd heard was in the church. We didn't have a stereo at home in the country and we didn't listen to the radio either. I went to school when we moved to Sydney, the big city, and they had a school band. I'd never seen anything like that in my life. It was a brass band, with cornets and euphoniums and tubas and trombones. It absolutely fascinated me because prior to that in school, the only music was when they put a record on and you play along to it with triangles and castanets and things. And the thought that this school band was making the music all themselves and there was no record and it was completely self-contained fascinated me. I decided I wanted to be in the band. You had to be seven to join and I was still only six at the time. My brother John, who still plays drums in my quartet, joined the band as soon as we arrived because he was two years older. So when he was out riding his billy cart I used to get his cornet from under the bed—actually I'd get *under* the bed where it was so I wouldn't get caught—and practice it. When I turned seven and went to audition for the band, I'd had nearly a year getting ready, and they didn't expect you to even know which end of the instrument to hold. You went for a musical aptitude test. I don't know how they were going to judge at seven years old whether you'd be a trumpeter or not, but the bandmaster gave me a few instructions on how to blow and said, 'Now see if you can make a sound.' Of course, I put the instrument to my lips and instantly reeled off a couple of scales!

"Around the same time, in that year when I was still seven, I first came into contact with jazz. That was when we became part of the local church. My father was an associate preacher there, part time, while he had his gig in TV, but the preacher was a trombonist and a jazz fanatic. He'd spent a lot of his time as a young man in the United States in black churches listening to gospel music, and he'd taken that back to Australia with him. And to this day it's probably still the only church in Australia like that. We just happened to live in the right neighborhood! So I heard jazz in the church, and here was the familiar sound of brass instruments that I'd become accustomed to, but they were being played a whole different way. As soon as I saw him play the trombone I said, 'Well, I gotta play one of those.' The thought never occurred to me that I would need to give up the cornet to play the trombone; it just seemed to me that now I wanted to play trombone, too. Fortunately, the local school had more instruments than players, so I was able to take home a trombone, then a tuba, and a euphonium, and a flugelhorn, and shortly after that I came into contact with a saxophone.

"I got a big band record and it was Harry James—that would have been my first record—and of course, the trumpet on it was great. I loved hearing that. But the other thing that fascinated me was hearing saxophones for the first time. I can't say who it was taking a tenor solo on one of the tracks, but I heard the tenor and instantly, right away, I was attracted to it. It wasn't until a friend of mine who knew I was interested in jazz—an older guy, I guess he would have been sixteen or seventeen and I was still, like, eight—said to me, 'Well, if you like jazz, have a listen to this. This is the real stuff.' And he played me Coleman Hawkins and I said, 'What's that? I want one of those.' I didn't even know what it looked like, the sound I heard. It didn't sound like the tenor saxophone on the Harry James record. And he said, 'That's a tenor saxophone,' and I said, 'Well, I gotta have one of those.'" James chuckled at the memory of his precociousness.

"So I instantly set about getting hold of a tenor saxophone. I borrowed one from someone at the church who wasn't playing any-more—there was always that sort of thing going on—and started playing the saxophone. And then, one of the older guys—I guess he might have been forty or fifty—in the church who played the trombone said, 'You should hear some other types of players. Have a listen to this.' He played me Erroll Garner, and my ears sort of popped out of my head. I said, 'Wow! How many hands has that guy *got*?' I said, 'That's it, I've gotta play the piano!'

"At the age of nine I said, 'I want to have a band so I can decide what tune we're going to play and how fast we're going to play it and what key it's going to be in and I can direct the music.' And so I started a band. My brother was on drums, he was eleven, and I guess most of the other guys were eleven or twelve. It was a traditional band. We did 'Fidgety Feet' and 'Maple Leaf Rag' and 'Bill Bailey' and we got a repertoire together of about half a dozen tunes and that was it; I couldn't wait, we had to have a gig. So we played down at the local shopping mall and we played any fair that was on, church fair or school fair, anything, any event that took place where I could possibly put the band on.

"I didn't have the players to draw on in primary school, but when I got into high school, seventh grade, I just got up when they had the morning assembly and announced, 'I'm starting a big band. Anyone who wants to be in a big band, come and see me.' I think I had nine trumpets, four saxophones, one trombone, and a rhythm section with two guitarists!

"I had started to get gigs when I was thirteen, in the middle of high school. Some of the older guys in the church were professional musicians. I must have been blowing okay and they said, 'Well, you want to come and do some gigs with us?' These were gigs playing at the local bowling club, the dinner dance on Saturday night, you know, and I learned a lot of old tunes doing that.

"I was listening to Oscar Peterson and Erroll Garner, and toward the end of high school I heard Dizzy Gillespie, and then I wanted to get all of *his* records. All of a sudden there were all these other notes. 'Where's he getting those notes from?'

"By the time I finished high school, when I was sixteen, I could put an arrangement together; I'd also worked out that there were five saxophones, four trumpets, and four trombones. About then, I got a gig in a jazz club for the first time. It was called the Paradise Jazz Cellar and it was in the middle of King's Cross—the red light district of Sydney and a bad part of town. I put together a quintet of guys that I'd known—my brother was still on drums—and some other players I met along the way.

"So all of a sudden I had an outlet for all that music. Looking back now, I can see the place was owned by the most notorious criminal and organized crime boss in Sydney. It was just one of his many clubs and he must have had all sorts of rackets going. I don't know what the real reason for the club was, meaning it could have been a front for him to run any kind of business out of.

"It didn't matter what we played in this jazz club; we could just play what we wanted. And it was time to play, just leap into it, and we played bop. We must have done some nights where we didn't do anything but just play bebop heads and play flat-out all night.

"But the musical thing that was happening in the club then was that I started to experiment. I heard people like Clifford Brown and 'round about then I heard Miles Davis for the first time. At that stage I had hardly seen anybody live. In the mid-to-late '70s there weren't a lot of people visiting Australia. It wasn't until '83, '84 that it became more common for people to include Australia—probably because by then Japan was becoming such a big market and it was more economical for them to come to Australia.

"The next big thing happened while I was still doing those gigs at the Paradise around 1970. I met Don Burrows, who was the most popular jazz musician in Australia. Everyone knew him and I had some of his records; he was a big star. I decided when I left high school I'd go to the Conservatorium of Music and do the jazz course they had there. Halfway through my time in the two-year course he came and took over as head of the jazz department. So I met him and he ended up asking me to join his group and form a quintet. He said, 'You want to come on tour with us?' That was probably the biggest—definitely in Australia— career break for me because he took me on tour around Australia to this massive audience he had.

"I toured with Don for the next six years, 'til I was about twenty-four, and in '82, he asked me to come back and teach at the Conservatorium. I did that for four years, which I thought was kind of funny since I didn't even finish high school.

"So I spent another few years and became quite popular at home. I started my big band again in '83 with my brother and we called it the Morrison Brothers. We'd seen Clark Terry and had an album of his, Clark Terry and His Big Bad Band Live at the Wichita Festival. So we instantly had the Morrison Brothers Big Bad Band back home. I wrote a lot for it and refined those skills I'd learned in high school. We played plenty of gigs at home, big concerts and all sorts of things, going from strength to strength.

"But we were both thinking, 'We've gotta get back to America.'" (James had made his first trip to the United States when he was seventeen. He was with a band made up from different high schools for performance at the Monterey Jazz Festival.) "John hadn't been there yet, and then the opportunity came when I was invited in '84. The Olympic games were in Los Angeles and there was a jazz festival at the Ford Theatre in that outdoor amphitheater with Willis Conover emceeing. There was an American big band and they invited guests to perform out in front of the band from all the different countries represented at the games. And I was the Australian invited. At the time I had thoughts of, maybe I'll never come back, maybe I'll be discovered while I'm there. I went and played with Benny Carter and, of course, I saw Albert Mangelsdorff live. I'd never even heard him on record and I heard him do the multiphonics and I said, 'Now there's something going on there!' I asked him how to do it and he was kind of strange; he said, 'This is just the beginning. The possibilities are endless.' And I'm going, 'Yeah, but how do you actually do it?'

"I didn't get to New York on that trip. We did the gig and then came back home. My brother John came along with me on that trip, just to see America. I said, 'Well, we're going to go back.' And a year later things were going so well at home—it seems strange to me now that we made this decision—we suddenly said, 'It's time to go to New York.'

"We sold everything, cars and whatever, and he sold his drum kit and said, 'I'll get another one over there.' And we got the tickets and put the rest of the money in the bank and said, 'That'll be enough to last; we're going to New York.' I don't even know what we had. Probably wasn't much. Then we just took off to New York, with no contacts, no nothing. And we just arrived in New York and caught a cab into town and found a hotel, booked in and said, 'All right, we're here, we're going to make it in the jazz scene.'

"We figured we'd stay for a year and see what happened. Can't live in a hotel for a year in New York; we'd go broke in a month. I didn't know how to go about renting an apartment or anything there, and I thought that sounded horribly expensive anyway. But I'd looked at the map and I said to my brother, 'Did you know that New York is five boroughs and four of them are islands? This is all surrounded by water. We'll buy a boat!' I had always been a boating fan and I had boating magazines from the United States and I'd seen the advertisements in them. The prices of boats were a third of what they were in Australia. I said, 'We'll buy a boat and we'll live on it! Because Manhattan's an island.'

"The first day—we arrived at midnight—we got up the next morning, it was a Sunday, and I got the *New York Times* and I went to the classified section, the boating section. I looked through it and I said, 'I've found it!' It was an Owings Cabin Cruiser and I said, 'That sounds great, I don't know what it is but it sounds great. The guy wants twenty-five hundred dollars for it. We can live on it for a year and we can sell it when we leave.' So we caught the subway and went to see this guy at Jamaica Bay. I shudder to think now that I had twenty-five hundred dollars in my pocket! We looked at this boat and said, 'Great!' and we bought it and sailed it back to Manhattan, still not realizing you can't just pull up to Manhattan and tie up.

"I'd read the paper on the Circle Line boat trip around Manhattan and I'd said to John, 'I'll look at the ads of the boats; you watch and if you see anywhere you think we can come back to, mark it on your map.' He'd picked the 79th Street Boat Basin—there's a marina there, on the West Side—so we came back to there and pulled in. It was about a four-hour sail into Manhattan and we'd named the boat the Koala Bear on the way there.

"Fate must have meant all of this to happen because it's probably the only place in Manhattan you can just pull in and tie up. The people there were very loose and will let you live on a boat there. It's unofficial but we pulled in there and said, 'Hi, we're from Australia.' And they looked at the boat and said, 'Wow! In that boat?' We said, 'Well, not exactly; we picked up this boat on the way.' We didn't elaborate and then we said, 'We need somewhere to stay' and they said, 'Sure, tie up.' They thought we meant for a couple of days and we said, 'Yeah, we'll see how we go,' and we stayed there for nearly a year.

"The boat was so small, I mean, it was tiny. We just had to get a little bar radiator and you had power from the dock and that would heat the boat and we'd turn the propane gas stove on and just let it go, to put heat around the boat, and it was okay. We put big canvas sheets over the boat for the ice and snow. Other guys who'd lived there for years gave us all the tips; they said, 'Do this, winter's coming, get some tape and do all the seams in the windows.'

"After a while we found out where you could sit in, like the Jazz Cultural Theatre and the Blue Note had a jam session, real late, and so on, but we didn't seem to be getting anywhere. After a while, I was fed up with it; we'd been there six months and still not had a gig. We were nobodies, and I said, 'What're we doing here? Back home we've got our own big band, we can put a concert on in Town Hall any time we like. Here we can't even crack it for a gig in a really bad club. What're we doing here?' And John'd say, 'Well, you know, this is where you've gotta be, what the song says, you make it here. We've gotta stay.' Then other times he'd want to leave. Lucky, we never hit the same mood at the same time. Even so, we kept our return tickets in a jar under one of the beds.

"Eventually, we inevitably ran out of money because we went to clubs like the Blue Note to hear people we wanted to hear. Art Blakey and the Jazz Messengers were on and then Max Roach or someone was on, so we just went. Of course, the prices of clubs up there, when you start going out every night, we ran out of money in no time. And then we'd play on the street and make money to eat and so on.

"Then we found a place down on Hastings Street called Arturo's. It was a pizza joint and had a piano and a snare drum and a hi-hat and they had duos play and then anyone can sit in. We'd go and play there for our dinner and it became a regular haunt for us. Then we're out at Bradley's one night listening to Kirk Lightsey and Ray Drummond and we're sitting there listening and a guy came over and said, 'Hey, you're the guy that plays the trombone.' And I said, 'Yeah,' and I thought, 'Wow! Who is this guy?' He was American, he didn't have an Australian accent, and he said, 'I heard you out at Arturo's earlier tonight. I was in there getting a pizza.' He said, 'You should sit in with these guys.' And I said, 'Well, sure, but I can't just—' and he said, 'I know them.'

"And it turns out his name was Angel Romero and he's an arranger and sort of producer for George Benson. He knew Kirk Lightsey, he knew a lot of the guys, and he went over and said, 'This is a kid here from Australia who plays the trombone.' Finally, I think more to shut him up than anything, Kirk Lightsey said, 'Okay, he can play a tune.' And I walked up with the trombone and played and we had a grand time and he said, 'Stay,' and I played the rest of the night with them. And then in the audience was a guy who came up after and said, 'Wow, who are you? I'm an agent,' and he got a contact number from us—it was the office down at the marina; they'd have to run around to the boat and get us—and he said, 'I'll be in touch.'

"And one thing led to another and he booked me on a big band with Cab Calloway doing a tour of Europe and then we got to go to festivals. I was actually not part of the big band; he put me as part of the act, like, Cab'd do his thing and his daughter would sing a few numbers and I'd come on and play a couple of numbers out in front of the band. That's all I did on the tour, but I got to meet a lot of people and the agent got me some more gigs. One thing led to another and I started to get invites to come to jazz parties here. I did Dick Gibson's Denver Jazz Party and I got to meet and play with Urbie Green and Ray Brown and a lot of the guys. And then, just like a snowball, one thing leads to another and I started to get more of a chance to come back here. But instead of coming back to the States a lot, maybe because that first tour was in Europe, I got to go back to Europe a lot doing festivals. The agent also looked after Adam Makowicz and booked me with him for the North Sea Jazz Festival. And then, from doing a gig at the Montreux Festival, part of an all-star thing, I got to meet Neshui Ertegun. He sort of took me under his wing and said, 'We'll put you on Atlantic Records.' And it was still this dual thing. Back home I could do what I liked and I was still making my way overseas and I still didn't come to the States much. Red Rodney heard me in Australia and said, 'Come and play with me in the States.' We did the Vanguard for a week and we did the Jazz Showcase in Chicago. I didn't follow it up with anything. I had to go back to things in Australia and so I still didn't really break into the American scene.

"This, really, is my first tour of the States—and a little bit low key, in a way. I'm not able to bring my own band yet; it's not financially possible. The next thing I know for sure that is happening is early next year I've got a tour with Ray Brown and Gene Harris and Jeff Hamilton. We'll start in Australia, go through Japan, through Europe, and finish up doing a tour of the States. That'll be a great boost. So that sort of brings us up to the present day."

One of the most fascinating releases of recent years was James Morrison's *Snappy Doo* on Atlantic, on which he overdubs all the instruments.

"Four trumpets usually—I think one or two spots I use five—four trombones, five saxophones—two altos, two tenors, and baritone. It's just like a regular big band. I did the piano because the only other guys in the album are Herb Ellis, Ray Brown, and Jeff Hamilton. We had a couple of days off while we were in Australia and I said, 'Let's get into the studio in Sydney,' and we put down the quartet tracks, and then I said, 'Now, some of the tracks I'm going to do some overdubs on,' and they said, 'Okay.'

"To me at the time it did seem a little bit amazing that they trusted me that much. Those guys have reputations and they can't just be on any old thing.

"I guess my motive was a couple of things," James Morrison summarized. "I've always wanted to put down all the horns in a big band. How many times have you sat in a big band, when you've written all the arrangements, and thought, 'They're playing it great, but would I have played it like this'? Then why not play it all? And the other thing is, I thought, 'What does a big band sound like when everyone in the band plays as though they wrote the chart and when everyone in the band has exactly the same concept of how the thing should go and how it should sound?' Short of getting seven or eight guys around a piece of manuscript, the only way to do it is to play it all yourself. What's really going on is, I'm hearing the whole band in my head right from the first horn, and as I put down, say, third trombone, I just cancel it, 'cause there's a real one. And then once that's down I've gotta put down the second trombone. By the time I get toward the end, maybe there's three trumpets left, the rest is real, and I'm still imagining those three trumpets as I put each one down. If you wrote the arrangement, you know it real well. And that's all I did, just as I put each real instrument down I could stop imagining an extra one, until I didn't have to imagine anything. It was all there.

"I had a big band concert in the Sydney opera house last year," James said. I reminded him that he has a reputation for sometimes unorthodox approaches to performance—for example, playing the trumpet with one hand and either flying his plane or scaling the sheer face of a cliff with the other. "I said, 'Okay, it's not very jazz to walk onto the stage. Everybody walks onto the stage. The audience knows the lights are gonna go down, that you're gonna walk onto the stage.' That's not jazz. Jazz is not knowing. And I said, 'Okay, the lights are gonna go down and it's going to become pitch dark. They won't even be able to see their hands in front of their faces. And then I'm gonna appear about a hundred and fifty feet above them on the end of a rope and I'll play the trumpet on the way down. As I play it, the lights will come up and there'll be a big band on stage that they didn't see when the lights went down, and the band'll start into this almost surrealistic-like Kenton when he was in his wildest thing. I'm gonna hit the stage and we'll instantly drop into the heaviest back-beated groove you've ever heard. People are just gonna go, "Ah-h-h-h-h!"'" Now, *that's* a *jazz* beginning to a concert. To me, the music was jazz, but the presentation was jazz, too. That's not to say that every jazz presentation has to be spectacular."

"I'm from Rio de Janeiro in a place called Copacabana," Joyce* began a conversation with me in 1991. She was doing a gig at Blues

---

* Joyce is the professional name by which she is known. Her full name is Joyce Silveira Palhano De Jesus.

Alley in the evening and we were talking that afternoon in the lobby of a hotel a block away. "It is a very popular neighborhood because of the beach and everything and I lived in the part of it that is almost a corner, going to Ipanema. Do you know Rio? Rio is all mountains and beaches. So the sea comes like this"—Joyce drew a line on the table with her finger—"and Copacabana by this time was the most famous beach in Rio. It still is. Ipanema's maybe a little more famous now because of the song, but at this time it was the most famous beach. And where it ends, it ends like this"—she drew again—"and then Ipanema starts, and it's exactly in this corner that I was born and raised.

"I believe that," Joyce responded when I mentioned that Rio is said to be one of the world's two most beautiful natural settings of a city; the other is Naples, where I lived for two years in the mid-1960s. "I have played in Naples, I know Naples. I would say—I beg your pardon—I would say that Rio is more beautiful. I love bays, I love places with bays, like San Francisco and Acapulco; those places, they're beautiful. I think that bays are the most beautiful settings for cities. I've never been to Hong Kong, but from the photographs it also seems to be wonderful. Naples is great, with *le grotte*, those places that you go into the rocks, they're so beautiful," she concluded, referring to Capri's Grotta Azzurra.

"My great-grandmother was a painter but that didn't mean much to my musical history. I always listened to a lot of music, especially Brazilian music. One of my older brothers was a musician. He worked professionally for some years in the bossa nova times, then he went to college, became a lawyer, and started working at a bank and made a business career. He kind of quit the music business, although he still plays at home. He was a good guitar player.

"So there was a guitar in the house, his guitar, and I always used to listen to him playing, and that is how I actually began to get interested and involved with music. I was a kid and he was fifteen years older than than I was. He always brought his friends to play at home. I was six years old, seven years old, and I was always listening to this kind of thing. His music friends were actually some real famous musicians from the bossa nova scene. So I had all those guys coming to my place and I could listen to them. Roberto Menescal, who's a very famous guitar player and composer in Rio; Leny

Andrade, a famous singer, a great singer; Carlos Lyra, also one of the master composers of bossa nova, who happens to be a distant cousin of mine, very distant. He was the author of many of the greatest songs of the bossa nova. So, people like that, then, lots of musicians. Eumir Deodato, who was the pianist in my brother's bands when they were all music students. I had those people walking around the house and heard them play a lot.

"When I was fourteen years old I started playing by myself. I was never taught; I just saw my brother play and his friends play and began to look at the chords and tried to figure out what they were. I learned fingering and all that later when I was already playing and teaching. I had a lot of nerve to do that, because how could I teach something that I had never learned before? But I was doing it.

"At eighteen I took my first classes on classical guitar, with a Brazilian concert player, very well known—Jodacil Damaceno. This guy taught me to put my fingers in the right positions and I started learning to read music and those things that I never heard of before. I was lucky, because it didn't take too long for me to do it. There was only four years between my starting playing and my starting to learn music. I felt that learning by myself was all right because the only thing I didn't know was certain technical details, like having the fingers right and making things easier for myself. But that didn't interfere much with the sound. I didn't have to have so much technique; it was just something to accompany myself while I sang. I was playing bossa nova stuff, which was really my beginning in music; that's where I started making, playing, and hearing music.

"I always sang. I remember singing since I was a little kid. All these musicians who would come to our house, at a certain point, would ask me to sing—like, 'Here comes that funny little girl to sing,' and they would accompany me. I also remember composing. I had lots of songs written by myself since a very early age.

"Actually, I started playing by myself. I always played solo. When I started professionally, then I started playing with other musicians, but only when I was eighteen, nineteen, around then. I started in music festivals, which were very popular in Brazil. When I was eighteen years old I had a song picked up for this huge music festival that took place in Rio in a large stadium with many famous artists. They would pick you by a number—they didn't use names—so you could be famous or anonymous. If they considered your song to be good, they would pick it up and have it in the festival. So that was my start of playing. Anyway, I was there and my song was played and then I got my first record deal and I did my first shows in places like small theaters. That was really the beginning of my career. I did two albums for Polygram at that time. That was my first record company. Now I'm back." Joyce laughed.

"And then I got married and had kids at a very, very early age—at twenty-two I was already a mother. I had two daughters, one after the other and I stopped making music for five years. And for ten years I didn't make a record of my own in Brazil. But after those first five years I went to Europe with Vinicius de Moraes, who was a very, very famous poet and song writer. He is one of the authors of 'The Girl from Ipanema.' He wrote the lyrics and [Antonio Carlos] Jobim wrote the music. He was incredibly popular in Brazil and in Europe and South America. He needed a singer who could play guitar also. So I worked with him for two years. We toured South America and Europe. I made albums in Europe. Then I moved to New York for a while. I made a record that never came out with Claus Ogerman as a producer and arranger. This was 1977. It had all the conditions to be a good album. We had great jazz musicians on this album like Buster Williams, Jeremy Steig, and great Brazilian musicians like Nana Vasconcelos and others who were not as well known.

"And then I went back to Brazil and a new moment of my career started, because all that was like a prologue to what was going to happen next. This was in 1978. I had a lot of material that I had written and I was always keeping this material for myself because I thought some day I might do a new record. After all that time, since 1970, I hadn't made any albums solo, just as a guest on other people's albums and the albums that I made abroad—nothing in Brazil. So I started distributing songs to everybody, to all the great Brazilian names like Elis Regina, Milton Nascimento, Maria Bethania, people who really sold lots of records.

"And everybody started recording my music. And then I really became popular as a songwriter. Then, in 1980, there was another festival and I went to it. It was huge with lots of television involved. I sent one very simple song that I had written to my kids when I was abroad, 'Clareana.' It was almost like a lullaby, a very, very simple tune, but it was just, like *vroom*! It was a popular hit, a national hit, and I found myself selling thousands and thousands of records and having my name everywhere and my music played on all the radio. Lots of people in Brazil think that that was my first record because that's when I really got popular in my country.

"After that I had many other albums, a different one each one-and-a-half years. I don't know exactly how many albums I do have. Should I count the albums that only came out abroad, like the two I made in Italy? Or should I count only the albums that came out in Brazil? I never know about that. Anyway, around seventeen albums, I think.

"When sometimes I can spend two weeks at home, which is great, I do mostly theaters. It's like almost every weekend. It's kind of crazy; I don't have a routine in my life. I travel a lot, especially when I have a new album coming out. Brazil is such a big country that going from one side to the other is like making a tour in Europe and starting in Portugal, for instance, and finishing in Russia. Brazil is huge, really a large country to travel. I'm doing a lot of traveling out of Brazil, too, so I'm going like crazy. I don't work much in South America outside of Brazil. I work a lot in Europe and in Japan."

Remarking that she has been a rather controversial figure in her homeland and that she has achieved some firsts in terms of being a professional woman, I elicited the following account.

"I think this would deserve a whole book. It's a very interesting subject. It's not only a thing in the last decade or two. Women have been very, very present in music since the last century, but they have always been hiding behind something. In Brazil, we are in the front line, in the front row, and there's a veil, a kind of a veil that covers them.

"We had this great Brazilian female composer called Chiquinha Gonzaga. She was a classic in Brazilian music in the nineteenth century. She shocked everybody; she abandoned her family, her husband, and her five children to be a musician and to be a conductor and an arranger and a composer. She was a big scandal in her time. After her, we heard about one or two women composers in Brazil, but not much.

"So when I came—that was in 1968, my very first appearance and first album, as a teenager—I had never thought about all that. I always thought of myself as being a composer, being a writer. It was very natural for me. Then, all of a sudden, when I do my first album, I hear the funniest, most incredible comments: 'Is she really the person who writes this?' 'She's a great guitar player—for a woman.' 'She plays like a man.' 'She writes like a man.' All those sorts of things.

"I was really mad at the very beginning, because it seemed so weird. I was very young then and I was writing my own material, and that seemed pretty strange to those guys from the press at that time. But ten years later you could see dozens of women composers appearing in Brazil.

"So, you see, I felt that I really opened up a way for those people to come. It was when I became popular, really popular with that festival story and everything. For some people, it may even seem that I was part of that feminine explosion of the '80s, which is not true because I was there much before. But that is when I became really, really popular, because my previous albums didn't have that much recognition or good press. Then after that, I got really popular in my country."

Agreeing with my comment that her country is a very male-dominated culture and society, she said, "Brazil still is. But in the music business people are different; they don't care so much about that. The resentment I felt, strange as it seems, was directed against me as the guitar player, the instrumentalist. The singer was okay, no doubt about that. The composer was acccepted, because the music was indeed good music; they couldn't say anything about that. Also, I wasn't trying to compete in their area because my subjects, as a writer, were so feminine. But when I started really playing the guitar, that kind of shocked some musicians. Once, in Argentina, when I was playing with Vinicius de Moraes, this Argentine guitar player was really mad at me. He came to me and said, 'I always knew that the Brazilian guitar players were great, but I can't take this from a woman.' He was really mad! I found this so funny! I mean, I had nothing to do with him, so why was he so mad at me? Just because he liked my playing so much? It was crazy!" She laughed at the recollection of the scene.

"The shower, actually, is one of the best places," said Joyce, laughing, as she began to describe her compositional methods. "My family already knows about that. They knock at the door and they ask, 'Are you composing?' when I'm taking too long in the shower. Anyway, sometimes I do words and music together. If not, I will probably do the music first, and then the words—put the words and phrases in. And there's always a certain time in the year when I'm about to make a new record or I'm trying to organize my life a little better, and I give myself a certain amount of time every day when nobody can disturb me. I will be locked in a room with just the guitar and a tape recorder and work on a song. I'm learning to do this because I just can't keep everything in my memory. I've lost so many good songs that I could have used for lots of different things that I can't afford to do this anymore. I made a promise to myself that I'm going to be very careful about that."

Joyce continues to perform in Brazil, throughout Europe, and in Japan. Her latest album is *Astronauta—Songs of Elis* on the Blue Jackel label.

"I was born June 6, 1944," said Monty Alexander as we took seats for a morning conversation in his hotel suite nearly a decade ago. The Kingston, Jamaica, native and his combo were in residence that week at Washington, D.C.'s, Blues Alley. "My mother had a piano in the house; she wanted to take piano lessons, and the piano attracted me because it's a fascinating thing. That started when I was three or four years old, my relationship with the piano. It's a part of me; the piano is connected somehow. For the music itself, I was able to pick up melodies from an early age, simple melodies. I was developing an ear and I guess that's one of my fortes, that I have a pretty good ear.

"But for musical development, I think of going to the movies and their fascination for me as a child. I would try to recreate that movie and I'd just imagine I was providing music in the background, like a film score. I found I could sound like a waterfall on the piano by running up and down the black keys, just up and down. I'd make sounds on the piano, that was my thing, and my folks saw that I had this interest. I could just put my arm on all the black notes and I would say, 'Hey, that's a melodic thing, it sounds nice!' I used to love the Western movies, the cowboy shows. I remember playin' cowboys with the kids. I'd go to the piano and play the low notes on the piano, so it would sound like a cowboy's gun"—Monty made the sound of a gun firing—"'I gotchou, I gotchou,' and I'd be at the piano shootin' people.

"I was pickin' melodies from a very early age. My mother said there was a Christmas party at our home and a calypso band and they had the band play these songs. The next morning while they were wakin' up they heard 'White Christmas' on the piano. I'm playin' 'White Christmas'; I'm pickin' out the melody. Then she said it dawned on her that Monty has got some little thing goin' here. I must have been about five or six years old.

"I was in kindergarden and Miss Betty Brown, halfway up the block where I went, she was the piano teacher. From the very beginning I had a problem sittin' there, with the discipline, and studyin', and practicin'—just hated it. So when I would have practice time, I'd just be sittin' there havin' my own kind of fun.

"Then I picked up on rhythm; I started playin' boogie woogie, simple stuff, but I did it with a sense of utter confidence. I was the rhythm section in this rhythm-and-blues sound. We had a lot of that in Jamaica. You heard it on the radio. I figured out chords, my own little simple chords, and I was rhythm on the piano from a very early age. Then there was the calypso music that I heard. I was able to pick out these old-time folk sounds like we've heard Harry Belafonte and Sonny Rollins play.

"So this is coming from all directions. I developed the desire to have a nice sound comin' out of the piano. From an early age I must have developed a sound, instead of bang-bang-bang. For styles in music, this rhythm-and-blues thing was in me, the melody thing was in me, and making up things—but jazz? I didn't know what that was.

"When I first heard about jazz, to me it was silly, stupid. We had a radio station that played just nice melodic music, songs, all those beautiful ballads in the '50s. I'm seven, eight years old. Gene Autry was my first idea of American songs and the guitar. And then I heard Nat King Cole and it was an easy connection from Gene Autry to Nat. It was something in the timbre, the sound of the voice, so I made that connection. It's all connections; it's all related.

"And then, pianowise, Eddie Heywood. His music was very digestible. I'm about eight, ten years old; years are goin' by, and I'm playin' Eddie Heywood. I'm gettin' that sound, that left hand on 'Begin the Beguine.'" He vocally simulates the repetitive boogie woogie bass figure. "'Canadian Sunset.' It's all about tappin' your feet.

"So it's all comin' together. Meantime, I gotta go study with Miss Trench, the lady from England. She's tellin' me what Bach and Mozart did—these guys, gee—and all this rigid stuff. Miss Trench, three o'clock in the afternoon. I was at boardin' school now. I'm about ten years old, boarding in the country because my mother wanted me to have the best education. It was a struggle financially, but it was 'Monty has to have a good upbringin' and go to boarding school.' There was a church connection, Anglican; it had a British tone to it.

"Another thing that happened to me, from an early age, was a certain interest in the supernatural—not in the mystical way but just the whole idea of the creator God and all this thing of 'H-o-l-y, h-o-l-y.'" He chants it in a deep voice. "'Man, this is something special, yeah, this is heavy!' I was in the choir; I'm singin', and bit by bit they got me pumpin' the organ, playin' the hymns when Miss Trench couldn't make it.

"My mother's side, everybody loved the old-time church music. The people from the earthy style of life, they had their Saturday night dances and we heard the New Orleans grooves. Professor Longhair, Huey Piano Smith, Fats Domino, Little Richard, that whole medium. Rhythm and blues was a part of life.

"There's this elitist thing that I addressed from an early age because I'm a cross-cultural kind of guy. I was hangin' out with the common folk. I enjoyed that. The local musicians took a liking to me; they saw my sincerity, and I was able to fit in because I had the ears. I bring color into this now, because I'm from a somewhat mixed family. Some of my family is dark-skinned, colored if you will; and I have Jewish relatives, I have Syrian relatives, I have Spanish in me. People in my family were aspiring to be with the high-class, elitist people. It's like tryin' to hobnob with the governor. If you can have tea with the governor, boy, you really made it. But I rebel against that; I was mixed.

"I just had a wonderful experience as a child, goin' in and out with different people. That's why today I consider myself very adaptable to all kinds of people. I remember when I first came to America and I was hangin' out with these hard-nosed Italian people, at eighteen years old—that rough crowd you see in movies. I've always been adaptable. And musically, the same thing happened. It's all good! Country-Western sounds, those melodies that linger on forever. Bap! That hit me just like anything else. I never had any barriers as far as music was concerned. A reverence for music came to me at an early age.

"I knew most of the church music by ear. I had paper in front of me as a guideline and I was scared some of the time, but I was able to keep up to that level of what the reading was. My dad, he got a kick out of seeing his litle kid Monty up there playing the piano with the musicians in the public place and he encouraged me to go to the local places where we had some terrific players. I'd take my accordion, which was the first portable keyboard. I have my accordion, the calypso band was up there, and they'd say, 'Come on Monty, bring the flutina'—this is Jamaica talk—'Come play with us.' And I'd be up there with Lord Power and Lord Kitchener, the calypso people. They were an incredible bunch; it's unfortunate that America doesn't know them. The first rappers, man. These cats had names that they took from the British, like Lord Nelson is a calypso singer. Got a straw hat on and gold teeth, two teeth missing. Aw, man, singin'—'I wa-a-ter the ga-ar-den,' and it's all risqué, naughty. I mean, we be on the road, you know, and the fun in music and people sitting around, and merriment, joy! Let's have a good time!

"But let's talk about the sophisticated thing now. I don't know what year it was, but I saw *The Eddy Duchin Story* with Carmen Cavallaro's music. He used to play 'Nocturne in E Flat.' Carmen Cavallaro was bad. He was playin' 'Whispering,' which is Dizzy's thing, and all these melodies. I had no fear of the piano. 'You're not going to rule me, Mr. Piano! I'm in charge of this stuff!' I had no fear about my technique; whatever I wanted to play, apparently I could play it. I'm going through a little development of 'How can I do this, how can I do that?' And I would apply myself and somehow I'd get it, I was able to express myself with different little directions I was going in.

"But for jazz, what is it that makes somebody make up notes? Jazz, what's jazz? For some reason, I didn't know what jazz was. I was sort of acting high and pompous with my religious thinking: 'That's the devil's music.' I was going through some changes in my personality. Eddie Heywood came to Jamaica and my father took me to see him at the theater and took me to meet him and I played for him. Eddie was very childlike and he got a kick out of comin' all the way to Jamaica to listen to a guy playin' his music. So that was great; I'm hobnobbin' with the heavy dudes now! Then I see *High Society*, with Bing Crosby, Frank Sinatra, Louis Armstrong. Armstrong! Kids love him, the jazz hipsters love him, people all over the world love him.

"Then I hear the Modern Jazz Quartet. I dreamed these things, and then I would see these musicians. A friend of mine had this album and there are these four black men with beards on the cover—looked like funeral directors, we used to say—and they're in tuxedos. Looked like death warmed over, man. What is this? And I hear on the record this minuet stuff, Bach, all these blues, man! This is the opposite of Louis Armstrong. Milt Jackson, who's my friend. Boy! Then I hear Louis Armstrong, simplicity. Erroll Garner! He was another one I heard! Nobody painted a picture like Erroll Garner. That's Ravel, that's Debussy. I heard Ray Brown on bass, that beat that he played. But joy is in the music! So these people attracted me.

"I remember seeing Nat King Cole at the theater in Jamaica. My mother went to the show and I got out of school enough to see the last two songs. I didn't know he played the piano! I didn't know! I think it was a white piano, of all things, and he's playin' the piano. He plays the piano! And it was that whole graceful smooth charm and that sound! I just loved Nat Cole. So Nat Cole is in there, too.

"Here's another connection. Still alive today, and well and thriving and playing—one of the greatest artists America has had, Ahmad Jamal. He's so gifted it's incredible. I heard 'Poinciana.' Now that's 1958 and I'm fourteen. In fact, Eddie Heywood is a big connection to Ahmad. If you hear those ostinato vamps and you listen to Ahmad Jamal, he's doin' that. 'Poinciana' was a big connection to me, because I heard this subtle thing with the piano, a guy who was Eddie Heywoodish, but behind him was a rhythm that sounded like the most furious jungle drumming you ever heard in your life. It reminded me of all the natural music in Jamaica, the

African polyrhythms, the calypso. I said, 'Man, this is another thing!'

"So this is what's happening: I'm at school, I'm a medium student, I'm good at history, terrible at mathematics and literature, but I'm the piano player, the mad kid on the piano. In fact, when I first went to high school, when you're a new boy, you gotta go through this discipline with the older students. You gotta sing for them, you know, this initiation thing that the British schools do. I say, 'Ah, I can play the piano a little bit.' He says, 'Play the piano, boy!' And I sit at the piano and I start wailing, man! From that moment they wouldn't leave me alone. I'm walkin' across the school ground with my books and somebody says, 'Alexander, commere! Come play the piano for me!' I would have to march into a room and play.

"So I'm playin' for the guys and I had a school band. Bunch of kids at school, the other guys who liked music, and we're tryin' to copy Little Richard, Elvis Presley. I wanted to be like Elvis—pull up my collar, the whole bit. Chicks liked Elvis, man. And I played the guitar, tuned it down sort of like a bass. This is before the Fender bass came out, or it was in America but we didn't have it. I was playin' the low notes on the guitar because the bass was crucial to me! It's still in my music. I hear my music from the bass up; I hear the melody down, and somewhere in there the chords come. So Derick on the other guitar, Teddy Smith on the drums, and other guys—we're playin' these songs. I'm tryin' to teach them! We all wore black pants and red shirts. So we're tryin' to play where the girls come, at the different school events.

"Another thing that happened, I made a record, a 45 rpm—'Summertime' on one side and the other side we made a tune called 'Dog It.' It got on the Jamaican Hit Parade! Now I'm getting public with my band; I'm gettin' bandleader chops, so to speak. So we had a band, a back-up band. I would sneak out of school and take the bus, hope nobody would see me. I'm goin' down to hire out with these guys, man, backin' up the local artists while they're singin'.' Most of it is twelve-bar blues. And Jamaica Ska, because somebody said, 'Let's call it Ska.' You know that beat, the one that go 'Ska-pit, ska-pit, ska-pit,' and they developed a dance. 'If Chubby Checker got his twist, we goin' to have the Ska!' So that's how Ska started. Ska is the forerunner of Reggae.

"For the next stage of my musical development, I'm at the piano all the time, playin' up and down like Carmen Cavallaro, rhythm-and-blues, or just tryin' to be hip with jazz. I'm developing that inner language of how to construct a jazz solo like Charlie Parker. I'm not quite there yet, but it's the willingness to allow myself to be free. This is what the classical people don't understand. They got so ingrained with avoiding mistakes that they don't begin to know what to say! I'm not sayin' all of them are like that, but they have a built-in barrier. But I didn't want that! I wanted to be free!

"As has happened at various stages of my musical development, there was some kind of a wonderful little key that would go in the lock, that would open up a new adventure for me. I don't know how I got the harmony I got, but I'm told by my colleagues that I'm a sophisticated harmonic musician. I hear Ravel, I hear Johnny Mandel, Art Tatum. Tatum is Michael Jordan; it's that level of heaviness. Art Tatum changed American music because Charlie Parker was in the wings watching him, getting into all that harmonic stuff. Buddy Rich was another kind of a guy, heads above the second best!

"My mother wanted to leave Jamaica. She had personal reasons. Something went down between my mother and father and they didn't want to be together anymore and she had friends in Miami. I'm seventeen years old now, didn't complete my schooling, had gone to New York once. So, I'm in Miami and it's like, 'What's next?' Okay, am I going to go back to school? This is like '61, '62, and she met some people in a hotel on the strip where we're stayin.' There are a few Jamaicans scattered around Miami and I longed for that kind of companionship. I'm lonely, so I start hanging out. I'm walkin' by a place one night and these five guys are standin' out there, all black American musicians, and they were friendly to me. 'Hey, man.' They liked being around a Jamaican kid. 'You dig jazz?' And I say, 'Yeah, yeah, man!' and they say, 'Man, how're you doin? You play piano?' This happened several times. I'd go up there and I started smokin' a cigarette, or smokin' I dunno what, and I went in with them one night, and they went up to play. Serious, groovin' stuff; I'm just havin' a ball, right? And I'm playin'. And this kept happenin'; I did it two or three times. One night I went in there and there's this man in the bar named Steve Stark; his father was Herman Stark, the stage manager of the Cotton Club. He sees me play, this seventeen-year-old at the piano, and he says to me, 'Hey, kid, we're gonna get you some work around Miami!' So he got me sort of illegally into the musicians' union. I had a couple of sort of illegal gigs and I brought home some money, I got my three hundred dollars and I put it on the table. I gave my mother one hundred fifty, and she says, 'Wait a minute! Monty, hey, this is great!'

"Steve Stark is gonna be my booking agent, my manager. So we went to New York and I met Duke Ellington. I didn't know about Duke Ellington. I knew about this guy and that guy, but I didn't know much. I'm already playin' little odd jobs around the Miami area with my own trio. I'm playin' these joints where the prostitutes are hangin' out, and the gangsters are hangin' out, late-night Miami, 79th Street Causeway, which is a very heavy place. But now I need to get secure and get my visa in America, and there's this joint in New York called Jilly's that Steve wanted to get me a gig in. But it didn't work; they wouldn't accept me; we didn't meet the right people.

"So I go back to Miami, and apparently Duke Ellington wrote a letter on my behalf to the U.S. Immigration Service, saying that I should be allowed a chance. Eddie Fisher even wrote a letter for me; somebody knew somebody and I met Eddie. And my mother, in her quest to get me in, went to the Fontainbleu Hotel in Miami and met Count Basie. She knocked on his room door and Basie came in his robe to the door and said, 'Yes ma'am?' and she said, 'Excuse me, but I'm from Jamaica; my son is very talented, and we're tryin' to get him in the country.' And Count Basie just must have seen the sincerity—the way my mother said it. He said, 'Well, any mother who is that proud of her son must be a very special mother.' Apparently, Basie wrote a letter, too. These letters went to the musicians' union and then to the Immigration Department—bob, bop, bop, I get my immigration card, I get my union card, I get my visa. Now I'm legal, and I'm playin' around Miami in these clubs.

"Six months later and I'm hangin' out with the wrong element of the musicians and I start smokin' the stuff, and I don't enjoy it. It's a big thing in Jamaica, but certain people don't do it. I did it and I never liked it. I couldn't play the piano; I couldn't hold a conversation. All I did was eat cookies and ice cream all night. I remember one night I got so high from the stupid thing that I thought I was gonna die. My heart was beatin' like *this*!" For the last few words Monty Alexander has speeded up his speech and rapidly snapped his fingers. "I didn't know what this guy gave me, but I remember I knelt down and I prayed. I went, 'I'll never do it again!' So I was spared from that.

"So I'm playin' this Miami club and who walks in but Frank Sinatra and Jilly Rizzo. Frank says, 'Who's the kid? He'd be good in the club.' Now, this is the place that *rejected* me! I'm playin' another club, in Hollywood, Florida, for Art Mooney, who had 'I'm Looking over a Four-Leaf Clover.' I'm backin' up the belly dancers. Art Mooney invites me to go to Las Vegas in his orchestra as the piano player. Gosh! 'Mom, can I go to Las Vegas?' 'Careful.' I go to Las Vegas. The job ended after six weeks and I'm just hangin' out in Vegas with a fast crowd; I couldn't be in the casino because I'm underage, but I got a job playin' bass and I'm backin' up some singer. Then another job came and I'm backin' up another singer, Johnny Bachelor, 'Mr. Wonderful.' And here come Jilly and Frank again. I got a phone call from New York and they sent me an airline ticket. I arrived that day in New York, and the next night I was at Jilly's, playin'. All these show people would drift in. I met Sammy Davis Jr.; I met Milt Jackson. Frank had combos back me and I would pick up the phone and call Ron Carter. I could pick up the phone and call Connie Kay to come play with me at Jilly's. And I had guys whose names I'd seen on records; they liked me, accepted me, 'Hey, man, you're swingin'.' I'm not tryin' to rub up and hobnob with these show people. I'm downstairs playin' dominoes with the cats in the band. I want to be one of them. So, that's how it started and that's how I got in with the big boys.

"It's all so amazin' because I'm just comin' from this little island country and another culture, you know. Jamaica never really got into the fray, especially the heavy, on-the-ground life. We didn't interact with Americans, so all this is like, *wow*!"

Several years ago I interviewed trumpeter and flugelhornist Ingrid Jensen. We were in her hotel suite down the street from Washington, D.C.'s, One Step Down, where she was performing that weekend. I had checked her out there the night before and had been as impressed with her virtuosity, creativity, and taste as I had been a couple of years before. That was when I saw her perform as a member of the trumpet section and a star soloist with Diva, the all-women's big band. They were playing at the Kennedy Center's first annual Mary Lou Williams Women in Jazz Festival. In fact, I was so blown away by her plunger-muted solo on "Caravan" on that earlier occasion that, never having before met her, I told her afterward that she was "ba-a-a-ad!" We both still chuckle over that moment.

And Ingrid *is* ba-a-a-ad. Listening to her recent album *Higher Grounds* on the Enja label, you can't reach any other assessment of the talents of this extraordinary artist. Quite simply, she is emerging as one of the most expressive trumpet players on the scene today. Although she's not yet a household name in jazz circles, my ears convince me that it won't be long into the third millennium before she is generally recognized as a major contributor to the ever-renewing perpetuation of the jazz art.

Ingrid Jensen has lived in New York since the mid-1990s, but it was in another country, far from the jazz Mecca, that she grew up and came to love jazz and decide to devote her life to performing it. She was born in North Vancouver, British Columbia. After her parents divorced when she was three or so, she moved with her mother and sisters (the younger one, Christine, would become a saxophonist) to nearby Cedar by the Sea.

"It was all very, very lush green country living that I was brought up in," she recalled, "nothing to do with the city and very little exposure to live music or things like that, except that in the house my mother was playing piano all the time. After working all day, she'd sit down at the piano and play some tunes, just to give herself peace of mind. So she was playing standards and Chopin and Debussy, all that stuff. And *tons* of records! I was listening to great musicians like Louis Armstrong, Jack Teagarden, lots of Bing Crosby, and Burl Ives, Rosemary Clooney, Oscar Peterson, Ella Fitzgerald—she really loved Ella. So we listened to some great music from when we're little kids."

The three sisters were "always messing around on the piano; probably as soon as we could climb up on the seat, we were playing. It was just sort of a natural extension of our environment. We lived in a very creative environment where television was not important; it was actually kind of discouraged. If it had not been for my mom

suggesting we go outside and play or make some music, who knows
what creative juices we would have allowed the tube to suck out of
us?

"My grandmother was a piano player, too, and she left these
things lying around, things from the 1920s and 1930s. I knew how
to read music because I'd been in choir when I was a kid. I remember the first thing I learned was the verse for 'My Funny Valentine.'
I would take a melody from a book and I'd just play off of it. I didn't
realize I was improvising. I just sort of played around with it, made
up my own version."

Piano lessons eventually followed, but the teacher engaged for
eleven-year-old Jensen was less than inspiring. "You'd go in her
house and it's a beautiful sunny day outside and the minute the door
closes you're in gloom; the windows are all shut and the curtains are
drawn and it's just a dark vibe. I was just really turned off from the
whole idea of music. So I just went back outdoors. I had a horse and
I probably was singing a lot of music. I had a Walkman at that time;
people were giving me tapes and I started buying records, like when
I was thirteen, fourteen."

Of the three sisters, Janet, Ingrid's older sister, was the first
instrumentalist in the family. She took up trombone in junior high
school but did not continue in music. In fact, Ingrid briefly went
through a stage of wanting to play trombone before she realized
that trumpet was the instrument for her.

"My younger sister Christine started playing saxophone a few
years after I had already begun and I would often force her to listen
to things beyond her ears, like Trane and Bird. She soon enough
figured out what was happening and what wasn't. She has become
one of my favorite musicians and sidepersons." In addition to performing and recording with her sister's band here and abroad,
Christine has contributed tunes to its book. She has also been a
member of the Joel Miller Sextet, played lead alto with the McGill
Jazz Orchestra, and led her own combo.

At thirteen, Ingrid took up the trumpet so she could join the band
at North Cedar Elementary School. "It came very easily in a lot of
ways; I think it was because my ear was so tuned in many ways to the
music and I had a very good feeling for it." The next year, at Cedar
Junior Secondary School, she continued, "We had a band teacher,

Norm Porter, who was a trumpet player and he gave us tapes. Everyone in the band who showed any interest, he would make them these tapes, a mix of all the great sounds from traditional Louis to Don Ellis, really great exposure things for us. Those tapes really turned us on to people. I would take one name from this tape that I was really into and buy all that person's records. It's very hard for me now to remember exactly my obsessive phases, but I really went quite distinctly from one player to another. I never listened to Clifford Brown and Freddie Hubbard at the same time. I don't know why, but I would just really get stuck in one sound, like the sound of their instrument, more than anything. So I went from Chet Baker and then into cool Miles, then it was maybe Lee Morgan. Then I discovered there was more Miles out there than just the cool Miles, like 'All Blues' and 'Kind of Blue'—that era, the Wynton Kelly thing. Then after Miles I discovered Freddie, and then Clifford. Then it really opened up and I started to hang out with a lot more musicians at that point, in early university, and started to listen to everything—Woody Shaw and a lot of Freddie, and a lot of later Miles. I played along with records a lot at home and I started transcribing some things, so I got a feeling for the music even better."

About barriers in the way of a young woman taking up the trumpet in the early 1980s in the Vancouver area, she said, "Well, first of all, right off the bat, there were no attitudes about *any* of us as being young women playing brass instruments. In fact, there was the opposite; there was support. We had the entire community behind us because we were doing something good. We were doing something that was going to take us into another zone of intellectual and spiritual development, and the people around us—our parents, our community—they all saw that.

"Of the three school bands I played in at Nanaimo District Senior Secondary School that were always very important to me, concert band was not one of them. I hated that. It was just the most boring, ugly, insensitive music I'd ever heard and I used to get kicked out of concert band every rehearsal. I'd just mess around. The ones that were really fun were Dixie Band—the traditional New Orleans thing—and the jazz combo and the big band. And this was all in a school out in the middle of the country. Pretty cultured stuff!

"For some reason the personality of our band teacher, Norm Porter, really drew out the strength in women, so his bands always had way more women in them than men. He was a trumpet player and a drummer and just a very well-rounded musician from the prairies of Canada. And he came out west and he just started up these great music programs and really did a lot of great stuff for the music scene. He had an *amazing* record collection, just amazing."

Incidentally, Ingrid Jensen points out, this was also the high school that Diana Krall attended. "She was ahead of me and I used to watch her when I was growing up. I was trying to emulate her presence and her seriousness. She was practicing a lot—and that was one thing I wasn't doing. I definitely had the will at that time to do it, but maybe not so much that environment that she had, which was a big house, a piano all to herself. So I used to watch her a lot and even try and be like her in many ways. And that's changed."

Pressed on what had changed, she explained. "Well, hopefully, with everyone, once you realize who you are, you stop trying to be like other people. You stop idolizing them; you stop looking for who you are in other people's images. I think that's one of the big dangers in this world today; there are kids who are just watching television or reading things, these magazines, and pretending that they're someone else rather than really digging into themselves to find out who *they* are and what *they* love. I think that's why music is one of the greatest gifts ever, because you have to be honest. Once you start putting the air through the horn or putting your fingers on the piano, you can't fool anybody. People are going to know what you're about. It's been the most exciting discovery in my life, that I want to play like me, like Ingrid Jensen. When I surround myself with really great musicians, I'm even more free to do that, because they're all supporting my individuality, as well as, of course, our respect for the music, which I think goes hand in hand. That's not always the case in a lot of music we hear these days. Sometimes it's very controlled by an image and by what people say it has to be. All my favorites never, never sound like they're playing by any rules; they're just playing themselves.

"So, back to the combo thing and the big band thing and the Dixie Band—very important. We'd do a lot of stuff—gigs at the Legion and at the mall, the local parades—and we used to go around campaigning for money so we could go on tour with the band and do festivals and things. We'd get in the back of a pick-up truck and put on these band uniforms that were twenty-five years old—so they were either too big or too small for us—and we'd drive around the neighborhoods of all these different suburbs of the Nanaimo area and do a bottle drive. We'd have three vans behind us full of kids and they'd all run in and get bottles for recycling and we'd play. You got five cents or ten cents a bottle, and we raised a lo-ot-t of money. Some people, if they didn't have bottles, they'd just give us money. 'Here's ten bucks.' So it was pretty happening.

"Also, there was a band called the NMA, the Nanaimo Musicians Association Band, combined of heavies, like all the professionals from the islands and the teachers. This band was really important in my growth because we played all the great swing music, really great Basie stuff and a bunch of Duke Ellington; we'd also do contemporary things. We rehearsed every Tuesday and we'd do concerts and a lot of dances. The dances raised money to buy more music for the band. So that's what we did—went out and played with the guys a lot. The whole principle of the band was to bring in the young, upcoming players who were in the school system and give them a chance to be immediately in a professional environment where they had to really carry their own weight. It was heavy; it was really challenging. Sometimes I'd be playing and I'd think, 'Wow! I just suck! I have no right to be here!' But I got in the band when I was sixteen, and then I played in it for a while, and my younger sister Christine was in it three or four years later. All the really great young players from the islands were in it." Also, there was Malaspina College. It was "right up the hill from the high school, which made things easier for those of us at Nanaimo District Senior Secondary School who were already filling chairs in the college big band, which met after our school got out."

Ingrid Jensen was also getting gigs as a leader, "sort of trio gigs here and there, hotels and some bookshops." A pivotal moment occurred when she attended the Bud Shank Workshop across the border in Washington State. "Phil Woods was there and Tom Harrell; all these guys were teaching there. I got to hang out with them and Hal Galper, and they said, 'Ingrid, you really have to go East; otherwise you're gonna stay here on the West Coast and you're not gonna grow as much as you can.' This was twelve years ago, July. In August, I was packed up and on a plane to Boston to study at Berklee. I had some scholarship money and I convinced my parents to give me money, and so I went there for three years."

To use a well-worn cliché, the rest is history. And what a history! *Higher Grounds* is Ingrid Jensen's third CD for Enja Records and she has played on several dozen more under the leadership of others. She has toured across the United States and in Europe and Japan, and she has offered clinics here and in her native Canada. At the age of twenty-five she was appointed Professor of Jazz Trumpet and Big Band at Austria's Bruckner Conservatory. She has also been Artist in Residence at the Berlin Hochschule and at Tufts University. The trumpet sections of Diva, the Maria Schneider Jazz Orchestra, the Vienna Art Orchestra, and the Netherlands' Metropole Orchestra have been graced by her presence, and her artistry has often been officially recognized. For example, in Canada, her debut album *Vernal Fields* won a 1995 Juno Award (the equivalent of a Grammy) and in Ireland she was the recipient of the 1996 Best Newcomer Award at the Cork Jazz Festival. The *Boston Globe* also honored the album and in Kalamazoo, Michigan, she won the 1995 Carmine Caruso International Jazz Solo Trumpet Competition. Having earlier been profiled in *Down Beat*, Ingrid Jenson was included among "25 for the Future, a Cast of Rising Jazz Stars," the feature article of the May 1999 issue of the magazine. That same month she appeared as leader of her quintet at the Fourth Annual Mary Lou Williams Women in Jazz Festival at the Kennedy Center, Washington, D.C.

Before closing my interview with Ingrid Jensen I inquired how she thought of her role in music, asking first how she felt about all-women combos and big bands. She offered her views and her musical philosophy.

"My problem with the all-women thing—the all-*any* thing—is that it tends to cause a problem artistically. It just does. To me, we need to try to figure out who works better with us. It's not like, 'Oh, well, this woman and this woman and this woman and this woman, I want to play with *them*.' If somebody said to me, 'Well, put your ideal band together,' I might have a Japanese guy on piano, an African American on drums, some Russian cat, maybe a girl, or maybe a guy, on bass, maybe some transsexual on flute. You know what I mean? It's just who I really conceivably can see in the best combination of personalities. Hal Galper, who's one of the wisest educators and one of the most incredibly deep personalities in checking out what's going on in the scene, said to me: 'You know, the only thing really left to change in this music is that there're going to be more women playing with the men and it's going to be more mixed.' There's not just the masculine side to this music; there's a *huge* feminine side that goes with it."

A short list of representative artists with whom she has performed here and abroad would include sit-ins with Clark Terry and Art Farmer and gigs and/or recordings with saxophonists Gary Bartz and Pat La Barbara, pianist Marc Copland, Austrian guitarist Karl Ratzer, Maria Schneider and her band, and French bassist/composer Helene Labarrierre. Looking back on this spectrum, Ingrid exclaimed, "I have realized how exciting it is to have these different energies and personalities and backgrounds mixing together. When you have a mix of humans who have all these different backgrounds and come from all these different places to express what they have to say, and do it as a group, it's the ultimate high. That's *it* ! I mean, what else *is* there?"

8

Blues

"You can't say, oh, because you're white or because you're black or because you're fifteen or because you're fifty, you can't do something. You just can't make those distinctions when it comes to what strikes your soul."   Rory Block

"I have a love for the blues. I feel that it's basic human emotional music, very direct, very applicable to almost anyone's life."   Dave Hole

I grew up around Lexington, Massachusetts," said pianist Dave Maxwell. "My mother was fond of classical music, some of the more romantic composers, Tchaikovsky, Beethoven, and I suppose that permeated my listening existence. I gravitated toward the music and my parents noticed that when I was four or five.

"I started taking piano lessons in grade school. In junior high I was listening to popular music, whatever was on the radio, and this would be mid-'50s. But I was never really exposed to black rhythm-and-blues stuff that early. I hated folk music and show music and it wasn't as though I was listening to all the doo-wop groups. I remember listening to Pat Boone, 'Love Letters in the Sand,' sappy stuff like that, and the Everly Brothers, 'Wake Up, Little Susie.' I eventually gravitated to more of the bluesy sounding stuff and was also into a little jazz as well—Dixieland and New Orleans—and I was attracted to the Dave Brubeck stuff. In junior high school there was a drummer, Doug Stewart—his father was a famous news broadcaster on WBZ here in Boston. I went over to his house and there was a book on *How to Play Boogie Woogie* on the piano. I remember reading through it a little bit and I was really struck by the whole idea of playing blues notes and some of the sounds that I was reading in the book. So that somehow made a certain impression on me. And then we kinda had a little band in junior high; we jammed, but we didn't really do any gigs.

"Then in Lexington High School there was a dance band playing stock arrangements and the jazz band, and I played piano in them. I played clarinet in the marching band, concert band, and orchestra. And then I was singing in the a cappella group and the chorus and I made All District Chorus and All State Chorus. Music was the reason I got through suburban life, really.

"I remember at that time my mother bringing home from the grocery store the RCA Victor *History of Jazz*. I think they were 10-inch LPs and they were coming out in the late '50s—twelve of them; you bought a new one each week for a buck. So I started to listen to all that stuff. Meanwhile, I was still listening to popular rock and more rhythm-and-blues and hanging around with some kids who were real interested in the more progressive jazz. The Brubeck kind of faded away.

"So I continued with the classical lessons and in high school my mother found a teacher, Saul Skersey, who was quite a good musician, classically as well as in jazz. He had taught at the New England Conservatory at one point but left to start his own school.

"Then there was a drummer in high school a couple of years ahead of me who used to have sessions over at his house. We'd kind of party a little bit, you know, have a few beers or some vodka, play music, and I got involved in those. And through those sessions I met Alan Wilson, who played the trombone, the same Alan Wilson who later was part of Canned Heat.

"We did standards and then we also were interested in the music of Bobby Timmons, Cannonball Adderley, and so-called jazz funk, and we used to play tunes like 'Dis Here,' and 'Moanin.' We weren't playing blues per se; it was more bluesy jazz and standards. I was studying with Saul Skersey, who was very accomplished as a player in the Art Tatum/Cy Walter mode. I had two sisters—one younger, one older—and he came over and gave us all lessons. He really encouraged me, he was very, very important in my development musically. I learned to improvise a little bit and learned about chords. And he also started me analyzing compositions in terms of structure and harmonic development. I listened to Tatum, Earl Hines, and the bop pianists, Bud Powell, and particularly Thelonious Monk, and I was interested in more far-out sounds. At that time Alan played me a record of Cecil Taylor.

"One time we went to a record store down in Roxbury, which was the predominantly black section of town, and we went into the back room of Skippy White's and Alan said, 'You gotta listen to this,' It was some John Lee Hooker on Crown, stuff he had done in '48 and '49. We were just flipping out over that stuff, particularly some of the instrumental numbers the sucker was doing. They were really just wild, that kind of sound he was getting. It was almost sort of Eastern sounding, the tones he was getting, just unworldly in terms of conventional blues or jazz. It was sort of raw and so penetrating and affecting. And of course his voice. To this day, John and I are very good friends; we talk all the time.

"I went to Club 47 when it was still on Mt. Auburn Street by Tommy's Lunch. That was the original Club 47, where Joan Baez first appeared. They were doing jazz occasionally. That's where I first heard Sam Rivers and Tony Williams, sitting in with Sam, when Tony was about eleven, in the mid-'50s.

"I went to the University of Rochester, to Eastman School of Music. I was there for two years, doing the music major bit, pursuing a liberal arts degree. I didn't enjoy it at all. I gradually became more familiar with blues and got into it a little bit more. I managed to do a junior year abroad in Paris and studied at the Ecole Normale de la Musique. I took counterpoint, theory, harmony, and piano, and I studied with a piano teacher who also taught at the Paris Conservatory. I met other musicians, American and French, and we played. It was still more or less jazz oriented. I was becoming very, very interested in Indian music, north Indian as well as south Indian. And this is also through the influence of Alan Wilson. My interest in world music or ethnomusicology persists today. So I came back to

Rochester and I realized that my credits didn't match up to what was expected of me and I quit school and came back to Boston. I took a few courses at the New England Conservatory and began accompanying modern dance classes and ballet classes, improvising music for that. I had kept in touch with Alan and we got together and all of a sudden he wasn't playing trombone anymore. He complained that he had lost his lip, so he put it down and was playing blues harp. We began to hang out a bit, listening to blues of all sorts—rural blues and prewar blues and then later the urban stuff.

"There was a blues show that played in Paris and I remember really being struck by Otis Spann, who played the hell out of the piano. The sound really stayed in me. Later when I heard Spann with Muddy, I realized this is something I had to get my teeth into. I became really passionate about it and began to hear more and more blues, get into it a lot more. At the same time I was starting to jam with different people in the Boston area. I heard Muddy Waters when James Cotton was still in the band. And eventually I screwed up my courage to ask Muddy if I could sit in—Spann was with him at the time—and that was my first introduction to Muddy. Over the years I continued to play with him—sat in or even did gigs with him.

"One time John Lee Hooker came to a coffee shop on Beacon Hill, just showed up with a battered guitar case, sat down in the chair, and played—and that was it. I asked him if he knew 'Crawlin' King Snake' and he gave me a funny look, like, 'How do you know that?' Later on he used to come to town and I would back him up. Also I was in the first J. Geils Band. By this time the blues had overtaken my life in a very passionate way. When blues guys came to town, I used to hang out with them. I would say my association with Otis Spann and later on with Sunnyland Slim and Pinetop Perkins were the most valuable as far as learning to play blues; also listening to all kinds of piano players—from Charles Brown to Ray Charles and Big Maceo and some of the earlier pre-war piano players, like Memphis Slim.

"I also backed up Big Mama Thornton and played with Albert Collins. I went to hear Freddie King and was completely electrified. I had never heard him before. I talked to Freddie the next night and told him I played piano and asked if could I sit in 'because I notice there wasn't anybody playing piano,' and he said, 'Sure.' So I sat in and he told me that he liked my playing a lot and asked if I'd be interested in joining him, going out on the road. So I went out with Freddie and that was quite an experience.

"After Freddie would be Bonnie Raitt, and that gig was over in April '74. I was also with John Nicholas, a fine guitar player and singer—everything from New Orleans to Cajun stuff—and then I was part of the house band at the Speakeasy in Cambridge. Over the years I played with so many different people, from Buddy Guy and Junior Wells to Otis Rush to Jimmy Rogers.

"But to really stress a point, it's that my musical interests are broad. Even though I'm intensely into the blues and play it with a lot of depth and feeling and invention, I also have strong interests in other music. I love jazz passionately, and I also love to play abstractly—pure shapes and forms and colors, so-called New Music or Improvised Music. I have an intense interest in certain ethnomusical stuff, especially Eastern music, Indian music, and music that's based on Turkish systems of microtones, music of that whole region, anything that's Islamic, particularly double-reed sounds. Recently I was in Morocco and hung out with Jajouka musicians, who play those double reed instruments, the ghaitas, and I traveled in Thailand and Indonesia, Java, Bali. When I travel I take a little tape recorder and try to document stuff. I'm interested in ecstatic religious music. Some of the music from those groups is pretty entrancing. Japanese music, particularly Gagaku music, the music of the Imperial Palace, some of the world's oldest orchestral music, going back to the twelfth or thirteenth century—it's just exquisite. And flamenco music, North African music, anything unusual or exotic really captures my ears. I've been more or less a devotee of John Cage and his whole frame of reference and composers associated with him, as well as many modern classical composers, including Ligeti and Messiaen."

I first met Rory Block two decades ago and continued to catch her whenever she performed in the Washington, D.C., area. In recent years, those occasions have been at her annual spring appearances at The Barns of Wolf Trap Farm Park for the Performing Arts in Vienna, Virginia. Many, including me, consider her to be the foremost living interpreter of the classic Delta blues style.

"I grew up in New York City," she told me, "and was brought up in a musical family. There was a lot of mostly classical music around me. When I was eight years old, I started playing classical recorder. When I was ten, I picked up the guitar and started teaching myself how to play it, trying to pick out melodies, and driving everybody mad with 'Froggy Went a-Courtin' and things like that.

"In 1962, when I was twelve, my father, Allan Block, walked into the house one day with this whole absurd story. He was always making stories up and you never knew whether what he was saying had any basis in truth or not. He said, 'I was walking down the street and I met this little old country guy, who happened to be in the city, and he came into my store and he had this violin with him and he pulled it out and started playing this wonderful style.' This was for the benefit of us kids, the myth of how he started playing country fiddle. Prior to that, he was a classical violinist, although he didn't play it when we were growing up. It was one of the things he had done when he was younger.

"So when my dad started playing this country fiddle style, I tried to back him up. I started playing in a kind of finger-pick-Carter-family style, and we did that for a couple of years. We recorded together, we did parties and festivals, and that began my professional career.

"There was this really interesting folk scene going on in Greenwich Village at the time, in the early 1960s. There were quite a few people who were fans of old-time country music and there were old-time country artists being brought through the area doing concerts and stuff. And there were country musicians and all flocking to my dad's sandal shop. On Saturday afternoons this fantastic jam session would develop, and really great players would be there, people like Eric Weisburg and Roger Sprung and Jody Stecker. There were musicians from down south, musicians from up north, and people who were getting inspired by watching it and becoming musicians themselves. And I was sitting there playing guitar. I really got into the middle of things and began to learn what country-style guitar picking was all about.

"Then I was in Washington Square Park one day, where there were all these big jam sessions going on during weekends. You'd have clusters of people all playing different kinds of music. It was crowded and I'd see this group of people and I'd go over and work my way into the circle and I'd find that I was hearing great bluegrass music. And then I'd go over to another group and find that it was ragtime guitar. It was Stefan Grossman playing this beautiful-sounding guitar style that I had never heard before and I was quite mesmerized by it. I stood there and afterward I started talking to him and he gave me a couple of blues albums, something called *Really the Country Blues*, with Robert Johnson, Skip James, Son House, Bukka White, Tommy Johnson, and I listened and that was it! I was in love with blues from that moment on. It just went straight to my heart.

"For some reason, at that time in my life I related to blues. I felt practically like a homeless person myself. I was running away from home; I hated school, I was really, really sort of in limbo and this music to me expressed my own blues perfectly. And I just loved it like crazy. I sat in front of the record player and the tape recorder for hours and hours for a couple of years of my life transcribing the old blues, note for note. I had a very strong feeling about retaining the original flavor and meaning. I didn't want to distort the music; I wanted to interpret it almost historically accurately. And for a long time I didn't sing because I felt, well, I was a white girl and it would be presumptuous of me to sing a black person's music from the 1930s in a whole different lifestyle. Although I could have sung it, I felt very shy about it at that time, and it took me maybe ten years.

"I met many, many people from the old-time country blues scene. I knew Mississippi John Hurt personally. And I also spent time with Skip James and I spent time with Son House. Stefan Grossman was studying guitar with Reverend Gary Davis. I never took lessons, but I was there and he came to our house. We'd sit around talking and playing together and we would travel with him. It was a tremendous inspiration.

"And then Stefan and I started traveling around together. I was definitely young to be leaving home and doing those things, but that's what was going on in my life at that time. I did run away from home when I was fifteen. We visited Skip James in Washington, D.C. There was a group of folks in Washington, D.C., who were also hard-core country blues fans. There was Nick Perls and John Fahey, who at that time was just starting to do what he does and he had a cult following. And we also visited Mississippi John Hurt in his home in Washington, D.C. And then we just went through the South. We went to Nashville and we went to a lot of guitar stores and pawn shops, and Stefan picked up a lot of fabulous old guitars that formed the basis of his truly great collection. It was a fascinating time for me in all these strange cities.

"Then, back in New York, Mississippi John Hurt came up north for concerts and that's when I got to meet Son House. Stefan used to stay at his parents' house in New York and the blues players would come and stay there. That was a time that I really felt I learned something deeper about blues. As soon as I heard it, I already had this very deep soul connection to it. It was as if it was somehow part of me. I had already done a tremendous amount of transcribing and figuring out the old songs. I had already spent maybe two years listening to blues all the time and learning how to play it and going deeply into it. But then meeting players *like* Son House and having him play in front of me and having his personality overwhelm me and just sitting in his presence and talking to him and having him say things to me—like he taught Robert Johnson to play guitar—were so awe-inspiring, were so immense to me. At the time I didn't think it was so immense because I thought everybody knew these blues players. I didn't realize, I didn't have the perspective to realize that it was such a precious moment. Not everybody would have the same circumstance happen to them and this *was* precious beyond words. At the time, it was just part of life; it was great, and it was something that seemed to me that everybdy who wanted it had access to.

"To tell you the truth, I already knew most of their music when I met them. One time Son House sort of turned around and said, 'Where did she learn these songs?' I was playing 'Future Blues' for him, and 'Walking Blues,' and he was impressed because I knew them and cared about them, having come from the period that he came from and the place that he came from and the climate of racism that was around when he first recorded blues. To come to New York City thirty years later and have a teenage white girl playing the old music to him was amazing.

"At the time I didn't see how it was so amazing, but now I understand. But I really believe it's a matter of souls—not in the traditional manner, like soul music, but something even more spiritual and even more intense. What inspires your soul never has any boundaries. You can't say, oh, because you're white or because you're black or because you're fifteen or because you're fifty, you can't do something. You just can't make those distinctions when it comes to what strikes your soul.

"I had some really rough years of gigs from hell, playing for the two interested people in the audience. It seemed to me that there were years and years and years when I was playing for my dinner, playing at unimaginable places in unimaginable circumstances. What happened is that somewhere along the line I began to learn how to perform, as a result of being under duress all the time. I actually began to learn how to carry on, no matter what. That's one of the first things I learned.

"Then, after a long period of time, some good things started to happen, bit by bit. Stevie Wonder played on one of my records. A good thing would happen here and a great thing would happen there. *Rolling Stone* gave me a fantastic review, the one where they said, 'Some of the most singular and affecting country blues any one man, woman, black, or white has cut in recent years.' The outward signs were that I was unknown and that I was struggling and that people were really not interested in what I was doing and it was uncommercial, it had no future. I was really indoctrinated with that. But I kept doing and I kept doing and, all of a sudden, these little good things would happen and I would have something to cling to and I would say, 'Maybe it's worth it.'

"And then, all of a sudden, one year it actually happened. My accountant told me how much I'd made that year and I said, 'No, that's gotta be wrong.' I mean, all of a sudden I had a financial identity. Now, I'm not talking about rich; I'm talking about going from impoverished to actually being able to pay my bills one year. And I suddenly realized that I was actually making a living and that began slowly to show me that this was somehow going somewhere. And it went from there, sort of indistinguishably, to a place where all of a sudden I realized that I was actually established, I actually was successful, I actually have a strong following, I could actually play in the types of rooms that I wanted to play in.

"When I first went overseas, the blues was very, very well

recognized and very well regarded. This is an example: Someone in Holland said to me, 'You're going to be on a radio show. Give him a list of four country blues songs you cover and he will play the originals when you're over there.' And I said, 'Well, he won't have those songs.' And he said, 'Trust me. Just give him the list.' And I kept thinking, 'This is impossible, he can't *have* Charlie Patton's "Moon's Goin' Down," he can't have all these old songs.' Well, I gave him the list and he had every one of them and everybody there had been hearing songs like that for years. Then I toured Italy, and they definitely were not that familiar with the music, they didn't even know the words I was singing, but they were *very* enthusiastic. And I toured Austria and I've done some tours in England. I did some touring in France. They were also *very* enthusiastic. I played in Poland once. When I'm in Europe I get promoters coming up and saying, 'We do concerts in Romania; you've gotta come to Romania.'

"I just won the W. C. Handy Award for Female Blues Artist of the Year. Musak has picked up one of my songs and Martin Guitars is using me to endorse their strings in a photo campaign. I'm on the same poster with Eric Clapton. I really feel very successful right now and I feel most grateful. I have come *way* further than I ever dreamed was possible. It just sort of slipped into place."

"I was born in Cheshire, England, just the other side of the Mersey from Liverpool," began singer and guitarist Dave Hole in 1993. We were in the bandroom of Washington, D.C.'s, Bayou, which was razed last year. He continued, "I moved to Australia with my parents at the age of four. My father was in submarines during the war and they used to call in to Perth and he began early on speaking with Australians. After he got married and had a couple of kids, he moved there. Perth is on the west coast of Australia on the river, and twelve miles to the west of it is the Port of Fremantle. It's a reasonable size city nowadays, approaching three-quarters of a million people. When I was a teenager it was probably 300,000. It's quite isolated—2,000 miles from the next city of any size and that is across desert. So it's an insider sort of community. I grew up in the hills suburb outside of Perth. It was only a little community, and I had a very pleasant childhood.

"Both my parents were music lovers. My mother plays a bit of piano, which she learned as a child—not exactly classical but she reads music. And my father always liked music. He was fairly broad; he liked all sorts of music, but he did have a bit of a leaning toward country music. Also, my father was in a little trio; one of his mates played guitar and the other played a drum kit. This was like a percussion thing—a snare drum and a bass drum and bottles half filled with water and all that kind of thing, so it was really funny. And my father was roped in to do the bass so he had a tea chest bass—just a wooden box with a broomstick and then a piece of fishing wire or thick catgut or something. You alter the tension by moving the broomstick. I wouldn't say my father was a master but he got by.

"So I was exposed to that at an early age and liked the idea of seeing them perform. I liked having them come around to our house and rehearse and have quite a few beers. It was basically English skiffle, Lonnie Donegan kind of thing. The guy who played the guitar had a voice along the lines of Pat Boone, so he used to do those crooning kinds of tunes as well. They didn't do a lot of performances and they never really charged. Wherever they'd go, I'd be there, from when I was about seven. The acoustic guitar was probably a big factor for me because I really liked that; it was the instrument in the band that I loved. The guitar player was Doug Lawrence and he's still playing today.

"My earliest recollection of being drawn to music is around the age of five or so. I just loved listening to pop music on the radio. Later, when I was about eleven, the things that were big were the Everly Brothers, Buddy Holly, Duane Eddy, that kind of guitar music. So it's late 1950s we're talking about. I'd hear Elvis Presley and all that kind of stuff and I wanted to learn guitar, so my parents bought me an acoustic. We had a gramophone, as they called them, and I remember my mother getting the Elvis Presley record 'Love Me Tender.' She thought that was fantastic and we played it a lot. I think it was just the sound of the guitar, that twangy guitar thing, that was appealing to me—on the radio as well. I loved the sound of the guitar on Buddy Holly's records.

"I didn't hear any blues at that time. Obviously there might have been blues influence in some of the things I was listening to, like Elvis, but I wasn't aware of that then. Radio was very mainstream and still is to this day, more so than you get here in your programming. The diversity is not big. It's a population thing, really; the market is not too big, so you can't cater to minority listening audiences. It's very much the pop thing and rock 'n' roll now. And then it was basically pop music and it was all the American stuff—Bobby Vee and Ritchie Valens, any of those things that you would have had here. We also got a fair bit, probably more than you, of the English groups, like Cliff Richard and the Shadows. The Shadows were a band that I really liked. They had a great guitar sound.

"I did play guitar for a short while. I got a cheap acoustic that my father bought for me. I think it cost thirteen pounds. I had some classical guitar lessons, but my heart was set on doing rock 'n' roll. I got a bit disillusioned with the classical lessons, but I was in love with the guitar and any person in the area who gave guitar lessons was a classical guitarist. So I just drifted and my parents probably thought it was just a phase. I played for about a year. The Beatles were huge and I liked their stuff; I loved the Animals, and the Rolling Stones also came on. Meanwhile, we moved down to the coast; I was in high school there and a friend of mine was forming a band to play Beatles and Stones. I was fourteen, a very impressionable age.

"I joined that band because they needed another guitar player. The guitar player they had could play chords and I had no idea how to play chords. So I was playing the single note leads and that sort of thing. We had every album from those British bands and at some point I also heard John Mayall with Eric Clapton and that was another great thing for me. I also heard the first Paul Butterfield album with Mike Bloomfield playing on it. And the Rolling Stones did cover versions of Muddy Waters, Jimmy Reed, and Robert Johnson, all that. So we practiced and thought, well, this is obviously the source of where they're getting material from. We were looking for Muddy Waters albums, Howlin' Wolf albums, and so on, and they were difficult to get. Because of the English bands that were more blues oriented—the Animals and so on—we started to lose our Beatles repertoire and became more a rhythm and blues band. But we had still never heard what you'd call the authentic original blues masters. I remember very clearly the day the other guitar player in the band turned up with a Muddy Waters album. It was wonderful; I immediately thought, 'Wow!' This was like another element to it—the intonation of Muddy's voice and his guitar playing—and all that really authentic blues feeling hit me. It was really powerful. The whole band felt the same way about this, so we realized we'd sort of tapped into the real roots of this thing. This was '65.

"We got more immersed in those black original blues players of Mississippi and Chicago. We were gradually moving more toward becoming a confirmed blues band and rhythm-and-blues band. We played a few high school functions and frat friends' parties. My last year of high school was '66 and then I went to university and continued playing in bands. The next five years I studied physics during the day and played semiprofessionally in a band at night. I graduated and was supposed to go back and do postgraduate studies, but I took a year off to enjoy myself and that's when I drifted into being a professional musician.

"I had my own band and we were earning money and having a really great time. If you think about that particular period—of the late '60s and the hippies and the flower power—it was a very loose sort of period of my life and of most people who were my age. We had a great time and were learning all the time.

"Traveling was just in the Perth area because it's really isolated. There are other towns in West Australia but it's a hundred, two hundred miles to travel to them and we didn't do that at that time. They're only small towns, in any event—little mining communities. There were clubs in Perth and what we call pubs, similar to bars here, although generally they tend to be a little bigger. Some of them are really quite massive, up to 2,000 people. There was quite a lot of work; I'm still constantly amazed at how much work is available for musicians there. I think that is because of the isolation; until fairly recent times very, very few touring artists came to Perth.

"I was listening to all the stuff that was popular at the time, but what always really impressed me and what was always my main source of inspiration was the blues. At that time I was getting more and more into the 1930s blues—guitarists from Mississippi like Robert Johnson, Charlie Patton, Son House, Tommy Johnson. It was just a pain trying to get records in the style of that time. I first got the Robert Johnson album from a young guy who came to live in Perth from South Africa and he had the reissues. I used to sit forever looking at that album cover. All we had about Robert Johnson was to look at the cover and listen to the album. No one knew anything else about him."

Dave Hole married a little later and he and his wife spent a year or so in London. "That fitted right in with my plans because I was so into the British blues scene. I played in a couple of bands, but the blues scene there was dying, so it was a bit disappointing to me. Pete Green was digging graves in Putney or something and Eric Clapton was hiding those two years. Mayall was living in Los Angeles. So I came to the right place at the wrong time. But it was still fun; there was still a lot more happening there than I was used to. I saw my first *real* blues performance in London and that was B. B. King. I was totally smitten with him. He was my ultimate hero. I'd studied the records, but the sheer power of the live performance was really overwhelming, just a fantastic experience.

"When I got back to Perth I put together my own band again, and from that point right up to the present day, having my own band has been fairly continuous. We've been touring in western Australia, those mining towns I always talk about, and that's quite an experience. You've got little communities that basically are starved for entertainment and very isolated. It's hot, dusty, and remote; people drink beer like water—wonderful people—and they treat you very well. In retrospect, I guess my whole career has been in Perth with very little playing experience outside of it."

Dave recorded an album at the beginning of the 1990s, which was picked up and released by Alligator Records. "So that was the start of what is now, I suppose, a serious career. The last two or three years seem a bit of a blur because of the things that have been happening. I've done three tours of Europe and we did two shows in Royal Albert Hall in London. That was just fantastic for me. A lot of my relatives still live in England and a few of them came, and that was a thrill."

When asked to talk about his devotion to the blues, Dave Hole said, "I have a *love* for it. Why that is, why I should relate to it, I don't really have an answer for, except that I feel that it's basic human emotional music, very direct, very applicable to almost anyone's life, except the details maybe are different. When I first heard

Muddy singing about some mojos and things, I had no idea what he was singing about, but somehow you know the basic emotions he's feeling. I mean, if your woman leaves you, it doesn't matter whether you're Italian, Australian, German, American, whatever, because basically we're all very similar. The blues has a universality. I really don't like to analyze it because I don't understand it. But I certainly feel it very powerfully. I enjoy it very much, and it's motivated me enough to want to have a go at it and to play it. Which is basically what I do."

"Well, I grew up in Los Angeles, and both my parents were involved in music," Debbie Davies began as we sat and talked in the backstage band room of the late Tornado Alley in Silver Spring, Maryland, in the early 1990s. She spoke first of her father, Alan Davies, who was an arranger and session leader for Ray Charles, Frank Sinatra, and Pearl Bailey.

"My dad was a professional musician and he worked in Hollywood. He was a singer who came out of the 1940s and was with a radio show called *Your Hit Parade* out of Chicago. The show was moved to Los Angeles to become one of the first television shows. So he came to Hollywood in 1949 and the timing was such that he ended up being a real major guy in the Hollywood recording scene for television and movies. I mean, he would even be flown occasionally to New York to do sessions because he could sight-read anything.

"My mother was a classically trained pianist who had been giving recitals since she was sixteen; she taught music in school. So we had music around the house all the time in one form or another. My dad had a lot of jazz albums and various pop things and I can remember maybe as far back as when I was two or three sitting in front of those big hi-fi speakers. Whenever it was on, for some reason, I had to sit right in front of it. I remember at one point realizing that I knew—I was really, really little—where the notes were in the song or whatever it was I was hearing. I knew where it was going, somehow, and yet I didn't know what that meant. But I liked it, I was attracted to it. And then I had some piano lessons and in school I always sang in the choruses and by the time I was seven I could harmonize pretty much to anything. So I was really into the singing.

"My dad had a collection of Ray Charles albums and I was also really attracted to him. And during piano lessons, I wasn't that into playing the classical. I liked boogie woogie, which drove my teacher crazy. We'd do this for one week and then go back to Tchaikovsky. So I was drivin' them all nuts because I wasn't doing the right thing musically. To me, the Beatles, the Stones, that was what was happening, and I really wanted to play electric guitar. But my folks wouldn't have any part of it because it was, like, the rockin' thing and to them that was real decadent—rock 'n' roll. They didn't like it as music because they were into classical and jazz, and I wanted to do this radical electric thing, electric blues.

"I just really coveted an electric guitar. I was one of those kids who cut a guitar out of cardboard from a big box that a refrigerator came in. I cut it out and I drew everything on there—the little knobs, the strings—and I took a piece of my mom's yarn and made the strap, and lip-synched and pretended I was playing to all my little records. I got very into Eric Clapton as soon as I heard him. I just loved him and I memorized all his solos, vocally. I could sing all his solos even though I didn't have access to an electric guitar.

"I got an acoustic guitar when I was twelve. I had some folk lessons but in a couple of weeks I could play everything the teacher knew. Folk and then Crosby, Stills, and Nash, Neil Young, the stuff that was acoustic that was out then, but it was sort of like folk-rock, which was real big. And Beatle songs, a little Stones, whatever I could *do* on acoustic. For me this was limited because I wanted to do all these things that you really needed lighter strings for to be able to bend and sustain.

"As I got out of high school and was sort of doin' the college thing and tryin' to figure out what I was doin,' I still had this desire to play electric guitar, and I started focusing on that again and focusing on what it was that I liked. I started reading articles that interviewed Eric Clapton, talking about all of the blues artists that he was trying to emulate. It was really a guys' club at that point—the '60s. The guys didn't want a girl sitting around playing with them; it was their *thing*. So, yeah, I played by myself or maybe with one or two other people, like one guy, a friend. And a lot of it was in my room, with my records. I even had a snare drum for a while and I was playing it to all my records.

"In college, at Sonoma State, at one point I just had this self-revelation that, well, I can do this if I want to. I'm working, I can take my money, and so I did. I bought myself an electric guitar and then started practicing in a whole way I never had on the acoustic. And there was a club in the town of Cotati there, where the guy loved blues, the guy that booked it. His name was Mark Bronsky and he had blues in there all the time—Buddy Guy and Junior Wells, Etta James, Albert Collins, Robert Cray. They were all doing that circuit, you know, so I was there every night! I don't know what I was doing for school because all I was doing now was practicing my guitar and going out every night and starting to buy blues albums, collecting them.

"Then I started playing rhythm and singing in a band, a blues band. Eventually it got to the point where I wanted to play lead, and a lot of the guys were not really into that. I mean, they couldn't take it seriously. So I had to break away and start a band with some other guys. As much as I could play, I'd play; I just kept learning stuff. Man, at that point I was just a fiend. I'd practice six hours a day; I'd listen, I'd go watch, and it just kind of evolved from there. I could be in better and better bands. I was up in the San Francisco area playing a lot in the North Beach area, where there're a lot of old blues clubs. I stayed in San Francisco for ten years.

"And I then decided to move back to Los Angeles in the early '80s and just get into the big pond, as a musician, and see what would happen. And as it turned out, I met a *lot* of blues players in Los Angeles; it surprised me. I ended up meeting the guitar player working with John Mayall, Coco Montoya, and he introduced me to John's wife Maggie, who was putting together an all-female blues band.

"I started going to all the blues jams and just meeting whoever I could meet, and I found there are a lot of really good blues players, a lot of good bands down there, so it was a pleasant surprise. I was taking gigs, jamming, ended up working with Maggie Mayall and the Cadillacs for two years. And John became a real important mentor for me; he's been very supportive. He took us on the road and he would have me sit in with him every night. He made some tapes for me from his personal record collection. He would have people up to the house and we'd play records and he'd tell some stories. I got to do a little recording on his album *A Sense of Place*.

"I also met Albert Collins during that period. Coco used to be Albert's drummer in the early '70s and he invited Albert to come hear us play in a little bar. Albert came down and sat in, and thrilled all the people in the bar. He really liked what I was doing and he invited me to sit in with him at the San Francisco Blues Festival. I did and he liked it, and then in April of '88 he called and asked if I wanted to go on the road. So that was, for a blues nut, a dream come true—to work a while with one of your idols. Albert became a real important mentor for me, and I traveled and toured and played with him for three years. I did his album *Iceman*.

"We did Europe and Japan and Brazil, and the States. In between tours with him, I would always be booking my own gigs, and a few times I got to open for him. He knew I was tryin' to get my thing together and was real supportive and we had a lot of conversations goin' down the road. I don't know if you know much about him, but he drives his own bus. I'd sit next to him and pour the coffee and look at the map and we'd talk for hours about all kinds of stuff. I just absorbed a lot bein' around him and that whole world. And then at one point I just left to go on my own.

"I think in some ways it's a little lonelier," mused Debbie Davies on what it's like being a blueswoman. "There's a camaraderie that guys have, a buddy thing, that to a degree I have with them, and then there's a point where I don't. But the main thing I would say about that is that it was tougher when I was tryin' to get started and tryin' to get people to take what I wanted to do seriously. Now it's turned around. Instead of a roadblock and a handicap, it's a selling point. Now all of a sudden I'm a player but I'm a different gender, so people take almost more interest in that than they would if I were a male. I guess it's been good *and* bad.

"There is a point where I think you have to prove yourself, but I don't really concentrate on that. I know that when I was with Albert Collins on the road, sometimes we'd show up at a club and the sound man and the people there didn't spot me as one of the players. They assumed I was, you know, one of the girlfriends. That's kind of a drag for your personal sense of pride or whatever, your humility. You just have to deal with that and realize that they don't understand because it's just something they haven't seen that much; they're not trying to be shitty, they just really don't know, and so they're jumping to a conclusion. They don't mean anything by it. So, you just, in your head, have to know all that kind of stuff."

Debbie Davies won the 1997 W. C. Handy Award for Contemporary Blues Female Artist of the Year. Her fifth album as a leader, *Tales from the Austin Motel* on the Shanachie label, was released last year. Albert Collins joined Debbie on her 1993 debut album *Picture This* on Blind Pig Records. Later that year Collins died of cancer at the age of sixty-one. "There will never be another Albert," Debbie said of him. "What I learned from him is that everything that comes out has to be totally wired to your soul, no matter what."

"I had to get a nap in" was the apology offered by blues guitarist and singer Roy Rogers. He had arrived a little later than the appointed time in the lobby of the Best Western, Alexandria, Virginia, late one fall afternoon in 1994. Roy was opening for Robben Ford at the Birchmere later that evening.

"Yeah, you've been out on the road." I said. "Where'd you come from just now?"

"Pittsburgh. We played Carnegie Hall there with John Lee Hooker one time. I was still on the road with Hook so it's gotta be at least eight or ten years ago." He paused, then reflected on the ongoing tour. "So we're out here, we're having a great time; we started out in Texas with Robben and his band, and we're going to end up in Canada."

"Okay, let's go back to your very beginnings."

"Well, I was always aware of music from my earliest rememberings. I don't know what age that would be. My mother, Luverne Rogers, played piano. She was not a professional musician but she was actually quite a good pianist. So we always had music in the house. I can't ever remember not having music in the house growing up, playing records. I used to go buy rock 'n' roll records when I was a kid.

"What kinds of music were in the house? What did your mother play?"

"Oh, she played some classical music, but mainly she played pop stuff, from the '30s and '40s—'Talk of the Town,' 'Darktown Strutters' Ball,' that kind of thing. She has a great left hand, that old-style left hand. She can play any key in the left hand, which I wish I could do.

"I started taking guitar lessons when I was twelve. I'd actually taken some piano and dropped it when I was eight or nine. I have an older brother, Bill, and my mother came to both of us when I was about twelve, 1962, and she said, 'Well, I'm going to take you guys to whatever concert you want to go to.' My brother was sixteen and said, 'Well, I want to go to the Kingston Trio,' so she took him to see them. And I said, 'I want to go see Gary U.S. Bonds.'" Roy laughed. "So she took me to see Gary U.S. Bonds, and it was heavy, it was mind-boggling. It was like going to church. It was too heavy for her, I'm sure, at the time. But that was *it*! People were standing on their chairs and going nuts and it was like, you know, *those rock 'n' roll times*! The energy was too much! It was at the Cow Palace in San Francisco. I still have the brochure. The Shirelles were on the bill.

"I'm a native Californian. I was born in Redding, California, but I went to school and was raised in the Bay Area in a town called Vallejo. My father worked for the Maritime Administration. He was in charge of the mothball fleets after World War II—the Victory Ships. I started playing guitar and I got in a band when I was thirteen. My guitar teacher, Joe Wagner, was extremely influential. I can't underestimate that. He used to play rhythm-and-blues with Sly Stone. So early on I distinctly got a blues direction, as opposed to a Chet Atkins or another kind of direction. He turned me on to Johnny 'Guitar' Watson and Chuck Berry, and I dug Little Richard from the git-go, all new stuff to a twelve-year-old. I immediately was enamored at an early age, learning guitar and learning that style. This was before the British Invasion.

"And that's how I was exposed to that music—other than hearing songs that I liked on the radio, like Chuck Berry's 'Johnny B. Goode' or something like that. I really was not aware of the distinction between blues and pop before that time. When I started playing in a band, obviously then I differentiated.

"Joe Wagner encouraged me to buy records and he brought records for me to listen to. We didn't have tapes at that time; that was nonexistent. So it was hard to find that stuff. He would have to loan me a record and then he would teach me a song. He would start out with something as basic as maybe 'Honky Tonk,' a Bill Doggett song, and you'd learn it in your band and *boom*! Next thing you know, you're learning something by Jimmy Reed. I did a little bit of reading music, but it was pretty much him showin' me on the guitar what notes, the pentatonic scale, stuff like that."

"Did you progress fast?"

"Pretty fast, mainly because I got in a band real early. I was playing with high school guys. All the players were older than me, sixteen, seventeen."

"How did your parents react to this, when you were in the band at thirteen? Were they supportive?"

"Yeah, they were supportive because, really, they had to be. I mean, I was just driven. Nobody told me to practice music; it just kind of came, one of those things. We all have those things in life that just come and everything facilitates you doing that. That was me playing in a band. I could not imagine, from that day forward, that band's not being a gas. The time periods that I was *not* in bands felt weird."

"So, what was it like?"

"Oh, we were playing gigs, we were playing dances. My voice hadn't even changed yet at thirteen, and we got in battles of the bands. First band was kind of a combo instrumentation, guitar, bass, drums, sax, and an old Wurlitzer electric keyboard."

"What kind of bag would you describe it as being?"

"Just an early rock 'n' roll, early '60s kind of thing. I mean, bands were everywhere! You didn't think about having a function for your church or your organization or your school without a band, good or bad. And so you played all kinds of music. We played everything from Chuck Berry and Little Richard to rhythm-and-blues stuff. We played some instrumental things, 'Harlem Nocturne,' 'Summertime,' the whole gamut. 'Honky Tonk,' all that kind of stuff. Didn't get into writing stuff at all. We were too much into learning the band, learning how to relate to musicians, how to present ourselves. We dressed in ties and suits, even had gold lamé jackets for a while. Oh, man!

"We were playing all around the Bay area, but mainly local kinds of functions. We didn't do any recording, unfortunately, or anything like that. Won a lot of big-time battles of the bands in San

Francisco. It went on until the guys who started the band graduated from high school, when I was about fifteen."

"And then what?"

"Well, along this whole time, of course, my musical perspective changed dramatically. I got more and more into the blues, in a very deep sense, when I was fourteen. From fourteen or fifteen, I got turned on to Robert Johnson when my brother bought this Robert Johnson reissue on Columbia Records, *King of the Delta Blues*. I had gotten more and more into B. B. King and other people, but up to that time none of my lessons or playing ever prepared me for Delta blues. That was just something that I explored. The whole open tuning style of guitar playing became a parallel path for me, as far as playing straight guitar in a band setting. Exploring Blind Lemon Jefferson, Bukka White, Robert Johnson—I couldn't get enough of that particular style. So by the time this band broke up, I wanted to play blues. I still would *play* other types of music but I wanted to play blues, because feel-wise and just the emotion of that music, that's what draws *me* to that music. The statement. So I wanted to just explore that in all ways."

I remarked that a box-set reissue of Robert Johnson's work had sold a million copies five years or so ago.

"Isn't that amazing?" exclaimed Rogers, astonishment in his voice. "Incredible."

"I make reference to that in my show some times. You know, that's really something, that a man could make a record in 1936, '37, and it sells that many copies today."

"Did you have an opportunity to hear any of your heroes in person when you were fifteen or sixteen?"

"Oh, sure. Bukka White, Mance Lipscomb, Muddy Waters, James Cotton, Lightnin' Hopkins. Saw B. B. King one weekend in Vallejo playing the Vet's Hall and the next week he played the Fillmore. John Lee Hooker and Jimmy Reed playing together. Bo Didley. I only saw Howlin' Wolf one time. He didn't come out to the West Coast too much. At a place called the Avalon Ballroom. Amazing impression, to see a sixty-five-year-old man up on stage going nuts, totally in control but going crazy, and doing his thing. It was so powerful, I'll never forget it." Roy laughed. "You just don't forget those kinds of things."

"No, you don't. Did you sometimes have any kind of an opportunity to say hello to these guys?"

"Oh, man, I remember one time when I was fifteen. Coming out of the Fillmore, I saw Muddy Waters walking in front of me and I was so surprised I said, '*Muddy Waters!*' I just kind of blurted it out and he turned around and I went—." Roy simulated a gasp. "I mean I'm just in shock. He says, 'Hello, son.' I couldn't speak hardly.

"I was playing with the same guys up until I was about nineteen and we were quite good, actually. I wish we could have recorded some of that. Just playing blues; I really wasn't writing. It was very much of a maturing time, playingwise—getting more and more into open tuning and exploring the whole aspect of that

"I got married when I was nineteen, like a dumb fool. And I was going to college, California State University at Hayward. I majored in history and was going to be a teacher. I wasn't going to be a professional musician and I was not interested in taking music in school. From my young perspective I was too much into playing and I thought maybe getting into the process of learning it would somehow interfere with getting in touch with whatever I was thinking that the blues was. I didn't want to delve into learning harmony and stuff like that. I started to play a lot of casuals, just pick-up gigs. People would hire me to play guitar in health clubs and stuff like that.

"Right after I graduated I played in a kind of a lounge act band for money, playing back-up guitar—not a fun gig, but it all contributes to your experience, backing up a singer and learning the pop schlock stuff of the day off the record and playing Holiday Inn kinds of things. I did that for about a year and a half. Hated it. I knew right then that I would have to play the music that I wanted to play. It was good for me to find that out because music is very precious to me. It's always been very personal; that's why I play it.

"Then I met a harmonica player, David Burgin, and we formed a duet. This would have been about 1973. We started opening up shows in the Bay area—Keystone, Great American Music Hall, nice things. Opened up for Bobby Blue Bland, Taj Mahal; went down to L.A., did some shows, went to Minneapolis for a short tour. The act became quite good. It was strictly a duet, sometimes with snare and brushes, not electric, only amplified acoustic, some 12-string guitar sometimes. And I was working day gigs, doing anything, digging ditches, working in an office, anything. We cut a record in '76 for a long-defunct label, Waterhouse Records, a pretty good record called *A Foot in the Door*. We'd become friends with Maria Muldaur and she did guest things with us.

"In 1980 I formed the Delta Rhythm Kings, my trio. I just wanted to explore what I'd been going for and wanted to just do a trio setting with slide guitar. I played mainly open tuning, anyway, at that point. I've had the trio ever since."

"I've been hearing music since I was a baby," Sue Foley told me as we sat at a table before the first set at Tornado Alley in Silver Spring, Maryland. She was twenty-three and had been a professional for about five years. "I'm from a real musical family. My dad's a picker and singer, so he played a lot around the house and he had me singing when I was a little girl. My earliest recollections in music are sittin' around the campfire or somethin' and him playin' country and Irish music, 'Frankie and Johnny.' Just guitar; he's just a strummer and a singer—entertainer, as he likes to call it. My brothers played guitar, too. I have three older brothers. They all played rock 'n' roll and stuff, but they don't gig or anything any more.

"I've always just loved music, whatever was on the radio when I was a little girl. I was just crazy about radio. My brothers were into Led Zepelin and my sister was into the Stones, so I was into them too. My family was not into jazz—or blues, for that matter.

"My parents split up when I was about eight. I changed schools every year after that and when I was thirteen we moved out to Edmonton, which is like 2,000 miles from Ottawa, and that pretty much severed every relationship I had in Ottawa. When I moved back, I was fifteen. I wasn't gettin' along with my mom, so I moved in with my dad in Ottawa and pretty much started over.

"When I was about fourteen I was crazy for the British Invasion, all that music, the Beatles and the Stones, David Bowie, everything from Britain. The Animals and the Yardbirds, all those bands. That kind of just got me into blues because the more I learned about them, the more I learned they were just tryin' to play blues. The Stones did Robert Johnson and they did some Muddy Waters and some Slim Harpo stuff, too. So, that's how I got into the blues. I just wanted to learn more about how they got *their* sound. I was trying to learn how to play a little blues at the time, just learn how to do a shuffle and some easy stuff. I was playing song book stuff, Beatles, and whatever I could follow the chords on.

"Then I read an article about James Cotton in the paper in Ottawa. I knew who Sonny Boy Williamson was and there was something about James taking off with Sonny Boy when he was a little kid. So I was reading it with my friend, and we said, 'Wow, this guy must be heavy!' He called himself Sonny Boy Williamson's adopted son or something in the article, so we said, 'We gotta go check this guy out!' And that was my first blues show. He just really put out; it was really happenin'—a lotta energy in the music, and, I thought, the *soulfulness*. It just reached me. After that it was like church or something, I'd been baptized, by James." She laughed. "I mean, I was just elated. I thought I found a home or something in music. I played guitar at the time but I didn't have any direction musically; but after I saw him I just said, 'I'm gonna play blues guitar, I'm gonna learn how to do what *he* did to *me*.' That was when I was fifteen. I've been playing since I was thirteen.

"It took me 'til I was about fifteen to start learning all the names. I used to just buy every blues record that I could get my hands on. I bought my Little Walter records and Muddy Waters and Jimmy Reed and all the people who played the older style, Robert Johnson and Memphis Minnie and a few compilation records that I really liked. I was really into the big blues belters. I got into Bessie Smith and the other old-style women singers. Alberta Hunter, I like her a lot. But there's not many women guitar players and that's why I like Memphis Minnie. She can really play guitar good. And Sister Rosetta Tharpe; I like her, she's a picker, *helluva* guitar player. Now, I don't even think *I* can play as good as her. She's a heavy guitar player.

"My friend, this horn player, kinda turned me onto Billie Holiday and Lester Young. When I first heard Billie I didn't like the way she sang. It just sounded sort of sweet, and then after I'd listened to her a few times I couldn't *stop* listening to her; I got addicted to her. She's been a real big influence on me. I don't know if you can *tell*, but she just *has*. T-Bone Walker kinda got me into the Swing Era and I followed jazz and Count Basie stuff and the big bands a little bit. I don't have any recent records, but I like Charlie Parker and bebop and I like Miles Davis a lot. And I like the piano players, like Thelonious Monk and Bud Powell. I used to have a tape with one side Thelonious Monk, the other side Bud Powell. I used to just love it and listened to it all the time.

"I was sitting in at the jams and I just really didn't have any other interest except learning about music. I mean, I was ferocious about the way I wanted to learn. I'd buy records; every penny I had would go into music, and every spare minute I had I would be listening to music. The blues scene in Ottawa was small, as you could well imagine, but I was fortunate that there were some really good players who are world class, as far as I'm concerned. Some of them have moved away, and some of them have moved back to Ottawa. I had some good friends there, that's when I made my first friends as musicians, and my first boyfriend, and stuff like that. I didn't really have any friends before that. So I went through all that, and played in my first band, got my first electric guitar.

"I was playing country blues for two years, from fifteen to seventeen. I played in a duo and a couple of trios, acoustic, and played Memphis Minnie and Robert Johnson and any old stuff we could uncover, even Doc Watson and stuff like that, country kind of stuff. I was skippin' school and practicin' a lot. I'd listen to music while I went to sleep and before I went to school and I'd practice at lunch hour and everything. I don't know if I was the weirdo; I was more like invisible. People didn't single me out to tease me; they just didn't really notice me. I had one friend in school who was into the same thing I was and we hung out all the time, did our thing. I didn't try to meet anybody or make friends. I'd moved around so much in my life that I didn't like to meet friends any more and start that whole thing because I'd just end up movin' away and losing track.

"A lot of players came through. There's a club that's still there called the Rainbow and I saw Koko Taylor and Albert Collins and Marsha Ball there. You don't get to meet them, though. They're passin' through on a one-nighter and they don't hang out. I was a kid, so my mentors are more people that were musicians in Ottawa, not really famous or nothin'. The main one is a horn player, a sax player, named Norman Clark, who's retired now; he's in his late fifties. He's retired because there's just not much work for him there, so he doesn't play any more. He played jazz and blues mostly, and rhythm and blues. He was really cool and he got me into Lester Young and we used to talk about music. There was another guy, Back Alley John, who I played with—a harmonica player. He's relocated to Calgary now, but he's from Ottawa. He was soulful, real soulful.

"I played until I was eighteen in Ottawa, and then I split for Vancouver by myself. Shortly thereafter I started jammin' there like I had in Ottawa and learned more, meetin' people and stuff. Then I formed my own band because I couldn't get in a band in town. It was just too tight a scene. So I just formed my own band after getting rejected by every guy band in town.

"There're a few good players I like in Vancouver. The whole Canada scene is small, so we started working slowly, tryin' to get gigs in town. It was hard. I had a little help from the welfare system up in Vancouver for about a year because there are no jobs there for people with no talent for anything but playin' music. And then we went on the road, went to Calgary about three times and did a cross-Canada tour that I booked partly myself and got an agent to do the eastern stuff. We went right across Canada, back and forth; it took about four months, a long tour. That was my first tour, sometimes two or three weeks in a town. The audiences were about the same as in clubs here, twenty-five to thirty-five, sometimes a little older, sometimes a little younger.

"I would have been twenty when we first came to the States. I remember I was too young to drink, I remember that. We started touring with [harmonica player] Mark Hummel from Berkeley. He picked us up and toured us through the States and Canada and we even went over to Denmark. We did that for almost a year. I stopped fronting my own thing and backed him up. That's how I met Clifford Antone. Met him in Memphis and he said, 'Send me something.' So we went back to Vancouver after a tour and did a demo tape. I sent it down to him and he called me right back. I'd just gotten off the road, a really long, outrageous road trip, eight months long in the van."

Sue Foley soon settled in Austin, Texas, and Antone's Records released four CDs by her. Presently she is with the Shanachie label.

"At Antone's I met more people than anywhere. Clifford's had me up at the last two anniversaries. I've gotten to play with Jimmy Rogers and Albert Collins, Earl King, Otis Rush, Snookie Pryor, Pinetop Perkins, Lou Ann Barton, Angela Strehli, Derek O'Brien. That's just off the top of my head. There's been even more people I've played with.

"This is the first summer we've been able to do festivals. We're doin' the Montreal Jazz Festival, the Winnipeg Folk Festival, and the Detroit Blues Festival, something in Toledo. We did this one in Tampa just a while ago."

I asked her how she feels about her art.

"I just find I can't say things, I can't express myself very well," Sue confided. "I mean, as a person. The only way I can is through playing guitar and singing. So it's kinda like something I have to do; otherwise, I just go crazy. Musicians, they just can't express themselves like the way normal people do, and I guess they have to *get it out*, or kill themselves. If you just live inside your mind, you go nuts."

9

Comedy and Jazz: Two Sui Generis

"This music belongs to us—and I'm talking about those of all colors—it belongs to America. It was discovered here, it was invented here."
                                                        Bill Cosby

"If you're going to compose, and if you have the gift, I would advise being born in the 1920s and '30s, because I don't know what the hell today's composers are listening to that's going to encourage their ability to create melodies."
                                                        Steve Allen

I became aware of good music, fortunately, in early childhood," Steve Allen told me about fifteen years ago. We were talking in the New York NBC radio studios after his short-lived show had concluded for that afternoon. He had reentered the world of radio a few months before but soon had to give up the program because of other commitments. During the show's run he had many jazz artists as guests, including Mel Powell, Joe Williams, Ann Jillian, Bobby Enriquez, Terry Gibbs, Adam Makowicz, and Sven Asmussen.

Steve Allen indicated that his early introduction to good music had been "partly by the good luck of being born at the right time. As your readers don't have to be told, unless they're very young, there was a real golden age of American music that lasted roughly thirty years—the 1920s, '30s, and '40s. So from the age of about five, which would have carried me into the late 1920s, I was aware of good songs. I heard them on the radio and my mother and other members of the family would sing them. I can recall driving across the country and there were no car radios, of course, so people sang; that was part of the early conditioning.

"My first instrument was actually the tuba. I later took piano lessons for two or three years but wasn't particularly good at it. Strangely, the gift of composition emerged right away. I was apparently genetically programmed to create music. No one ever explained anything to me about music theory. What little music I learned to read was about the equivalent of what you learn to read in words when you're five years old. I began to compose, I would say, at nine or ten. There were songs they teach children, like 'Tweedle Dum and Tweedle Dee,' so I began to write songs of that sort.

"Then, when I was a bit older, fourteen or fifteen or so, a piano player named Eddy Duchin was a big attraction. His style of creating introductions to arrangements is still imitated by many American teenagers. He played just popular music; he had no connection whatever to jazz, nor did his orchestra, but there was good musicianship. There were, in fact, a lot of good bands in the early '30s that did not play jazz but were fine orchestras. Hal Kemp's band was one and there were others.

"Under the influence of Eddy Duchin, I began to write in the pop tune vein, songs of the sort I was hearing on the radio—more original but in that style. So if you're going to compose, and if you have the gift, I would advise being born in the 1920s and '30s, because I don't know what the hell today's composers are listening to that's going to encourage their ability to create melodies. They're hearing a lot of great rhythm sections now, a lot of great drummers, and a lot of good bass players and guitar players, but damn little melody.

"When I was seventeen I attended a high school in Chicago—Hyde Park by name. There was a fellow who's still a friend of mine who played trumpet then; his name was Niles Lishness. I've used his name in a thousand comedy sketches since then so a lot of people have heard his name. He and some other guys had already become aware of jazz, and people who are interested in anything in common tend to gravitate toward each other.

"The jazz-oriented guys had a lot of recordings that I had never heard much before. I had heard a certain amount of Erskine Hawkins and Fletcher Henderson and of course I'd heard Duke Ellington. So I began to brainwash myself with their jazz records. I had none of my own since I had no equipment on which to play them. Once I had been exposed to that, I concentrated on finding it on the radio. That was quite easy then and I listened to the band remotes featuring Jimmy Dorsey, Tommy Dorsey, Benny Goodman, Count Basie, Charlie Barnett, Woody Herman, Bob Crosby, Ellington, and others. I used to go down to the old Sherman Hotel, to the College Inn, and listen to them in person.

"I began to play little neighborhood dates, fifty cents a night, sometimes three dollars on a weekend. Some of these involved jazz and some of them did not; they just involved dance music. That's how it started for me. Somebody calls you up and you either accept the job or you don't. A friend would say, 'Hey, they need a piano player at this saloon at 63rd Street this Saturday night. It just pays a dollar and a half. Do you want it or not?' Generally, I would accept all offers.

"I was at some disadvantage in that I didn't read. I could read chord symbols; I could interpret them. Most popular tunes and jazz arrangements are limited to a few standard keys. One night I got a call at the last minute. Some regular piano player had fallen out and this job paid five or ten dollars, something like that, which was to me a lot of money. I had to travel to a part of Chicago I'd never been to before and I got there about ten minutes late on the street car. I rushed in and to my horror discovered that the band was playing polkas. I had nothing philosophically or psychologically against polkas, although I had no great interest in them, but when I sat down at the piano and opened the book to read the guitars I saw that everything was in sharp keys. Outside of a G, I'd never even played the scale in the other sharp keys before, so I think I played tonic chords all night long." Steve chuckled at the memory. "It was not one of the great nights for me, musically, but it was exposure.

"There were little neighborhood bands and they would play little neighborhood gigs. Mel Tormé was one of the good drummers in the school and there was a kid named Pete Crow and another fellow named Tommy Franklin and they were pretty good drummers. Nobody had a standard orchestra. It was always the first ten or twelve guys you could get together, and we played all the stock arrangements—'Tuxedo Junction,' 'Song of India,' 'One O'Clock Jump'—all those things that even in the late '30s had become standards. You could buy them for about three dollars. So all the bands seemed to play the same music.

"When I got to the college level—Drake University in Des Moines—a couple of years later I finally began to make better money. And, of course, I was playing better, and I began to insert a certain amount of singing. I earned a little extra money on weekends, playing and singing as a cocktail pianist and vocalist at a local joint. It was mainly playing old songs people wanted to hear and I got a kick out of doing that. I also played with campus bands. I remember the name of one orchestra, Dick Andrews. He was just another kid in the school; he played clarinet, and he organized a band. I played a few dance jobs with them. Sophomore year, I was at Arizona State Teachers College in the Phoenix area and played with various bands around town. So all that experience helped."

That experience has piled up by now to better than six decades in show business, dating from those teenage neighborhood gigs as a piano-playing Chicago high school student in the late 1930s. Indeed, Allen's long career, perhaps more than that of any other performing artist, confirms the centrality of jazz in our culture. A polymath and a man of enormous creative energies, Steve Allen simultaneously works on dozens of projects, a number of which always have a connection with the music he began listening to as a youngster. Take his 1950s hosting of *The Tonight Show*, which launched one of the most long-lasting and popular television programs of all times.

"One of the good things about the show," he reminisced, "for which I can take no credit because I was doing it for purely selfish reasons, was that we booked every jazz guy who was in town, because I love 'em.

"I remember the night Lester Young came. He walked in the back door of the Hudson Theatre and I recognized the hat and the tenor case and stuff and I went right over to him and said, 'Lester, welcome; I'm Steve Allen.' And he looked at me for a minute and then he moved up very close to me and in a very soft voice said, 'Many eyes.' First time I'd ever heard that expression.

"And then somehow it became a custom where they would roll out another piano and whoever the guy was—Erroll Garner and I or whoever—we would do some four-handed stuff, trading choruses. To me, it was just an honor, and we always had good rhythm sections, so I guess I didn't hang them up too much. I played one night with Art Tatum in a two-piano set-up. So now there's a twenty-year jump and I meet a guy at an airport one day and he says, 'Hello, Mr. Allen, I just heard your album with Art Tatum.' I figured he had been drinking. I knew I had never made an album with Art Tatum. I wouldn't be qualified if the offer had come through. He said, 'Well, I did hear it, sir. In fact, I'll be glad to send you a copy.' So he did and, sure enough, it consisted entirely of various radio and TV shows and there's a really romping ultra-fast treatment of 'Fine and Dandy' with Tatum and me. I guess the fact that I was in such company made me play at least at whatever my best is. So I was giving Tatum no competition but I didn't disgrace myself.

"I wish somebody had kept a list," Steve Allen lamented and reeled off from memory the names of some who made appearances on the show. "Miles Davis, Ella Fitzgerald, Mel Tormé, Anita O'Day, Sarah Vaughan, Thelonious Monk, Lambert, Hendricks and Ross, Willie the Lion Smith, Charles Mingus, Terry Gibbs. The studio orchestra included Sweets Edison, Lou McGarity, Yank Lawson, and Bobby Rosengarden, and Peggy Lee was the house vocalist."

Steve's career can be traced from those early days in Chicago and at college through his beginning radio work in the 1940s and subsequent stardom on *The Tonight Show*, to the lead role in the 1955 film *The Benny Goodman Story*, to the present day when he can still be caught in club engagements and heard on newly released CDs. Add to all of this his lyric writing and composing of more than four thousand songs, his authorship of forty plus books, his journalism, his emceeing and guest appearances, his teaching, and that foray back into radio that brought us together in the fall of 1987. I even caught Steve a couple of years ago in a supporting role on the television series *Homicide*. Around the same time I checked him out at a Border's book signing, where he talked of his life and career, played some piano, and sat at a little table to autograph his new children's book.

Steve Allen is in the *Guinness Book of World Records* as the most prolific composer of modern times. His first hit song was "Let's Go to Church Next Sunday Morning" for country and Western singer Jimmy Wakely. "Then Nat Cole recorded a song of mine called 'An Old Piano Plays the Blues,' and the fact that it was a jazz-oriented tune and was recorded by Nat opened up doors. The next big break-through was the lyric I wrote for 'South Rampart Street Parade.' That was recorded very quickly by Bing Crosby and the Andrews Sisters. So with these successes, whatever I wanted to show somebody, at least they would listen.

"Just for the hell of it I got an idea to do an album and I got a good rhythm section together and then I wrote some very stuffy scholarly notes, purposely dry notes, of a sort that do exist in one branch of criticism, and I drew up this imaginary character called Buck Hammer. I had an artist sketch a black gentleman who looked a little like Fats Waller or one of those heavy-set piano players, cigar in his mouth and big stubby fingers. The story line was that he had made only this one album and was a little strange personally, a little inhibited emotionally. Some jazz players had met him over the years as they would move through Mississippi and Alabama, and they would encourage him to join their groups, but he was too shy. He avoided the big time, he wanted no glory, he lived a very simple life, and after making this album he had in fact passed away.

"It's a very touching story," Steve said, laughing. "I was recording a lot with Bob Thiele at the time and we put the album out. And *Down Beat* gave it three and a half stars and the *New York Herald Tribune* gave it a real rave and said, 'Hammer's death was a tragic loss to the world of jazz.' And it got a couple of other nice write-ups around the country.

"And then, finally, [jazz critic] Ralph Gleason listened to it carefully and realized that on some of the tracks what he was hearing was not physically possible, because I had double-tracked and so had two hands going in the bass and two going in the upper register. So he smelled a rat and called Bob Thiele, who confessed the truth right away. And then *Time* wrote something about it and it was finally exposed.

"Emboldened by that success, several months later I did it again," he continued, laughing. "This time the album was entitled *The Wild*

Piano of Mary Ann Jackson. I took what sounded like the name of a black player, since many American blacks have Anglo-Saxon names, for reasons obvious in our history. And in this case we were even more devious. We had a wonderful woman who was our house-keeper at the time. She's now dead. Her name was Mary Sears, and I told her what I had in mind and she loved the idea. She put on one of Jayne's wild dresses and a pair of Jayne's earrings and posed for the picture. Mary knew nothing about music but she put her hands on the keyboard and smiled. So that was Mary Ann Jackson, and if you saw the album you'd never have any reason to doubt there really was such a person. There was her picture and she was at the piano. And, again, I wrote very stuffy scholarly liner notes explaining that this Mary Ann Jackson was not known to many people in America because she had played chiefly in Paris in recent years at Mars Club, which is an actual club there that I had visited not long before. The notes said that some people had commented on Mary Ann's style, that she played like a man, and that was neither praise nor a put-down, just an observation that she had a crisp, hard attack. It's no wonder since I was the piano player.

"I hired a great rhythm section, just guys around the studios in L.A., and when we got to the recording session they said, 'What're we playing, what tunes?' I said, 'None, actually, nothing you know, nothing even *I* know. We'll just deal with each track one at a time and won't worry about what the next is going to be until we get to it. What we'll do is I'll establish a tempo and you guys play and we'll agree on a starting key. And then after that it's every man for him-self. Follow me as best you can, but I'm going to deliberately make some meaningless changes, I won't modulate; I'll just jump from, like, C to A flat or whatever—any two keys. And I won't make it sensible; I will deliberately make it *non*-sensical as a jump and there'll be rhythm changes in a tune.' They immediately saw what I was doing. I said, 'I'm not putting on some of the guys who play ultra-modern, but some of the critics who claim to understand what these guys are playing.' In both cases, Buck and Mary Ann, it was really aimed at critics, not at anybody else.

"So we made twelve tracks for the Mary Ann Jackson album and it got quite a respectful review but I forget the name of the maga-zine. It was quite a good magazine and I felt a little guilty about putting them on because they were making a lot of sense about jazz. They cared about it, and they were supporting it, and their reviews were generally quite reasonable. But nevertheless, they gave her a pretty respectful review, although there was some little criticism.

"So I carried the joke even further. I had my secretary go out and order some feminine-looking stationery, blue paper, that said 'Mary Ann Jackson' at the top of it. Then I had my secretary write in her hand, so it looked like a woman's handwriting, taking issue with a point the critic had made about I don't know what the heck, and they printed the letter and commented on it. Except that I've discussed this publicly a few times, it never finally was exposed the way the Buck Hammer one had been. It just faded off into the mists."

Returning to an earlier topic, I asked Steve Allen to indicate how he goes about composing.

"This is a very mysterious process," he began, "and I shouldn't say 'this,' I should say 'these,' because I write in different ways at different times. In some instances—and the most dramatic and most mysterious way in which I conceive a tune—it's when I'm asleep. In fact, my most successful song, 'This Could Be the Start of Something Big,' was dreamed, and thank God it was dreamed during, I guess, those few minutes before I wakened in the morning. I often dream melodies but hardly ever can recall them, partly because, I suppose, I dream them at midnight and don't wake up until ten o'clock, and after ten hours, who can remember?

"So in this case, I had been assigned to write the score for a musical and my brain was already at work on a large problem of providing a dozen or so tunes. For this one, I recalled the full melody and the first few lines of the lyric, all of which I created in the dream. The idea was there's something very unpredictable about love or physical or sexual attraction. You don't look down a list of ten women and rationally select number nine as the likely object of your attentions; it just happens. Very often, one could spend twelve years on a psychiatrist's couch trying to figure out why, and most people never do. So, in speculating about that sort of psychological reality, it occurred to me to say that love can come anytime; you're walking along the street or you're at a party or else you're alone, and then you suddenly dig. So who the hell knows how you write a song asleep? I don't and neither does anybody else. I wrote another melody as good as any melody I've ever written, for the score of *Alice in Wonderland*, which I did for CBS. It's a very sad, very depressing French-like dirge sort of melody, very emotional. And, again, in a dream.

"Then there's a separate category where sometimes in connection with a lyric idea I think of words and music when I'm not at the piano. Generally, the harmonies are simpler in those cases. The biggest hit I had in that category was a song in the 1950s for Jerry Vale. I still play it with symphony orchestras. It's an Italian-type song called 'Pretend You Don't See Her'—very Italian, very emotional, sob in the throat and all that. I wrote that in a car driving across country. Just about five minutes and it was all finished up, words and music.

"Then at the piano, I write in a third style, much more harmonically rich. I've been in that phase of writing since I was about seventeen. In fact, recently on this radio show I played a song I wrote when I was seventeen. It sounded—and when I say this I don't mean it sounded as good as what he wrote, that's not my point—like something Cole Porter might have written. Not because it was a beguine, because you could write four hundred beguines and they could all be lousy; but without repeating a note he had written, it was definitely in his style. And it occurred to me one day when I was feeling out some chord relationships.

"So I guess there are those three methods: sleep, working to provide a melody with a title or a lyric idea, and then better harmonic constructs created at the keyboard while listening to what I'm doing. Sometimes you can spend three weeks trying to think of a good rhyme for the last line of a tune. But the melodies come out complete.

"But there's never any difficulty. Whenever I see old movies where they show a songwriting team and there are guys throwing pieces of paper away and breaking pencils and hitting notes, either this is total crap written by a guy who knew nothing about songwriting or, for all I know, maybe other songwriters have that trouble. All I can say is *I've* never had that trouble. I write all my songs in a minute or two." Steve Allen died in November 2000.

The performance of comedy and jazz have something in common. This was made clear to me a decade ago when I was concluding an interview with Bill Cosby at his TV studio in Queens, New York. I had brought along a photo of my then seven-year-old son Neale, who had been a "stone" fan of *The Cosby Show* for several years. My objective was to walk away with an autographed photo of the comedian for my youngster.

I handed the snapshot to Cosby and said, "I thought we could make an exchange." He glanced at the photo and, as quick as the snap of a whip, responded, "I'm sorry you don't like him."

It was such a fast comeback, I didn't know what hit me!

And isn't that the way with jazz? I mean, here are musicians on their feet and planning a few seconds ahead—all the while improvising—what they are going to next say on the instruments at their mouths or at their hands.

If you've seen Bill Cosby do stand-up comedy, you already know how fast he is on his feet. While much of the material he presents during the usual two-hour show is stock, there are many, many moments when you know that he has spontaneously come up with a new idea that he then proceeds to work, much as a jazz artist composes anew as he or she plays. Then there are the riffs he employs, most memorably for me the one he uses in the course of his dentist and patient routine—the garbled line, "I hope so," mumbled in response to the doctor's repeated assurance, "I'll fix it."

On that day when he zapped me about trading children with him, we took up the similarities between jazz and comedy. I suggested that they were especially closely related in timing, improvisation, and audience feedback.

"But not only that," Bill Cosby said, picking up the theme, "it's playing notes and emotions, coloring things, and what you say. That's why when people used to look at monologues that I had written, if they didn't know me well enough—of course, they know me now—or know my work, they'd look at the piece and say, 'You know, I can't do this. I mean, it's not funny. Where is the funny?' And then I would have to do it for them. Then they'd say, 'Well, yeah, it's funny when *you* do it.'

"That's because I start with what you call the 'head.' I got a beginning, a middle, and an end. When I start a story, I can go any place I want to go, but I keep in mind that this is supposed to be funny, and people are laughing, and that's what I want. So I build them the same way the musicians build their solos and bring it to laughter, maybe two or three laughs, one behind the other, and then off again to build on something else.

"You have some brilliant writers come out of this. What do you think of Jon Hendricks? Able to take *a* note, put a word or prefix to a solo that someone else played with a horn, and make those words work in telling a story. My lord, how fantastic! And that's who *I* am. I do consider myself under that label, talking."

Bill Cosby has been one of the best friends the jazz idiom has ever had. *Down Beat* recognized his "cheerleading" for jazz and his "active encouragement of jazz musicians" by naming him the recipient of its 1991 Lifetime Achievement Award. The citation was awarded as Bill was about to launch the seventh season of *The Cosby Show*, the popular saga of the Dr. Heathcliff Huxtable family, whose domestic adventures frequently involved jazz luminaries. They appeared both as actors and in jazz performance, thus bringing the music to perhaps the largest audience ever to view jazz in action.

No question about it. Bill Cosby had been for six years raising the jazz consciousness of the general populace to a degree, I think, that no individual had heretofore even attempted, and he accomplished that without executing a single note or beat of music. Think back over the eight years of *The Cosby Show*. Who are some of the jazz and blues and gospel greats who turned up on the series? There was Dizzy Gillespie, Betty Carter, Max Roach, B. B. King, Slide Hampton, Jimmy Heath, Art Blakey, Mavis Staples, Nancy Wilson, Joe Williams, Sandman Sims, and Frank Foster conducting the Count Basie Band.

"Then we did a whole thing about Little Jimmy Scott," he reminded me. "And let's not forget there was a wonderful scene where Cliff and Clair had had an argument and they weren't feeling too good about it. Then in the reconciliation, Cliff called her at the office and pushed the button on the cassette player, and there was Coltrane's 'Dear Lord.' Cliff put the phone down and let it play for her. I mean, that's a wonderful, wonderful way of scoring and showing what happens with music. Then we had the one with Big Maybelle's 'Candy'" (which Clair lip-synched to, unaware that Cliff was watching her).

For me, one scene looms as especially brilliant. Cliff is tossing and turning in bed with indigestion. He dreamed that he awoke and, sitting up in bed, was greeted by a performing combo right there in the bedroom. Daughter Vanessa, decked out as a Lester Young look-alike, porkpie hat and all, was blowing tenor with a rhythm section behind her. And she was *cooking*! Dr. Huxtable, incredulous, asked her how in the world she had learned to play like that. She replied that she had just picked up the horn and played. Cliff took the saxophone from her, put it to his mouth, and blew. Instead of his daughter's swinging and searing lines, he got only squawks and screeches, and he handed the instrument back to her.

The author vividly recalls Cosby's cameo emceeing appearance at the first benefit concert for the Thelonious Monk Institute in Washington, D.C.'s, Constitution Hall in 1986. Clark Terry had persuaded him to attend the sold-out star-studded four-and-a-half-hour event, and Bill spoke eloquently when it was his turn on stage.

"The musicians you've already seen tonight," he somberly began, "and those you'll see later are coming back from across the Atlantic and Pacific ponds where they are considered technicians, highly talented musicians, and geniuses, and where people flock to see them. They come home not to play in ball parks and stadiums and concert halls as they do overseas to audiences of seven, eight, and ten thousand, but to play in nightclubs with clinking glasses and cigarette smoke. This music belongs to us—and I'm talking about those of all colors—it belongs to America. It was discovered here; it was invented here." He closed his remarks with a plea to "bring your children to see these musicians."

I could cite many other instances of Bill Cosby's support of the jazz idiom. He invited Sonny Rollins, Wynton Marsalis, and the Modern Jazz Quartet onto *The Tonight Show* when he was guest host; he has long been the emcee of the Playboy Jazz Festival; he lent his support to Newark's WGBO and other jazz radio frequencies and often has perfomed benefit concerts for such deserving jazz causes as the Apollo Theatre; he has conducted Beacons of Jazz concerts at the New School in New York and has hosted an all-star benefit celebration of Charlie Parker at the Village Gate. His attendance at jazz performances of all styles has been consistent and frequent and he has been ubiquitous at national forums that have recognized jazz, America's lone indigenous art form.

"This music has always meant something to me, deeply. In the 1940s, as teenagers, we *danced* to Tiny Bradshaw, Cab Calloway, Charlie Parker. We *danced* to those songs, so that 'Confirmation' was not only a tune with a great solo, it was something to dance to. Miles Davis's 'Blue Haze' was a slo-o-ow dance for us. 'Sister Sadie' and 'Room 308' by Horace Silver and 'Night in Tunisia' done by Art Blakey, we danced to those. Those of us who are now in our fifties, we danced to those things. When you play them for people now, they don't know what to do with them. But we had developed a dance that was all across the United States."

Bill Cosby was not sure when his first exposure to jazz occurred. He tentatively dated it to his contact with bassist Spanky De Brest and drummer Lex Humphries when he was ten or eleven years old. Of course, there is the brief but priceless anecdote he related at that Monk benefit mentioned above. He was taken to see the Duke Ellington Orchestra when he was seven.

"I don't want to see no duke!" he recalls wailing. "I want to see the Lone Ranger!" But now he says, "Hey, when I was seven I went to see Duke, man!

"I remember my whole junior high school knowing the words to James Moody's 'I'm in the Mood for Love' before I even knew what they were singing. I mean, my *whole* junior high school class, the girls, the boys knew it!" It's no wonder, really, considering that Bill's classmates and friends included James De Priest, Archie Shepp, Bobby Timmons, Lee Morgan, Reggie Workman, and alto saxophonist Tony Williams. A few years later he became a friend of John Coltrane. He subsequently played drums for a spell in trumpeter Charlie Chissom's Philadelphians and filled in for drummer Donald Bailey in Jimmy Smith's organ combo. He joked about being fired by organist Groove Holmes "for playing too loud." In the 1960s and '70s Bill fronted his Bunions Bradford Funeral Parlor Marching Band on recordings and in concert.

For several years beginning a decade ago, Cosby threw himself into composing, arranging, and CD production, beginning with the 1990 *Where You Lay Your Head*, the initial release of three albums for Verve.

"What I hope to do is grow as an arranger, a conductor, and a writer," he explained. "Everything that says 'Bill Cosby' is really

mine. Someone else may have written it, but this is my interpretation." All five of the tunes on the album were composed jointly by
Bill and his long-time musical associate Stu Gardener. Bill offered
some illustrations from a later session of how he applies his creative
powers to the work of others.

"For instance, 'Trinkle, Tinkle.' When Monk and Charlie Rouse
played it, they played it together. I thought it would be wonderful to
have the piano and the horn trade, which gives it a different answer-
talk-question. Well, that's a different approach, whether you like it
or not, but it's still a guy saying, 'Listen, this is *my* interpretation.' I
mean, that's what it's all about.

"Then we took this 1930s song 'If I Had My Way' and I had the
woman sing it *naked*. Not with her clothes off; I mean, without any
dressing of instrumentation. And then what I *tried* to do was have
my musicians score her, have the bass bow a harmony with what she
was doing, the piano player play harmony with every note she was
singing, as if these two instruments were other singers."

Among the musicians Bill recruited for the first CD were saxo-
phonists David Murray and Odean Pope, pianists Don Pullen and
Harold Mabern, guitarist John Scofield, and drummer Al Foster.
Bill provided percussion on three tunes.

"It isn't on automatic, nothing is on automatic," Bill insisted,
"because I'm wandering that studio bothering people while the
music is playing. And let's not forget the humor. This is not something where, even though I'm serious, there is no humor. In the
recording session there is an awful lot of laughter. There *is* tension,
because the guys want to be correct. And there really isn't anything
on paper other than the head arrangement, and then we move off
from that, trying to capture things at the moment.

"Now, the musician that I'm looking at has to read my face and
body language and then play the chord that way," he continued,
clarifying his role as conductor and on-the-spot arranger, "which is
why we have an awful lot of fun. Certain faces have certain notes to
them, and the body English that goes with it as well takes it somewhere. The more a musician gets to know me, the more that musician can lock into really what I want. And this is *while* the music is
playing. So it's on the moment.

"There are certain signals. Ben Riley was playing and I pointed to the top of my head with my index finger, and he took that to mean, we're going to the *top* again, see. And the clenched fist means something, and a hand flat parallel with the ground waving to the right or the left or across the neck, sweeping across the neck, means something." Bill paused and then mused on the potential usefulness of providing his musicians a visual manual of his variety of signals, facial expressions, and body language, "as opposed to the notes on the paper."

Bill Cosby invited me to hang out a few months later for the two-day recording session of his second CD, *My Appreciation*, which featured arrangements he and saxophonist Bobby Watson made of compositions by Ellington, Monk, Miles Davis, and others. I took an early morning train from Washington, D.C., and walked from Pennsylvania Station to Studio 900 on lower Broadway, arriving there about 11 A.M. Taking the elevator to the ninth floor, I pushed the buzzer. The door was opened a few inches by one of the musicians. "Oh, he's all right; he's from Washington, D.C.," Cosby assured the doorkeeper. "How you doing?"

Bill and I sat and talked for a few minutes before the session started. "I want you to have a ball," he said, and then warned, "I may have to charge you for this."

The musicians were on opposite sides of a glass wall: the horns—trumpeter Rebecca Coupé Franks and saxophonists Jimmy Heath, Ralph Moore, and Bobby Watson—in the control room; the rhythm section—pianist Mulgrew Miller, bassist Peter Washington, and drummer Ben Riley—in the studio proper. Cosby, in the control room, interrupted as the band kicked off the Miles Davis classic "All Blues."

"No, no, take it from the top!" He scatted the melody, "Doodle-li-di-do!" Then he was on the other side of the glass, headphones on, instructing the rhythm team, occasionally gesturing in a conducting mode. He stared intently at Rebecca Coupé Franks as she alone played the melody. Then he was back in the control room in a semi-crouch, cigar in hand. He looked like he hadn't shaved for several days. He gesticulated to Rebecca, raising and lowering his arms. She returned his intense gaze with one of her own. Bill was clearly on top of everything that was transpiring. At some point one of the musicians observed of Bill, "He can sing anything he hears."

"It'll sound like the two of you have been playing together for nine hundred years," he said to Rebecca after this first take. "You're in the pool now. Swim!" There was general laughter all around the control room.

The two-day session continued along the loose lines laid down by Bill Cosby and it produced some of the most swinging bop playing that I had heard. To capture a moment on the second day, before they recorded "Wholy Holy I," Bill approached Rebecca Coupé Franks and instructed her, "Now you stay in here and listen, because you're going to be naked on the next chorus. I want you to capture the feeling of this. I want you to experiment. Try not to be perfect."

During her solo, Cosby crouched behind her, waving his posterior in a swaying motion to the music, totally absorbed in what she was laying down and clearly delighted.

All stood in silence as the playback ran. Rebecca's solo drew attention. It was beautifully conceived, stunningly economical in its choice of notes, and deeply moving. For me, thoughts of the gorgeous sound of Bunny Berigan came to mind. It was a gut-wrenching personal statement that brought tears to the eyes.

Sitting on the couch next to her a little later, I told her that it was a very strong solo "and will be noticed." She looked at me with an expression of disbelief about what was happening to her.

"We have this running joke," Bill Cosby had confided to me toward the end of that interview at Cosby Studios a few months before. "My daughters say, 'Please don't get caught in the house with Dad if he's just finished recording, 'cause he'll make you sit and listen to his music that he's very, very proud of.'"

Acknowledgments

Thanks to all the musicians profiled here for giving me their time and effort toward compiling this volume of their vital musical history and of the Americana that their accounts provide.

Thanks to the photographers whose splendid art is featured in the book.

And thanks to the many who have lent me help over the years in my endeavors to document in words the great American art form of jazz. In addition to the list contained in the Acknowledgments of my earlier book, *The Jazz Scene: An Informal History from New Orleans to 1990*, I would add these: Larry Appelbaum and Patricia Willard of the Library of Congress, Giovanni and Flavio Bonandrini of Black Saint and Soul Note Records, Ralph Camilli of Blues Alley, Congressman John Conyers (D-Mich.), Jacqueline Corbett of the Smithsonian Institution, Al Dale of the National Parks, Helen Oakley Dance and the late Stanley Dance, Wilma Dobie, John Dunlap, Trish Shuman, and Tracy Walmer of Wolf Trap Farm Park for the Performing Arts, Leslie Gourse, Mary Johnson of the Kennedy Center, Jerry Kline, Janis Lane-Ewart, Nancy Ann Lee, Don Lucoff of DL Media, Howard Mandel of the Jazz Journalists Association, Don Peterson, Tony and Denice Puesan of HR 57, Jack Sohmer, Catherine Stuart of the One Step Down, Kelly and Maze Tesfaye of Twins, and Scott Yanow.

I would also like to especially thank the following: Ellen Gross, formerly of Cates and The Nest, for her long-time encouragement, as well as public championing, of my writing efforts.

Judy Edelhoff for making it possible for me to put the finishing touches to this book in Rome.

My brothers Bill Stokes and Turner Stokes, my very first fellow jazzophiles, and Jud Henderson, my first jazz mentor.

My faithful canine companion for the past dozen years, Sparky, whose "big ears" have absorbed a whole lot of hip music in his time at his master's feet.

My sons, Sutton Royal Stokes and Neale Hartmann Stokes, for their patience in so often pausing and listening to yet another jazz story from Dad's seemingly bottomless repertoire of such improvisatory riffs and for lending ears to myriad recordings he has pulled off the shelf and spun for them.

My editor at Oxford University Press, Sheldon Meyer, who has no peer in providing encouragement to authors and in shaping the final form of a book on jazz. Other persons at Oxford deserving of my thanks include Penelope Anderson, Joellyn Ausanka, Sarah Hemphill, Patterson Lamb, and Russell Perreault.

And last—but most—my deepest appreciation goes to my wife, Erika Else Stokes, without whose constant and unwavering support neither this volume nor much else of my writings since the early 1970s would have ever seen print.

Rome   W. Royal Stokes
August 1999

Index